International Theory
and European Integration

International Theory
and European Integration

CHARLES PENTLAND

THE FREE PRESS
A Division of Macmillan Publishing Co., Inc.
NEW YORK

The Free Press
A Division of Macmillan Publishing Co., Inc.
866 Third Avenue, New York, N.Y. 10022

First published in England by Faber and Faber Limited

Library of Congress Catalog Card Number: 73-10832

Printed in the United States of America

printing number
1   2   3   4   5   6   7   8   9   10

To the Dragon

Contents

Preface

This book is not about the Common Market, or what North American newspapers insist on calling 'the ECM'. At least, it is not primarily concerned with that organization. Rather, it is about European political integration, a process in which the European Economic Community has played a dominant role in the past fifteen years, but which involves many other institutions besides the EEC, many more countries than the Six and many issues beyond economics. More specifically it is about what has become a flourishing literature on European political integration.

It is not my intention to provide a history of European integration, nor to offer a theory to explain it. Instead, what follows is an essay in interpretation, arising out of a state of mind fairly prevalent among students of integration – namely, the feeling that this literature lacks theme, pattern and direction. This essay is an attempt, in both criticizing and reformulating the theoretical literature on European integration, to set it in the broader context of international relations theory. Since integration theory has important prescriptive as well as analytical purposes, this exercise involves tracing the relationship between the theory and the practice of integration in postwar Europe.

For encouraging my early interest in problems of international theory, international organizations and integration, I am particularly grateful to Professor K. J. Holsti and Professor M. W. Zacher of the University of British Columbia. This book is an extensively revised version of a dissertation written for the Department of International Relations at the London School of Economics and Political Science, in the preparation of which Mr. Paul Taylor provided unsparingly of time, patience and valuable criticism. For their comments and guidance both in the preparation of the original dissertation and in the process of revision, I am indebted to Mr. Michael Banks, Professor G. L. Goodwin and Professor F. S. Northedge. For what appears in these pages, of course, I alone am responsible.

PREFACE

I am very grateful to the Canada Council for its financial support in the preparation of the original dissertation. For a meticulous job of typing the manuscript I owe considerable thanks to Maureen Bates, Merilyn Dasil, Donna McVicar and Fanny Morales.

Finally, for her editorial assistance, her inspiration and, above all, for her patience with a cranky and preoccupied author, I am indebted to my wife, Carol Ann – her contribution to this book has been immeasurable.

Kingston, Ontario
August, 1971

International Theory
and European Integration

1 Introduction

The language and methods of theory in international relations have changed dramatically over the past few decades. Many of its central problems, however, have not. One set of problems with which students of international relations, whether in the idiom of theology, classical jurisprudence or general systems theory, have continually been concerned, has to do with the political structure of world order. They have inquired into the stability of the present order and the likely direction of change, attempting as they go to sharpen and refine their tools of description, explanation and prediction. They have questioned the value of specific forms of world order, whether emergent or purely speculative, as ways of meeting human goals and needs. And they have attempted, through prescription and policy-analysis, to bring about or to influence change in the structure of world politics.

The realm of international politics, however, can prove intractable and perverse to participants and observers alike. Consequently, many of those concerned with the political structure of world order gradually become disenchanted with its present condition, frustrated at their own seemingly ineffectual efforts to influence change and, most fundamentally, uncertain about the empirical validity of the propositions most central to their theories. The real world of politics all too rarely permits the scholar the satisfaction of testing his grander hypotheses; he rarely has before him a manageable case or set of cases in which he can, over a reasonable period of time, observe the emergence of radically new political forms.

To these generalizations, the study of political integration is something of a happy exception. As a field of political science, it has a new self-consciousness and a new terminology; its roots, however, run deep in the history of political thought. Advocacy and prophecy of world government or regional (usually European)

13

unity are an ancient tradition of Western political thinking. Of similar vintage is a closely related analytical literature on the unification of states, the rise and fall of empires and the maintenance of peace. But as a systematic study directed toward empirically-based theory, political integration has been a major concern of political scientists for less than two decades. During this brief period the scholarly production of case studies, concepts, terms, models and hypotheses has been prodigious. Moreover, contemporary history has obliged students of integration by providing numerous cases in which they might test and compare their explanations and seek to apply their prescriptions.

The difficulties which the study of political integration is now beginning to encounter are of a somewhat different order. It would be surprising if a field in such a formative period were not characterized by an intensity and fertility of theoretical work. But formative periods, in which the outlines of theory are at best dimly perceived, also abound in baffling contradictions, lack of scholarly consensus on basic concepts and methods, and general uncertainty about the criteria for judging the relevance and limitations of various approaches.[1] One writer sums up the resulting sense of both promise and malaise as follows:

'As a contributor to the European integration literature I have more and more come to feel as if I were excavating a small, isolated portion of a large, dimly-perceived mass, the contours of which I could not make out. I know that there are others digging there too, for I can sometimes hear them, but we seldom meet or see each other, and we have seldom organized so as to combine our efforts. What we see as we confront the ever-growing literature on Western European integration is a multitude of events comprising the total economic, political, social, and intellectual life of six countries and the product of their interactions, and a profusion of theories from a variety of disciplines seeking to order these events and make assertions about presumed patterns of persistence or transforma-

---

[1] On these qualities as characteristic of the 'philosophic' stage in many fields of science, see K. W. Deutsch, *The Nerves of Government* (New York: 1966) pp. 3–5. Deutsch's notion of the 'philosophic' and 'empirical' stages of a science resembles Kuhn's description of 'pre-paradigm' and 'normal' science respectively. Cf. T. S. Kuhn, *The Structure of Scientific Revolutions* (Chicago: 1962) esp. pp. 10–11, 16–19 and Chs. 3 and 5. For a provocative application of Kuhn's ideas to political science, see S. S. Wolin, 'Paradigms and Political Theories', in P. King and B. C. Parekh (eds.) *Politics and Experience* (Cambridge: 1968) pp. 125–52.

tion. But the theories hardly ever confront or complement each other or even appear in any clear relationship to each other.'[1]

Integration studies, then, are still in their 'Hundred Flowers' period.[2]

Many scholars have been energetic and imaginative in devising remedies for this condition. There is no shortage of prestigious candidates to provide an overall framework for the study of integration. Essentially each of these proposals centres on a single organizing concept, from which is derived a macro-analytical framework.[3] The assumption seems to be that once the necessary semantic and conceptual readjustments have been made, it will be possible for theorists to combine their efforts, thus introducing an era of 'normal science' in which legions of scholars carry out detailed empirical verification and elaboration of the basic 'paradigm', sustained by a common view of the problems and a consensus on concepts and methods.[4] In this view, then, the sort of order the field requires for further progress toward theory will be obtained through the standardization of concepts, variables and measures – a methodological synthesis rigorous enough to permit causal analysis and prediction by such means as computer simulation.[5]

This book arises from a similar concern with the state of integration studies. It is foremost an essay in interpretation, offering a

[1] L. N. Lindberg, 'The European Community as a Political System', *Journal of Common Market Studies*, 5: 4, 1967, p. 345. Lindberg's remarks, limited to the problem of studying Western European integration, seem even more apposite when the additional concern of integration theorists with comparative studies of regional and global organizations is taken into account. This naturally serves to multiply the problems to which he refers. See, for example, E. B. Haas and P. C. Schmitter, 'Economics and Differential Patterns of Political Integration', in *International Political Communities: An Anthology* (New York: 1966) pp. 259–99; E. B. Haas, 'International Integration: The European and the Universal Process', in *ibid.*, pp. 93–130; J. S. Nye, Jr., 'Comparative Regional Integration: Concept and Measurement', *International Organization*, 22: 4, 1968, pp. 855–80; and A. Etzioni, *Political Unification* (New York: 1965).

[2] L. N. Lindberg and S. A. Scheingold, in the Preface to *International Organization*, 24: 4, 1970, p. vii. This is a special volume on theory and research in regional integration.

[3] Examples are Deutsch's communications-models, most extensively developed in his *Nationalism and Social Communication* (Cambridge, Mass.: 1966) and *The Nerves of Government*; Lindberg's systems-model, developed in 'The European Community as a Political System', *op. cit.*; and the process-models developed by Haas and Schmitter, 'Economics and Differential Patterns of Political Integration', *op. cit.*, and Etzioni, *op. cit.*

[4] See Kuhn, *op. cit.*, Chs. 2–4.

[5] E. B. Haas, 'The Study of Regional Integration: Reflections on the Joy and Anguish of Pre-Theorizing', *International Organization*, 24: 4, 1970, pp. 644–6.

perspective on what has been done in the field, and some proposals as to the direction of future work. It proceeds from the belief that to seek the kind of order described above in the study of integration may be, at best, premature and, at worst, misguided. What integration studies need least at the present stage is to be integrated.

Accordingly, no such overarching conceptual scheme is advanced in the chapters which follow. Instead, an attempt is made to determine not only the areas of compatibility but also the points of difference between the major approaches to integration theory. Beyond a very general notion of what the problem of integration concerns, these efforts are based on no central, organizing concept around which a macro-analytical framework might be fashioned. Contention, after all, may prove more productive intellectually than consensus. That is, at this stage in the development of the field, it would seem potentially more fruitful to identify, acknowledge and sharpen the fundamental differences between various approaches, so that they can be tested through confrontation in the empirical world. Through this procedure scholars may in time converge on the most useful approach, agreeing on its superior theoretical productivity. On the other hand, just as physics supports the existence of two conflicting theories of light – each useful within a certain context – so we may come to have two or more co-existing theories of integration.[1] But by drawing the disorderly collection of approaches we now have into recognizable lines of battle, we can at least suggest where the most important points of contact will be.

What exactly is an 'approach' in this sense? According to one scholar, an approach performs three main 'intellectual functions'.[2] In the first place, it acts as 'a rather systematic and consciously developed set of criteria and procedures to help with the problems of perception.'[3] That is, it guides the scholar in selecting his data, telling him what is of interest, and where and how to find it. Karl Deutsch's concern with the communications process in integration gives him more interest than most theorists in data pertaining to the flows of trade, information and population between countries. This approach, at the same time, leads him to pay comparatively little

---

[1] On the principle of 'complementarity' in the natural sciences, whereby two mutually exclusive theories may be used to explain fully a given phenomenon, see F. W. Matson, *The Broken Image* (Garden City: 1966) Ch. 4, esp. pp. 131–40.

[2] O. R. Young, *Systems of Political Science* (Englewood Cliffs, N. J.: 1968) pp. 8–12.

[3] *Ibid.*, p. 10.

16

attention to the behaviour of interest groups or to the growth of international institutions as elements of the integrative process.[1] The second function of an approach is to provide a framework for the 'intellectual organization' of perceptions.[2] It does this by establishing boundaries of relevance, emphasizing certain variables, ranking data in importance, and generating hypotheses. For example, Etzioni's 'paradigm' postulates that certain sets of variables are more important at one stage of the integrative process than at others.[3] Similarly, Lindberg and Scheingold's systems-model provides a set of interrelated categories into which data about European political processes may be organized, and which, in so doing, incorporates certain prior judgements about the role of each variable in those processes.[4]

These two functions comprise the purely psychological dimension of an approach. In this sense, an approach is a broad intellectual orientation, which may suggest or be associated with certain models, metaphors or analogies, and within which certain conceptual frameworks and methodological predispositions may be characteristic. It thus makes up the cognitive structure, or 'image', through which any individual scholar deals with the world around him.[5]

The third 'intellectual function' of an approach, however, adds an important sociological dimension to the foregoing. An approach provides a common language or framework of communications for those engaged in research. In Young's words, there must be a 'minimal standardization of word meanings, concepts, categories and patterns of explanation' among those accepting a given intellectual orientation.[6] In integration studies, the groups of scholars who draw their inspiration from the work of Deutsch or Haas respectively, seem to an increasing extent to be characterized by this sort of shared symbolic system.[7] An approach, in short, is not simply one man's image of the world, but an intellectual outlook shared by a community of scholars who both cooperate and compete in developing it into a more systematic theory.

The theory to which these communities of scholars aspire is usually seen as some kind of logically interrelated set of general statements capable of empirical testing. It provides descriptions, explanations and often predictions about the empirical world, with

---

[1] See *infra*, Ch. 2. [2] *Ibid.*, pp. 10–11. [3] *Infra*, Ch. 5.
[4] *Infra*, Ch. 4.
[5] See K. E. Boulding, *The Image* (Ann Arbor, Mich.: 1956) esp. Ch. 1; C.A. McClelland, *Theory and the International System* (New York: 1966) pp. 6–16.
[6] Young, *op. cit.*, p. 11. [7] *Infra*, Chs. 2 and 4.

reference to which it is constantly being refined and reformulated.[1] Whether such 'scientific' theory can or ought to be the sole aspiration and preoccupation of political scientists has been, and remains, a contentious issue. Most students of integration quite willingly leave the debate over a 'general theory' of politics to others, and simply assume that it is both necessary and possible to develop islands of 'middle range' theory in such areas as theirs. Whether we can build bridges between these islands and arrive at, say, a general theory of political change which incorporates, among other components, a theory of integration, is a question which ought logically to await the emergence of a body of falsifiable general propositions about integration. Each of the approaches discussed in the following chapters can therefore legitimately be assessed as to its potential in this respect.[2]

Few integration theorists, however, would accept that explanation is the sole or sufficient purpose of theory. Indeed, normative positions are rarely, if at all, disguised in their writings. Integration itself is assumed to be a good thing – a proposition which is understandable if not exactly self-evident. From such general propositions and assumptions, numerous prescriptions flow, although theorists differ considerably as to the emphasis they place on policy-advice. In functionalist writings the advocacy of solutions for specific social and political problems is usually the main object of argument, but it does not necessarily follow that an explanatory theory of integration cannot be found there as well.[3] Conversely, the most self-consciously 'scientific' approaches, such as those of Haas and Deutsch, do not

[1] On the nature of theory see K. R. Popper, *The Logic of Scientific Discovery*, revised edition (London: 1968) esp. Chs. 3 and 4. 'Theories are nets cast to catch what we call "the world": to rationalize, to explain and to master it. We endeavour to make the mesh ever finer and finer.' (p. 59). Cf. E. Nagel, *The Structure of Science* (New York: 1961) Chs. 2, 5 and 6, esp. pp. 90–7; and A. Kaplan, *The Conduct of Inquiry* (San Francisco: 1964) esp. Chs. 8 and 9.

[2] For a rigorous definition which takes the essence of theory in political science to be explanation, see A. Brecht, *Political Theory* (Princeton: 1959) pp. 14–15, 501–2. On the uses and possibilities of theory in international relations, see McClelland, *op. cit.*, Ch. 1, esp. pp. 15–16, and the articles by Rapoport, the Sprouts, and Hoffman in J. N. Rosenau (ed.), *International Politics and Foreign Policy* (New York: 1961) Chs. 5, 7 and 48. For a sceptical view of the claims of scientific theorists, see H. N. Bull, 'International Theory: The Case for a Classical Approach', *World Politics*, 18: 3, 1966, pp. 361–77. Cf. R. Aron, *Peace and War* (New York: 1966) pp. 11–15. On levels of generalization, see C. A. McClelland, 'The Social Sciences, History, and International Relations', in Rosenau, *op. cit.*, pp. 33–4, and Hoffman, 'International Relations: The Long Road to Theory', *ibid.*, pp. 421–37.

[3] See *infra*, Ch. 3.

preclude (and often in fact encourage) the derivation of policy-advice by those engaged in the politics of integration. In short, the normative foundations and prescriptive uses of theory are a part of the total fabric of an approach, and to examine them critically may aid an understanding of its explanatory components.[1]

The analysis and interpretation in the next four chapters proceeds on the assumption that there are three main sources for the development of theory in any approach, each of which suggests a distinctive critical method. The first source is what might be called the 'intellectual environment', by which is meant the tradition of thought in a particular field, as well as certain ideas in related disciplines. The appropriate critical method here might be called 'genealogical', and is, of course, familiar to students of political theory, literature and the history of ideas. It involves tracing the antecedents of concepts, assumptions or explanatory patterns either in the history of a discipline or in fields with which it overlaps. In its conservative vein, this critical method can be used to place seemingly new approaches or radical ideas in perspective by showing their debt to some venerable line of thought.[2] In a more radical vein it can be used to point out suggestive analogies linking two fields of study, thereby underlining the potential of an interdisciplinary focus.[3]

The second source of theory is in the 'internal' development of the concepts and their logical relations. As has been the case with economic theory, and, to a lesser extent, with some branches of sociology, testable explanatory propositions can be developed by the manipulation of conceptual variables and their relations by means of a logical or mathematical calculus. The appropriate critical method is of the same order, and seeks to point out inconsistencies, redundancies and other logical or structural flaws in the argument. To do this, it is necessary to trace and make more explicit the line of reasoning in a theoretical system. Such exercises, of course, are common in political and social science. In the study of international organization, a classic model of this critical method can be found in the work of Inis Claude.[4]

[1] On these points, see Haas, 'The Study of Regional Integration', *op. cit.*, pp. 608–10.

[2] A good example is the argument that behavioural theorists of international relations owe much to the rationalistic optimism of the Enlightenment or to nineteenth-century liberalism. See K. N. Waltz, *Man, the State and War* (New York: 1959), esp. pp. 73–4.

[3] Such an intellectual operation is fundamental to the relatively young discipline of cybernetics. See Deutsch, *The Nerves of Government*, esp. Ch. 5.

[4] I. L. Claude, Jr., *Swords into Plowshares*, 3rd edition (New York: 1964).

The third source for the development of a theory is in the 'real world' – that is, in the experience of attempts to explain, predict or act on the basis of the theory as it stands at a given time. This process of theoretical growth through 'feedback' has two related aspects. The first concerns application of the theory in the sense of testing, as in a laboratory. In this case, predictions are drawn from the theory, juxtaposed to observed events in the real world, and either confirmed tentatively or falsified – the latter outcome calling for revision of the theory.[1] To criticize an approach in this sense involves judging the significance of any such tests already carried out, and the extent to which its dependent propositions are testable and hence scientifically useful.

The other aspect concerns the pragmatic test, which is particularly relevant for the social sciences. This test has to do with the experience accumulated from attempts to carry out prescriptions derived from the theory. Again, this experience may modify the theory itself. That these two operational aspects of theory are interrelated, is perhaps best illustrated in the history of economic thought.[2] But the latter aspect, that of practical relevance, is especially important for a field such as integration theory, where the object of study is a process of political change often consciously being engineered by governments or international organizations.[3]

The first part of this book is an attempt to trace out a pattern of order in the field of integration studies by identifying, interpreting and criticizing several approaches which have in them the promise of theory. Clearly, from what has been said about the state of the field, to accommodate even a limited number of its theorists in such a framework will require a rather broad working definition of integration.

One of the symptoms of the current fragmentation of the field is the proliferation of definitions of integration which, although presented in general terms, turn out on closer examination to be rather narrowly focused. Such a proliferation is not undesirable in itself. What is unfortunate is that groups of scholars tend to equate the

[1] Popper, *op. cit.*, Chs. 4 and 6.

[2] See W. J. Barber, *A History of Economic Thought* (Harmondsworth, Middx.: 1967) esp. pp. 11–15.

[3] This suggests useful comparisons with the study of such processes as economic development or conflict-resolution, where there is (or ought to be) a particularly strong interplay between theoretical knowledge and practical experience. On the problem of 'relevance' in international theory generally, see A. A. Said (ed.), *Theory of International Relations* (Englewood Cliffs, N.J.: 1968) and J. C. Farrell and A. P. Smith, (eds.), *Theory and Reality in International Relations* (New York: 1967).

progress of the field with the progress of their own particular approach and to ignore scholars whose work begins with different premises and definitions. Integration studies thus proceed along a number of parallel tracks, and passengers rarely transfer from one train to another. In such a situation of mutual incomprehension, productive scholarly debate – let alone cooperation – is hardly possible.

Rather than complicate things further by suggesting yet another *a priori* definition, then, it might be useful to start from what seems to be the lowest common denominator among the many views already well developed. That common denominator appears to be very low indeed. All it seems possible to say is that international political integration is *a process whereby a group of people, organized initially in two or more independent nation-states, come to constitute a political whole which can in some sense be described as a community*. Clearly such a definition is not, by itself, very enlightening; it does, however, offer some clues as to how we might set about identifying the major approaches to integration theory.

Even on this level of generality, it is possible to ask two fairly concrete questions. First, to what sort of political whole or community is this process of change expected to lead? And secondly, what are the major conditions which bring the process about? On the basis of their answers to these two questions, it is possible to group most of the important writers on international integration into four general approaches. A pattern – albeit a rough one – becomes discernible in the field.

Let us take the question of the end-product first. In the literature on international integration it is possible to isolate two broad types of political whole or communal relationship in which theorists expect the integrative process to culminate. These can be termed the 'state-model' and the 'community-model'. In strictly institutional terms, the state-model is more specific and more demanding than the community-model. Federalist writers, in particular, emphasize the need to arrive at a particular type of constitutional arrangement before a system can be described as integrated. Neofunctionalist writers, while not always insisting on federalism, generally envisage some form of supranationality. For others, the emergent political community has many attributes of a highly centralized state.[1]

In the 'community-model', on the other hand, more stress is placed on the character of the relationships between the peoples – both the elites and the general publics – whose states have been

[1] See, for example, Etzioni, *op. cit.*, p. 4.

involved in a process of integration. The emergence of political institutions is considered less important than the growth of certain common values, perceptions and habits. For some writers the growth of this type of community can be compatible with the continuation of the nation-state system, and merely alters the way in which states deal with each other. For others, such as the functionalists, the emergence of a community is accompanied by a new, flexible type of organization which does away with the nation-state as a political form.

The second question arising from our definition has to do with the conditions contributing to the process of integration. To put it another way, we can distinguish writers on integration according to the types of independent variables which they use to explain the process of change. Again it is possible to discern two broad groups of theorists. In the first of these, interest tends to focus directly on political variables – on problems concerning the power, responsiveness and control of political elites, and on the political habits of the general public. Much of the analysis is pitched at the level of the states, which are seen as the main units on whose disposition the progress of integration depends. The writings of the 'pluralists' and the federalists tend to fall into this category. The other group, by contrast, focuses on the economic, social and technological factors which, by much less direct processes, are said to bring about political change. The functionalists and their intellectual descendants, the neofunctionalists, share this image of an incremental process of political change based on the need to resolve social and economic problems. Here the analysis tends to be pitched at the level of the integrating system as a whole.

On the basis of the minimal definition of integration suggested earlier, it is possible, therefore, to arrive at a two-fold classification which accommodates a broad range of writings on integration. Because these two types of classification cut across the field in different ways, it is perhaps most useful to represent them schematically as follows:

		END-PRODUCT	
		STATE-MODEL	COMMUNITY-MODEL
INTEGRATIVE PROCESS	DIRECT – Political Variables	Federalism	Pluralism
	INDIRECT – Socio-Economic Variables	Neo-functionalism	Functionalism

It will be argued in the next four chapters that each of these four cells represents a distinctive approach to the problem of international political integration. In each cell there is a core of values and assumptions, a concept of the purpose and product of integration, an explanation of the process of change, and an identifiable community of scholars whose ideas and exchanges constitute the nucleus around which the approach is centred.

The purpose of this book, however, is not simply to identify, interpret and criticize these approaches separately, but also to show the compatibilities and contradictions between their views of integration. In this way, it might be possible to show where they can re-inforce each other, as well as where they are bound to produce conflicting hypotheses which can only be sorted out through empirical testing. For the purposes of this exercise in comparison, each of the four critical chapters is constructed in a similar manner. The first section concentrates on the concept of the end-product, or the political whole which integration is said to produce. The attempt is made to relate this concept to the intellectual traditions and sources of the approach, and to the values and assumptions about political life on which it is based. The argument as to the distinctive quality of each approach thus turns on a genealogical and conceptual criticism of the way in which its practitioners derive their view of community.

The second section of each chapter is an examination of the dynamic part of each approach – its explanation of the integrative process. Here again the two critical methods – genealogical and conceptual – reinforce each other. As in the first section, the links are explored between integration theory and international relations theory generally – both classical and behavioural.

Clearly one of the main problems in integration theory has always been the need for a scheme in which to order the multitude of variables which from time to time have been adduced to explain the process of change. A useful method, suggested by the work of a number of writers on international relations theory, would be to classify them according to the level of analysis at which they seem most appropriate.[1]

The first level of analysis is that of the group of states as a whole, viewed as a system. Just as some theorists explain war as the inevitable product of an ungoverned, decentralized international system, so integration can be described as occurring because a certain pattern of communications or a certain common social need pervades the system, or because this system possesses the attributes of a rudimentary polity. The second level of analysis is that of the states taken as separate entities. Here, just as wars have been traced to the existence of certain types of states – autocracies, capitalist states, fascist states, underdeveloped states, dissatisfied states – so integration is often claimed to be more likely if a certain type of state, having, for example, a developed liberal economy and a pluralistic society, is involved. A third level of analysis, finally, is that of the individual. In integration theory, the equivalent of tracing the source of war to the minds of men is to explain the emergence of 'community' as a product of some kind of 'social learning' whereby individuals change their attitudes and behaviour toward their neighbours.

In each approach it is possible to find major theoretical assumptions or propositions on all of these levels of analysis. On the whole, as suggested above, integration theory (like international theory generally) has placed most of its stress on the first two – the system and the states. But the four approaches differ considerably as to which variables they employ at each level, and as to which level merits the most attention. The third level has to date received comparatively less emphasis. As the social psychology of international relations develops, however, many of the implicit propositions of integration theory at this level are likely to appear in testable form. Comparing the four approaches on each of these levels allows us to see where they confront each other on specific issues of explanation.

In the third and final section of each chapter, we turn to criticize

[1] On the 'level-of-analysis' issue, see J. D. Singer, 'The Level-of-Analysis Problem in International Relations', in K. Knorr and S. Verba (eds.), *The International System* (Princeton: 1961) pp. 77–92. Cf. Waltz, *op. cit.*, Chs. 1, 2, 4, 6, 8, and K. J. Holsti, *International Politics: A Framework for Analysis* (Englewood Cliffs, N.J.: 1967) esp. pp. 15–17.

the operational features of the four approaches, that is, their adequacy in explaining integration and guiding the policies of those who would bring it about. As was observed earlier, theorists of integration are increasingly turning to study and compare regional organizations in many parts of the world. Undoubtedly, as our understanding of these cases grows, our views about the adequacy of each approach will change. In the meantime, however, postwar Europe, and Western Europe in particular, remains the richest source of historical evidence by which to judge theoretical explanations and prescriptions. An unrivalled concentration of analysis and documentation, dealing with a wide variety of attempts to integrate groups of states, makes Europe an invaluable testing-ground for these approaches.

In none of the four chapters does this last section constitute an historical sketch or a detailed institutional analysis of the European integration movement: that in itself is a task worth several volumes. The focus here is rather different. Some European organizations, movements or policies can be traced directly to one particular theory of integration; others, clearly embodying compromises between representatives of two or more approaches, can be read in several ways; others still, growing out of more haphazard, pragmatic political arrangements, are difficult to attribute to any approach, although their subsequent impact may have been considerable. This section, then, is intended as an interpretive exercise, to trace the relationships between the development of each approach and the fate of its explanations and prescriptions in the post-war European context.

The first part of the book, as a critical comparative analysis, naturally is concerned with what has been achieved to date in understanding integration. In imposing a rough form of order on the field we become better able to judge where the vital theoretical issues lie. The second part of the book turns to consider some of these issues. It represents an attempt, not so much to synthesize a new approach, but rather to show that the four approaches are to some extent complementary – that they deal with different facets of a total phenomenon whose shape we can only dimly discern at present. A sense of this complementarity, and an indication as to future research areas, arises if we set a number of the explanatory propositions most frequently found in the literature in a broad framework employing the three levels of analysis. This framework also draws in sharper relief the major theoretical issues where the approaches often clash. Here the wider literature of international relations theory is helpful in suggesting ways to resolve these questions.

PART I
Approaches to Integration Theory

2 The Pluralist Approach: Integration as the Growth of a Community of States

The Pluralistic Community

International political integration is frequently identified with the circumvention, reduction or abolition of the sovereign power of modern nation-states. It is somewhat surprising and paradoxical, therefore, to discover that one of the oldest and most widespread views of integration reaffirms the nation-states as the bases of international life and envisages the emergence of an international community through improvement of the ways in which they regulate their relationships with each other. The advocates of this view find valuable many of those characteristics of the international system which, according to other theorists, are the prime candidates for elimination.

In this approach, integration is seen essentially as the formation of a 'community of states', defined by a high and self-sustaining level of diplomatic, economic, social and cultural exchange between its members. The states are engaged in a continuous process of sensitive adjustment to each other's actions, supported usually (although not necessarily) by the socio-political behaviour and attitudes of their populations. There is, however, no suggestion that those common institutions which might emerge to facilitate international cooperation and communication, represent the embryo of a supranational state, or are able to act independently of the will of the constituent states. International organizations, rather, are assigned the sort of role described by Inis Claude: in short term, lubricating the management of power by states in a system of more or less stable equilibrium; in the longer term, perhaps helping 'to limit the abusive aspects of state behaviour which balance of power operations may otherwise entail' and building the economic and social basis for new forms of international order.[1]

[1] I. L. Claude, Jr., 'The Management of Power in the Changing United Nations', *International Organization*, 15: 2, 1961, p. 235. See also his description of the UN as a 'synthetic neutral', in *The Changing United Nations* (New York: 1967) p. 121.

Such an image of international community is clearly a felicitous combination of the values of national self-determination on the one hand, and international peace and security on the other. This, no doubt, accounts for its continuing popularity both among statesmen and among academics. It dominates one of the earliest and most important systematic approaches to a theory of international integration.[1] It finds expression in the policies of most Western European states, and in the assumptions of most policy-makers about international life. And finally, it has a pedigree in the history of thought on international organization which reaches back to the era of the Greek city-states.[2]

Among the major theorists of integration, Karl Deutsch perhaps best represents this approach. In the oldest tradition of international theory, he has concerned himself foremost with the problem of developing peaceful relations among states. At the beginning of his major study of integration, he writes: 'Since our study deals with the problem of ensuring peace, we shall say that any political community, be it amalgamated or pluralistic, was eventually successful if it became a security-community – that is, if it achieved integration – and that is was unsuccessful if it ended eventually in secession or civil war.[3] What is essential for integration, then, is not a particular kind of formal institutional change, but the attainment of peace and security in the international system.

The emphasis on integration as the disposition of states to resolve their difficulties without recourse to arms, rather than as some new formal characteristic of the international system, is particularly strong in the basic definitions from which Deutsch's study departs: (1) a 'security-community' is a group of people which has become 'integrated'; (2) 'integration' means the attainment, within a territory, of a 'sense of community' and of institutions and practices strong enough and widespread enough to assure, for a 'long' time, depend-

---

[1] For the seminal works in this approach, see K. W. Deutsch, *Political Community at the International Level* (New York: 1954) and K. W. Deutsch, *et al.*, *Political Community and the North Atlantic Area* (Princeton: 1957). The theoretical essence of the latter book is reprinted in *International Political Communities: An Anthology* (New York: 1966) pp. 1–91, from which the citations which follow are taken.

[2] Useful historical surveys of thought on international organization can be found in F. H. Hinsley, *Power and the Pursuit of Peace* (Cambridge: 1963) and A. B. Bozeman, *Politics and Culture in International History* (Princeton: 1960). For a discussion of Hellenic concepts of integration see esp. Bozeman, *op. cit.*, pp. 77–89.

[3] Deutsch, 'Political Community and the North Atlantic Area,' *op. cit.*, p. 3.

able expectations of peaceful change among its population; (3) 'sense of community' means a belief on the part of individuals in a group that they have come to agreement on at least this one point: that common social problems must and can be resolved by processes of 'peaceful change'; (4) 'peaceful change' means the resolution of social problems, normally by institutionalized procedures, without resort to large-scale physical force.[1]

Deutsch's concept of the 'security-community', then, refers to a type of international system – not simply one whose members are highly interdependent, but one whose members do not contemplate resolving their conflicts of interest through violence.[2] Integration has to do with the 'ultimate task' of converting the world into 'a pluralistic society marked by high adjustment potential – by the existence of component parts which are susceptible of regulation in their relationships with each other and with the whole, through the process of political accommodation.'[3]

Not all theorists who see integration similarly – as a condition of the international system compatible with formally uncompromised sovereignty – necessarily accept the primacy of the 'peace and security' problem. One writer, for example, defining integration simply as 'an instrumentality of the modern multi-state system', sees it very broadly as the methods and forms of cooperation among nations.[4] Clearly such cooperation could be for may purposes besides security in the military or political sense. It could be manifested in such arrangements as confederacies, where institutions are set up through which 'individual governments, acting on behalf of their own countries, accept certain procedures for arriving at joint decisions which they are prepared to carry out afterwards through their own

[1] *Ibid.*, p. 2. An earlier form of this definition of integration can be found in R. W. Van Wagenen, *Research in the International Organization Field*: *Some Notes on a Possible Focus* (Princeton: 1952) pp. 10–11.

[2] In some of his more recent writings, Deutsch rather contradicts his earlier concept of integration. Any system, he suggests, is integrated because, by definition, its units are interdependent. Political integration is a relationship in which the political behaviour of one unit is modified by the behaviour of another. A relationship of integration, or 'community' thus exists not only between cooperative and mutually responsive states, but also between states locked in conflict: K. W. Deutsch, *The Analysis of International Relations* (Englewood Cliffs, N.J.: 1968) pp. 158–61. This formulation also seems inconsistent with the operative notion of integration underlying the last four chapters of Deutsch's text. See *ibid.*, pp. 158–202.

[3] I. L. Claude, *Power and International Relations* (New York: 1962) p. 284.

[4] E. Plischke (ed.), *Systems of Integrating the International Community* (Princeton: 1964) p. 5.

31

instrumentalities.'[1] As Beloff notes, such an idea is at the heart of the Gaullist vision of Europe.[2] While the Gaullists have stressed the issues of foreign and military policy, they have not hesitated to put forward their confederal model as appropriate for areas of European policy less directly concerned with security.

In general, however, peace and security are the prime political ends for which integration of this type is advocated. As is made clear in Deutsch's chain of definitions, the basic criterion of integration is the sense of community and the persistence of peaceful methods of conflict-resolution among states. An international system with such qualities may, by the standards of many other theorists of integration, appear rather primitive,[3] since the restraints on national autonomy are neither legal nor institutional, but political, and since the persistence of community depends less on the development of a specific form of common political institution than on the continuing capacities of the individual states to regulate their interactions.

For the purposes of peace and security, then, a 'pluralistic' rather than an 'amalgamated' security-community may well suffice and prove less costly politically. Much of the North Atlantic study is devoted to description and comparison of the conditions necessary and sufficient for each form of community, and indeed Deutsch does not discount the possibility that, as in the cases of Switzerland (1848) and the United States (1787), federal institutions may eventually emerge from looser confederations. But although he is aware of the advantages of these more centralized models of integration, he finds persuasive the evidence that pluralistic communities often emerged and survived under far less favourable conditions than those required by amalgamated communities.[4] Fewer of the 'essential conditions', in short, proved necessary to achieve the basic ends. The findings of the study, based on analysis of historical cases of integration, tended 'to bring out the very considerable potentialities of pluralistic security-communities for overcoming even partially unfavourable background situations.[5] For those who, like Deutsch, are mindful of the tenacity of the nation-state and concerned primarily with preserving peace in the international system, the less ambitious but

[1] M. Beloff, 'International Integration and the Modern State', *Journal of Common Market Studies*, 2: 1, 1963, p. 58.

[2] *Ibid.*, p. 59.

[3] See, for example, the comments of A. Etzioni, *Political Unification* (New York: 1965) p. 6 n.

[4] Deutsch, 'Political Community and the North Atlantic Area,' *op. cit.*, esp. pp. 10–12 and pp. 44–8. [5] *Ibid.*, pp. 47–8.

more stable pluralistic form of community must seem both a pragmatic and realistic aspiration.

It is not surprising that the Gaullist vision of Europe, deriving from similar assumptions about national sovereignty, the primacy of security and the need for diplomatic and strategic cooperation of a classic type, should be limited to the similarly pluralistic forms of 'political union' or 'l'Europe des Patries'. Occasionally, as with Deutsch, it is suggested that pluralism of this kind may be merely a way-station or a means to some federalist form in the speculative future. 'L'Europe des Patries', in the words of one slogan, may gradually give way to 'une Patrie européenne.'[1] De Gaulle, in his usual delphic fashion, hinted at a three-stage process of 'equilibrium', 'cooperation' and 'union'.[2] These stages could be taken as corresponding to, first, the classic balance-of-power system, second, the sort of pluralistic security-system proposed in the Fouchet Plans, and finally a full 'political union', perhaps even of a federal form. It hardly needs saying that the values and assumptions of Gaullist thinkers, and indeed, of most European policy-makers at the present time, do not encourage speculation beyond the second stage. There is a close affinity in this respect between these policy-makers and the 'realist' school of international theorists, who deny the viability of supranationalism in the face of states engaged in the struggle for power, and who attack the illusions and pretensions of those who see European or world government emerging from international organizations. In the eyes of the political 'realist', the conditions that render anything beyond pluralistic integration possible are likely also to render it unnecessary.[3]

Despite its lack of strong central institutions, the pluralistic system espoused by these theorists as the feasible and desirable goal of integration is often described as a 'political community' or 'political union'. In Gaullist usage particularly, the latter expression most often refers to 'one particular kind of institutional arrangement which would, through consultation among the six governments, facilitate the adoption of common positions on foreign and defence policy'.[4]

---

[1] Quoted in C. Johnson, 'De Gaulle's Europe', *Journal of Common Market Studies*, 1: 2, 1962, p. 166.

[2] Ambassade de France à Londres: Service de Presse et d'Information, *Excerpt from the Press Conference Given by General de Gaulle* (Paris: 21 February 1966) p. 2.

[3] For classic arguments along these lines, see H. J. Morgenthau, *Politics Among Nations*, 4th edition (New York: 1967) Chs. 27–9; I. L. Claude, Jr., *Swords into Plowshares*, 3rd edition (New York: 1964) Chs. 18 and 19; R. Aron, *Peace and War* (New York: 1966) Ch. 24.

[4] S. J. Bodenheimer, *Political Union: A Microcosm of European Politics 1960–66* (Leyden: 1967) p. 18.

Politics, in this sense, has primarily to do with the diplomatic and strategic spheres. It deals with the security of the state or the preservation of its capacity for autonomous decision. For Deutsch, politics is essentially 'the area of enforceable decisions or, more accurately, of all decisions backed by some combination of a significant probability of voluntary compliance with a significant probability of enforcement. . . . '[1] Now the international political system consists of a number of nation-states, or decision-centres with a high degree of self-determination and a generally high probability that their decisions, internally, will meet with compliance or be enforceable. But between nation-states, habits of compliance and means of enforcement are far less regularized or certain, and international politics, for a state, tend to be more centrally concerned with problems of influencing the behaviour of other states while resisting encroachments on its own decision-making autonomy.[2] In practice this tends to narrow the notion of the political, on the international level, to what Aron calls 'diplomatic-strategic' action or what Hoffman has referred to as 'high politics'.[3]

This concept of politics, implied in Deutsch's writings, central to the 'political realists', and most explicit in the common association of 'political union' with cooperation on matters of national security and foreign policy, differs fundamentally from that generally accepted by theorists in the neofunctionalist and federalist traditions. For most of these writers, politics is not associated with a particular type of subject or issue, be it economic, social, military or diplomatic. If anything, 'political union' connotes the formation, in a group of states, of a common, democratically-controlled system of institutions for making decisions on a whole range of issues.[4] The denial of this latter idea of politics by the theorists espousing more pluralistic forms of integration is clearly of a piece with, and essential to, their

[1] K. W. Deutsch, *The Nerves of Government* (New York: 1966) p. 254. For an elaboration of this 'dualistic' concept of politics see Deutsch, *The Analysis of International Relations*, pp. 17–20.

[2] K. W. Deutsch, 'The Impact of Communications Upon International Relations Theory', in A. A. Said (ed.), *Theory of International Relations* (Englewood Cliffs, N.J.: 1968) pp. 90–2.

[3] Aron, *op. cit.*, pp. 5–8, 88–93. S. Hoffman, 'European Process at Atlantic Crosspurposes', *Journal of Common Market Studies*, 3: 2, 1965, pp. 89–91.

[4] A forceful argument for this view is in U. W. Kitzinger, *The Politics and Economics of European Integration* (New York: 1963) pp. 62–3. Good statements of the difficulties arising from confusion of these two notions of political union are in M. Camps, *What Kind of Europe?* (London: 1965) p. 89, and in D. Sidjanski, 'Federal Aspects of the European Community', in J. D. Montgomery and A. Smithies (eds.), *Public Policy*, 14 (Cambridge, Mass.: 1965) pp. 417–18.

argument that no smooth progression can be guaranteed between cooperation in technical or 'low-political' areas and cooperation on matters of 'high politics'.

The priority of international peace and national security, and the association of politics with diplomatic-strategic action, are thus two important premises of the pluralist conception of integration. As suggested, these ideas complement a third important premise – the belief that the nation-state is both the central fact of modern political life and the central focus of all political analysis. This belief may be presented as the outcome of clear-eyed empirical observation of the hard realities of international politics; it may also verge on a more mystical, emotional attachment, such as has been expressed well, but by no means exclusively, by General de Gaulle.[1]

Few of these writers look upon the nation-state without some feelings of ambivalence – a kind of tragic sense which seems to derive from an underlying philosophical pessimism. For, despite its virtues as a political, economic, social and cultural unit, the nation-state has also been associated with an era of warfare on an unprecedented scale of destructiveness. Even in the work of Deutsch, where there flows a strong stream of the rationalistic optimism of social science, this ambivalence is present. A concern with the sources and development of nationalism and nation-states coexists throughout his writings with his concern for international order; it is clear from his recent writings that he is not optimistic about the trends he has discerned toward further national preoccupations and away from international community.[2] Nevertheless, if their feelings about the nation-state are often mixed, the pluralists base their analysis of integration firmly on an awareness of its dominance as a political form in recent history and in the foreseeable future.

From this emphasis on the nation-state both as an analytical unit and as a political value, several consequences follow. In the first

[1] See, for example, the well-known passage in C. de Gaulle, *Mémoires de Guerre*, Vol. 1 (Paris: 1954) pp. 5–6. Cf. Kitzinger, *op. cit.*, p. 91. Good discussions of the Gaullist doctrine concerning national states can be found in A. Grosser, *French Foreign Policy under de Gaulle* (Boston: 1967) and D. Pickles, 'French Foreign Policy' in F. S. Northedge (ed.), *The Foreign Policies of the Powers* (London: 1968) pp. 187–220.

[2] Deutsch, 'The Impact of Communications Upon International Relations Theory', in Said, *op. cit.*, pp. 87–92: see also Deutsch's 'Introduction' to the paperback edition of *Nationalism and Social Communication* (Cambridge, Mass.: 1966) pp. 1–4. This book, first published in 1953, before he turned to the study of international integration, remains the basic source for his ideas on the growth of nations and other political communities.

place, as pointed out, integration tends to be defined as a condition of the international system in which the nation-states are preserved. Indeed it is argued that international peace and security on the one hand and the full development of the nation-state as a political form on the other are not, as is often suggested, contradictory goals but are in fact complementary. In an integrated international system, or 'community of states', national diversity, autonomy and development on the one hand, and international stability on the other, would be mutually reinforcing.

For the pluralists, then, part of the solution to the problem of war lies on the national level. Peace, or integration, will be enhanced, not by the elimination of states, but by their development. Such, however, is not the whole answer. Many of these theorists also note that wars have occurred repeatedly in the most developed regions of the world. Hence, a second aspect of the problem is to improve the conduct of relations between these developed states. It is not the existence of the multi-state system as such that is taken to be the source of war, but the persistent malfunctioning of that system. The key to improving the system is sought in quantitative and qualitative change of the interactions and communications between its units.[1] Integration thus involves the end, not of the states, but of the 'state of war' among them.

It should be clear from this that the pluralist approach to integration draws on a number of traditions of international thought. In the first place, it has close affinities to the 'realist' school, which rejects dramatic therapeutic approaches to peace and places, instead, a great premium on the traditional virtues of diplomacy. Both the struggle for power and the conflict of diverse national interests being unchanging ingredients of international politics, the maintenance of peace and security requires, on all sides, the seasoned diplomat's skill in blending his instinct for national advantage with his desire for the pacific settlement of disputes. This image of international life probably has its origins in our somewhat stylized picture of the diplomatic systems of Renaissance Italy or eighteenth-century Europe. According to this picture, for the diplomat seeking national advantage, war is simply Clausewitz's 'policy by other means'; for the diplomat seeking pacific settlement, it is an unfortunate breakdown

---

[1] In this respect, pluralist theories of international order have equivalents in some recent writings on the problem of political stability in culturally diverse national societies. See, for example, the theory of 'Consociational Democracy' developed by Arend Lijphart in *World Politics*, 21: 2, 1969, pp. 207–25.

or failure of diplomatic skills. In neither case is it regarded as the product of more fundamental social or economic ills which the state is no longer adequate to handle. For although he may accept that the nation-state as a political structure hinders global welfare, or that the international system is inherently a threat to security, the pluralist agrees with the 'realist' that, men and their political forms being more or less imperfectable, it is on balance less misleading to rely on prudent statecraft for the preservation of peace, than it is to rely on the hope of dramatic structural changes.[1]

Having concurred with this 'realist' position, however, many pluralists would then go on to argue that it no longer suffices simply to assume that diplomatic skills will somehow evolve to meet the need: the functioning of the international system can be improved, and a community of states created and maintained, by the application of social-scientific knowledge in certain areas of foreign policy and diplomacy. Much contemporary work on international relations – particularly that associated with 'peace theory' or 'conflict-research' – operates on the assumption that integration can be brought about by developing the capacities of states to handle information about their political environment and to adjust to each other's behaviour. Deutsch's emphasis on the role of social communications in integration, as well as his use of information theory in analysing decision-making, thus serves to link integration theory with the work of such writers as Boulding and Burton.[2]

Not only this close relationship with peace theory, but also their preference for models of integration which do not compromise the essential sovereign power of states, puts the pluralists in probably the oldest tradition of thought about international order. The history of European peace plans is replete with confederal, cooperative or pluralistic models designed to end internecine wars or enhance European security against external forces without infringing on the self-determination of the states concerned. Most of these plans – such as those of Dubois, Sully, Penn or St. Pierre – envisaged no federal structures or majority voting, but were more like alliances, collective

[1] Morgenthau, *op. cit.*, Chs. 31–2; Aron, *op. cit.*, Part IV; Claude, *op. cit.*, Ch. 19, esp. pp. 402–6. After exhaustive criticisms of various approaches to international order, each of these authors turns finally to rely on the quality of statecraft and diplomacy as the soundest source of peace.

[2] Cf. K. E. Boulding, *Conflict and Defense* (New York: 1962); J. W. Burton, *International Relations: A General Theory* (Cambridge: 1965). Peace theory, of which these books are representative, often expresses a pluralist viewpoint, taking the nation-states as irreducible entities and concentrating on developing habits of adjustment and conflict resolution between them.

security systems or periodic conferences of scrupulously equal heads of state.[1] In many cases, these plans were thinly-disguised attempts to set up formal groupings of states which, while nominally based on sovereign equality or on the principle of 'influence according to contribution', were in effect instruments to ensure the hegemony of one state in Europe. That most of these plans came from French pens reflects the long-standing dominance of that state in European politics and provides something of a perspective on current French proposals for 'political union'. In any case, the advocates of confederal schemes or systems of collective security share with the pluralists the belief in the persistence of national sovereignty not merely as a legal fiction but as a political, economic, military and technological reality to be accommodated in organizing the peace.

To sum up, then, the goal of political integration, according to the pluralist writers, is an international system of developed nation-states which, while it lacks anything resembling common institutions of government, is marked by a high degree of communication and 'mutual responsiveness'[2] between its members, such that the resolution of conflicts through violence is inconceivable in the foreseeable future. Clearly, if it is to mean anything, the pluralist model must refer to something more than the minimal, truce-like forms of peace by which, historically, most international systems have been characterized. There have been numerous pacts, leagues, confederations and treaties of cooperation which have foundered on the rocks of national interest, discovered afresh by one or more signatories and invoked through such established doctrines as *rebus sic stantibus* or, more crudely, through unilateral denunciations. To be truly integrated in the pluralist sense, then, the states would have to form a 'community'. That is, their sense of obligation to one another would have to be rooted in deeper soil than international law or the traditional sources of international compliance. It would have ultimately to be rooted in what Deutsch calls 'we-feeling', or a sense of common culture based on intense interactions and communications between all levels of the societies in question.[3]

The existence of this sort of underlying 'sense of community' and of national interests that are fundamentally compatible would also

[1] For details, see Hinsley, *op. cit.*, Part 1, esp. Chs. 1–3.
[2] For an attempt to operationalize the concept of responsiveness, see B. M. Russett, *Community and Contention* (Cambridge, Mass.: 1963) esp. p. 39.
[3] Deutsch, 'Political Community and the North Atlantic Area', *op. cit.*, pp. 17–18.

seem to be a necessary assumption of those who would emphasize the integrative effects of skilful diplomacy or of efforts to improve the information-handling capacities and the responsiveness of states. In the classic notion of diplomacy, there is a certain antagonism between the values of international peace and national advantage, the resolution of which depends very often on whether the state concerned is a 'status quo' or a 'revisionist' power.[1] Diplomacy as an instrument or expression of integration is clearly to play the former, conservative role, concerning the preservation of peace and order in the international system. Its success, however, assumes some agreement among the states as to the basic values and the type of system they wish to preserve. Similarly, an increase, on the diplomatic level, of information about, and responsiveness to, other states, would be unlikely to lead to integration unless it were based upon, and revealed, deeper compatibilities of interest and of cultural traits.

Thus the 'community of states' envisaged by the pluralists as the goal of integration is not simply a dressed-up version of the Grotian 'society of nations.'[2] Nor can it be described fully in the standard diplomatic vernacular which refers to 'close', 'cordial' or 'friendly' relations between states. Nor, finally, do the notions of '*détente*' (as between the United States and the Soviet Union) or '*rapprochement*' (as between France and Germany) imply anything as deep as a 'community'. All these latter terms merely mark (or mask) temporary conditions in the ebb and flow of diplomatic relations, whereas a 'community of states' requires a firm basis of social, economic and cultural ties unlikely to be dissolved rapidly. The familar term which perhaps comes closest to describing this sort of community is 'special relationship', which evokes a sense of the intuitive partnership, and of the total inconceivability of war, between the states so described.

The Integrative Process

Having examined the notion of the integrated international system as conceived by the pluralists, and drawn out some of the values and assumptions on which it is based, we must turn now to analyse their

[1] A classic illustration is the difference between Bismarck's diplomacy before and after the Franco-Prussian war. See D. Thomson, *Europe Since Napoleon* (Harmondsworth, Middx.: 1966) p. 524.

[2] See H. N. Bull, 'The Grotian Conception of International Society', in H. Butterfield and M. Wight (eds.), *Diplomatic Investigations* (London: 1966) pp. 51–73.

explanations of the process by which a group of states evolves from Hobbesian anarchy to Deutschian community. These explanations of the integrative process can be examined in terms of our three levels of analysis – the system, the states and the individual.

i) The System: Communications and Interaction as Structure

On the systemic level, the relevant questions concern how the patterns of relationships between states affect the level of integration between them, and how increased integration becomes evident in these patterns. In the view of one major exponent of the systems approach to international relations, 'integration' is a regulatory process in the international system in which units merge or cooperate to satisfy 'system needs' (i.e., the needs of the system as a whole, or of individual subsystems).[1] The importance of integrative processes and the 'integrative role' varies with the type of system: it is least in the 'unit veto' system, slight but evident in the 'balance of power' system, active in many directions in the 'bipolar' types of system, and most pronounced in the 'universal' and 'hierarchical' systems.[2] Integration, it seems from Kaplan's work, may transform a system to one of the last two types; generally, however, it need not imply such a major structural change but may simply serve to regulate the functioning and enhance the stability of the type of system in which it occurs. Thus even in a classic 'balance of power' system, it is possible to discern various integrative processes taking place and various integrative roles being played.[3]

Kaplan's view of integrative processes in the international system complements and indeed resembles the pluralist view: integration is a process of mutual regulation of behaviour among independent 'subsystems' in an international system. Just as the pluralists allow for the possibility of more centralized forms of system evolving from the 'community of states', so Kaplan suggests that systems can in principle change toward the hierarchical or universal forms. In both cases, however, the more centralized types of system are presented as purely hypothetical or speculative possibilities. 'Real' or 'historical' international systems are firmly based on the states as dominant units of decision. In such systems, the task of coordination is

---

[1] M. Kaplan, *System and Process in International Politics* (New York: 1957) p. 89.

[2] *Ibid.*, pp. 145–6.

[3] *Ibid.*, pp. 113, 116.

accomplished, not by its delegation or assumption by a superordinate body (i.e., the Hobbesian solution) but by 'communications and responses among a plurality of autonomous components.'[1]

If integration is viewed in the latter sense, it is theoretically measurable in terms of the communications and interactions between states. 'Mutual responsiveness', in short, is potentially quantifiable. Such a possibility was suggested some years ago in the pioneering work of Quincy Wright, who distinguished eight measurable aspects of the 'distance' between states: technological, strategic, intellectual, legal, social, political, psychic and 'expectancy'.[2] From these, he suggested, it was possible to assess the probability of war between any two states. Conversely, these measures could also be described as the basic dimensions of a potential 'community of states'. As Deutsch acknowledges, Wright's formulation of the problem in these terms has had a powerful and lasting impact on peace research and integration studies.[3]

Traditionally the first assessments of the probability that a system of states might integrate have been based on geopolitical observations. Particularly if the historical analogy of international integration with the emergence of nation-states such as Germany and Italy is accepted, it is tempting to examine geographical regions such as Western Europe to see if there exist the sorts of 'core areas' around which a process similar to the growth of nations can occur.[4] This geopolitical emphasis in predicting the growth of 'political community' is often intuitively and empirically satisfying. Clearly, despite the modern technology of communications and transport, geography remains a major factor in the crystallization of international 'regions'. But many theorists of international relations, following up Wright's approach to the measurement of international affinities, have suggested that regions and potential political communities can be defined by a number of other criteria.

One writer argues that, by defining international relations as transactions and mapping their flows, one can discern the dominant structure of the international system and so determine which states

[1] K. W. Deutsch, 'Communications Theory and Political Integration' in P. E. Jacob & J. V. Toscano (eds.), *The Integration of Political Communities* (Philadelphia: 1964) pp. 58–61.

[2] Q. Wright, *A Study of War*, abridged edition (Chicago: 1964) pp. 332–3.

[3] K. W. Deutsch, 'Quincy Wright's Contribution to the Study of War', in *ibid.*, pp. xv–xvi.

[4] For Deutsch's concept of the growth of communities around 'core areas', see *Nationalism and Social Communications*, Ch. 2 esp. pp. 39–41, 63–4, and 'Political Community and the North Atlantic Area', *op. cit.*, pp. 18–20.

are in fact (if not always in geography) 'closest' to each other.[1] He specifies diplomatic exchange, trade and common memberships in international organizations as particularly revealing indices of patterns of coherence between states, arguing that such flows of international communication and transaction have a 'substantial' influence on the perceptions and images of statesmen, and hence on their behaviour.[2] A former student and colleague of Deutsch has examined the relations between Britain and the United States, using quantitative data on transactions in order to measure their 'mutual responsiveness'. He has since used factor analysis to delineate several 'regions' or clusters of states in the international system, according to their similarities and levels of interdependence.[3] Several massive projects have also been undertaken to gather statistical data not only on the characteristics of nations (for comparative purposes) but on their patterns of exchange and interaction. Here again it is hoped that by induction scholars will be able to arrive at a more accurate picture of the 'true' patterns of community and coherence in the international system.[4]

✓ The assumptions behind this transaction analysis of international systems seem to be that the formation of a 'community of states', besides being manifested in the ways the states communicate and interact, is in turn conditioned by these patterns. In the first place, the greater the volume and frequency of communications and inter-actions between states, the more 'salient' each is to the other, and the more aware each becomes of the other's actions and interests. Furthermore, the more that these transactions are perceived by each state as beneficial, the more its relations with the other become imbued with trust and confidence. This in turn encourages new expansion of communication and interaction between the states; in this way the integrative process soon 'takes off' and becomes self-reinforcing. In essence, then, the mutual responsiveness and peace-

[1] S. J. Brams, 'Transaction Flows in the International System', *American Political Science Review*, 60: 4, 1966, pp. 880–98.

[2] *Ibid.*, pp. 881–2.

[3] Russett, *op. cit.*, and *International Regions and the International System* (Chicago: 1967). The groups of variables according to which he determines the existence of a 'region' are: the number of common memberships in international organizations, trade patterns, geography, major social and cultural characteristics, and the political attitudes of governments. For an attack on the inductive, statistical methods used in the latter work, see O. R. Young, 'Professor Russett: Industrious Tailor to a Naked Emperor', *World Politics*, 21: 3, 1969, pp. 486–511.

[4] For a prospectus of one such programme, see K. W. Deutsch, 'Toward an Inventory of Basic Trends and Patterns in Comparative and International Politics', *American Political Science Review*, 54: 1, 1960, pp. 34–57.

able propensities of states are held to be sustained by the intensity of their social and political communications and interactions.[1]

A number of qualities found in particular international systems have been suggested by the pluralists as being favourable to such an integrative process. In Deutsch's North Atlantic study, six of the twelve conditions isolated as 'essential' for amalgamation are qualities of the interdependence of states (that is, the system itself) rather than of states viewed individually. These are: unbroken links of social communication, both geographical and societal; mobility of persons; multiplicity of ranges of communications and trans-actions; interchange of group roles; and mutual predictability of behaviour.[2] By examining such characteristics of international systems, then, it is possible to arrive at descriptions of the flow of goods, services, population, information and symbols between states, and from these to state the probability of their integrating.

In such a perspective the preoccupations of other theorists of integration are given a secondary position. Economic integration, for example, which is stressed by neofunctionalist writers as the key to political union, is judged by pluralists to be effective only in so far as it has a favourable influence on communications flows and hence, on mutual images. International institutions, too, which are relied upon heavily by most theorists, are here seen primarily in their role as processors of the information flowing between states. To the extent that they aid and do not distort these patterns, they may increase integration in the system. The structures that are important in integrating the international system are, from this perspective, not the formal legal and political institutions, but the less visible and informal patterns of 'intense, enduring and rewarding transactions', whose quantitative densities provide a picture of the mutual rele-vance and political cohesion of the states in the system.[3]

There are, of course, many problems with this sort of analysis. In the first place, as Haas has pointed out, some of the variables which Deutsch and others use to indicate a state of integration serve also to define the process and this makes it difficult to determine cause and

[1] For a brief and clear explication of these arguments, see Deutsch, 'Com-munications Theory and Political Integration', in Jacob & Toscano, *op. cit.*, pp. 46–74.

[2] Deutsch, 'Political Community and the North Atlantic Area', *op. cit.*, pp. 37–8. Cf. P. E. Jacob & H. Teune, 'The Integrative Process' in Jacob & Toscano, *op. cit.*, pp. 1–45.

[3] See H. Alker & D. Puchala, 'Trends in Economic Partnership' in J. D. Singer (ed.), *Quantitative International Politics* (New York: 1968) p. 288.

effect.[1] For example, is a high level of trade between two countries to be seen as a factor favouring further integration, or as evidence that some integration has already occurred? If it is taken to be both, then a circular process is postulated, the causal dynamics of which it is still incumbent on the theorist to explain. Moreover, some studies in this vein, such as Merritt's analysis of the integration of the thirteen American colonies,[2] which shows that the growth of social communications and a 'sense of community' preceded any serious institutional amalgamation, suggest causal relationships only at the risk of appearing either tautological or *post facto*. That is, the social communications and the 'sense of community' were only made significant by subsequent institutional change, and only historical hindsight is able to correlate them with an 'integrative process'. Predicting on the basis of such indicators is another matter.[3] This is perhaps best illustrated by the debate between Deutsch and Inglehart, who, on different readings of similar or identical data about attitudes and social communications, arrived at opposite conclusions about the prospects for integration in Western Europe.[4]

On the whole, then, it is clear at present that the pluralist approach, in so far as it restricts itself to analysis on the systemic level, has far more capacity to describe the development of integrative links between states than to explain or predict the process. If one accepts the definition of community in terms of communications and interactions between autonomous units in the system, the problem of description reduces to the technical one of mapping these patterns sensitively and accurately. For explanatory and predictive purposes, however, exclusive reliance on the systems perspective affords much less sure footing. For example, to place a great deal of emphasis on the self-reinforcing nature of integration via communications and mutual responsiveness would seem to preclude much possibility of dramatic reversals and to suggest a semi-autonomous, cumulative

[1] E. B. Haas, *Beyond the Nation-State* (Stanford: 1964) p. 27. Some pluralists, like Alker & Puchala (*op. cit.*, p. 288) make it clear they see transactions only as partial evidence of community and not as causal elements. Others, like Deutsch, are less clear on this point.

[2] R. L. Merritt, *Symbols of American Community, 1735–1775* (New Haven: 1966) esp. Chs. 8 and 9.

[3] That prediction of 'more spectacular political actions' from the 'mute forces of history, the societal shifts' is the aim of communications analysis is made clear by Deutsch in Jacob & Toscano, *op. cit.*, esp. pp. 51 and 74.

[4] K. W. Deutsch, 'Integration and Arms Control in the European Environment: A Summary Report', *American Political Science Review*, 60: 2, 1966, pp. 354–65; R. Inglehart, 'An End to European Integration?', *ibid.*, 61: 1, 1967, pp. 91–105.

and determined process. It is hard to reconcile this with pluralist assumptions about the continuing self-determination of states. Such an emphasis also makes the blithe liberal assumption that there are no really fundamental conflicts of interest between states. At worst, then, the logic of the systems perspective will lead the pluralist to some rude awakenings about the process of integration. More frequently, it leads him to overlook the possibility that integration may in fact proceed through the confrontation and resolution of conflicts.

ii) The States: Autonomy and Responsiveness

If we turn now to the second level of analysis, that of the states, we find more persuasive efforts to explain, and not simply describe, the integrative process. Pluralists, it has been argued, tend to see national development and international integration as mutually enhancing rather than conflicting processes. To the extent that states develop their administrative and political capabilities and are economically advanced or expansive, it is claimed, they are likely to engage in the types of international communication and interaction favourable to integration.

This proposition, basic to the pluralist view of integration, derives from earlier theories about the origin and prevention of war, and particularly from the tradition of liberal nationalism. As Kedourie points out, nationalist revolutionaries in the nineteenth century argued that the full flowering of national self-determination throughout Europe and beyond would put an end to war, 'for all these nations would be *ipso facto*, pacific and just.'[1] The very diversity of nationalities was to be valued, since it provided a natural and vigorous harmony. But there were variations on the question of how this diversity was to be expressed, different writers offering different prescriptions about the kinds of states most likely to be peaceable. Cobden called for the overthrow of despotisms, Mazzini for national self-determination, Woodrow Wilson for a sort of populist democracy and Marx and his successors for various kinds of socialist states.[2] Similar thinking seems to underlie much of the now-thriving field of development theory, which holds as an implicit goal a world

[1] E. Kedourie, *Nationalism*, 3rd edition (London: 1966) p. 106. For penetrating analyses of the assumptions underlying liberal nationalist ideas of world order, see esp. Chs. 4 and 6. Cf. K. N. Waltz, *Man, the State and War* (New York: 1959) Chs. 4 and 5.

[2] Kedourie, *op. cit.*, pp. 130–3; Waltz, *op. cit.*, esp. pp. 8, 83–4, 118, 143–4.

of industrialized, democratic, and therefore peaceful, nation-states.[1] One recent theorist, having explored the relationship between the internal social characteristics and the external behaviour of states, concludes 'that the nineteenth-century sociologists were correct in predicting an end to wars through industrialization, though their utopia of modernized society is farther away than was anticipated.'[2]

But the general argument that the multiplication of a particular type of state will lead to permanent peace, or, in the pluralists' terms, integration, is clearly open to serious challenge. At a sufficient distance, the states of Europe that went to war in 1914 or 1939 appear economically, culturally, socially and even politically to have been remarkably uniform compared to the rest of the world. If viewed closely enough, on the other hand, no two states seem similar enough to be guaranteed peace by such criteria. The point is simply that it is necessary to have some consensus among observers as to the important objective qualities by which such comparisons can be made, before they can have any meaning. It is just this consensus that has not been achieved as yet.

It does not necessarily follow, however, that those adopting the pluralist perspective on integration should confine themselves to a lengthy and perhaps unyielding comparative study of national characteristics before deciding on the prospects for integration. In the end it is the similarities perceived by the decision-makers, and not those determined 'objectively' by the social scientist, which will propel or limit the integrative process. If states act toward each other in the belief that their basic values are compatible, their economic and social systems similar, and their interdependence high, it matters little that the students of comparative politics do not concur. The reverse, of course, also applies: statesmen determined to be hostile to each other because of deep, or even superficial, conflicts of interest are unlikely to be impressed by the similarity of their countries' social structures.

In short, then, for the pluralist the progress of integration depends primarily on the nature, perceptions, and actions of those making

[1] For a discussion of such assumptions, see L. Pye, *Aspects of Political Development* (Boston: 1966). Cf. Deutsch, *Nationalism and Social Communication*, pp. 82–5.
[2] M. Haas, 'Social Change and National Aggressiveness 1900–60', in J. D. Singer, *op. cit.*, p. 244. Also of this species of thought would be the 'convergence theory' whereby, as American and Soviet societies evolve toward a similar pattern, relations improve between the two states.

policy for the states in the system. The central problem, then, concerns governments' capacities to handle information, to make decisions and to respond sensitively to each other's demands and to events in the international environment. What are the institutional and ideological limits of such capacities in different kinds of states with different forms of government and society? It seems clear that as yet there is no indication that any one particular type of state – democratic, developed, socialist or whatever – is necessarily more open and flexible (and therefore more amenable to integration in these terms) than any other.[1]

What can be argued, however, is that a model of foreign policy behaviour which focuses solely on the responsiveness of states to the international environment runs the risk of ignoring the possible limitations on integrative behaviour imposed by the domestic political and social systems. Indeed, it is an awareness of these limitations which leads most pluralists to reaffirm national autonomy vis-à-vis the seemingly inexorable march of integration when viewed from the systemic perspective alone. Because within each state there is an important reserve of political and social life which, generally untouched by international intercourse, may nonetheless be a prime influence on the images and decisions of statesmen, the possibility always exists that integration will be halted or undone.

According to the pluralists, then, the growth of a 'community of states' is potentially limited not only by the political will and capacities of national governments, but by a significant and persistent core of national identity in each state, in whose service governments may feel obliged to act in ways unproductive for integration. Clearly there are both normative and empirical judgements mixed up in this sort of proposition. President de Gaulle spoke of the 'absolute imperative . . . for a great people to have the free disposition of itself', and of course the norm of national self-determination (or at least the autonomy of accepted states) is basic to contemporary international society.[2] But whatever the normative position, the fundamental empirical question of the continuing ability of states

---

[1] For the best analysis of the general problems of information and responsiveness in government decision-making see Deutsch, *The Nerves of Government*, esp. Ch. 9. Cf. Burton, *op. cit.*, for an interesting but not entirely happy attempt to apply Deutsch's concepts to foreign policy.

[2] Ambassade de France à Londres, *Seventh Major News Conference Held by General de Gaulle*, 14 January 1963, p. 9. In Deutsch's theoretical work, the notion of self-determination also has a normative flavour. See esp. *The Nerves of Government*, Chs. 8, 12 and 13, esp. pp. 128, 219–23.

to act autonomously is certainly open to more debate than national-ists and political 'realists' would acknowledge. In the vital field of security, for example, the nation-state has recently been described by different writers as 'penetrated', 'permeable' and 'conditionally viable'.[1] In the fields of economic and social welfare, functionalists have long described it as bankrupt and as counterproductive in the face of increasing international interdependence. Increased inter-national communication, too, may be reducing even the core of national cultural and social identity. In short, it may be that to describe the internal identity and autonomy of the nation-states as continuing limitations on integration is not as 'realistic' as it is claimed to be. It may beg the basic question, which is whether or not international life is evolving in such a way as to make the states interdependent not only in their political capacities but in the very social, economic and cultural spheres which have traditionally been the sources of their separate identities.

iii) The Individual: Social Learning and Community

If we turn, finally, to the third level of analysis – that of the in-dividual – we find a very important component of the pluralist explanation of the integrative process. The expressions 'community', 'mutual responsiveness', 'we-feeling', 'perceptions' and 'images' which have recurred throughout the foregoing discussion, suggest an important social-psychological dimension to this approach to integration. They suggest, in other words, that changes in the political attitudes and behaviour of individuals may be central to the creation of a 'community of states'.

One critic of Deutsch's work, in fact, argues that he has developed a theory not so much of political integration but more of 'social or moral community' which, while interesting and suggestive, 'ignores too much that is politically relevant.'[2] For Deutsch, however, the 'sense of community' or 'we-feeling' that exists among the populations of several states, and the perceptions and images of their policy-makers, while not necessarily the fundamental sources of decisions

---

[1] The terms are respectively those of: J. N. Rosenau, 'Pre-Theories and Theories of Foreign Policy', in R. B. Farrell (ed.), *Approaches to Comparative and International Politics* (Evanston, Ill.: 1966) pp. 63–5; J. H. Herz, *International Politics in the Atomic Age* (New York: 1959) Chs. 6 and 8; and Boulding, *Conflict and Defence*, Ch. 13.

[2] L. N. Lindberg, 'The European Community as a Political System', *Journal of Common Market Studies*, 5: 4, 1967, p. 345.

and actions or the full extent of what is 'politically relevant', are nonetheless a crucial set of intervening variables in any decision. Deutsch, like many of those engaged in peace-research, sees a distinct relationship between the images of policy-makers and the probability of war between their states. Analysis of these social-psychological components thus becomes a theoretically parsimonious way of explaining and predicting integration. Moreover, drawing on his studies of national integration, he tends to see the essence of a 'political community' in the ability of people to communicate, which requires that they understand language and perceive the world in similar ways.[1] Again, this is not to argue that all political behaviour is 'determined' by images or that all conflicts which develop between states are based on faulty perceptions. The argument is simply that as images shape, and are shaped by, actions, they are useful sources of theory about such actions as they affect the growth of community.

The concept of 'social learning' is central to Deutsch's theory of political change, of which his theory of international integration is an extension. In studying the emergence of modern nations, he began from the proposition 'that both society and community are developed by social learning, and that a community consists of people who have learned to communicate with each other and to understand each other well beyond the mere interchange of goods and services. . . . Experience and complementarity may . . . continue to reproduce each other, like the proverbial chicken and the egg, in a syndrome of ethnic learning, that is, a historical process of social learning in which individuals, usually over several generations, learn to become a people.'[2] At the present time, the empirical evidence suggests that this sort of process is still working in favour of national communities. There is, however, no logical reason why 'social learning' cannot operate to create broader political communities in the future. As Deutsch observes, 'the same processes which made nationalism probable may soon come to turn against it.'[3]

This concept of 'social learning' as the central dynamic of integration is, of course, difficult to render operational and, apart from Deutsch's own efforts at historical and quantitative analysis, very little work has been done in this area. In one study, the growth of communal awareness in the thirteen American colonies was described

---

[1] Deutsch, *Nationalism and Social Communication*, Chs. 2 and 4; *The Nerves of Government*, pp. 150–1, 176–8.

[2] Deutsch, *Nationalism and Social Communication*, pp. 91, 174.

[3] *Ibid.*, pp. 190 ff.

as resembling the pattern of a 'learning curve' – that is, the analogy, crucial to Deutsch's theory of politics, between the communications systems of individuals and of societies, was held to be useful in explaining the growth of a collective consciousness.[1] In a somewhat more Pavlovian formulation, another theorist defines integration as the process by which people learn to respond to stimuli in the same way and to 'respond to each other as relevant stimuli.'[2] The major problems in rendering these ideas more manageable have to do with the ways of inferring a 'sense of community' from verbal behaviour (as Merritt did with content analysis) or from patterns of social communications and economic exchange. In many cases the 'fetish for measurement' of these 'hard' data and the lure of pure induction have left many questions about theoretical relevance begging.[3]

For those wishing to bring about international integration more rapidly, there is little in this concept of 'social learning' to offer encouragement or tactical hints. Not only is the process seen as long and gradual – occurring over several generations; it is also essentially circular or self-reinforcing and, beyond socio-political manipulations on an unprecedented and rather sinister scale, it is difficult to see how the process, once set in motion, might be directed or arrested. Certainly the growth of community through 'social learning' will be enhanced by certain geographical, economic, social and political background conditions – the French and the Germans probably have more opportunity to form such a community than, say, the Chinese and the Americans. But such background conditions are also, by definition, rather difficult to manipulate.

More immediate conditions, however, can be exploited to encourage 'social learning', even though their effects are little understood. The interactions of elites in intergovernmental negotiations, economic transactions and less formal contacts, as well as the social and spatial mobility of the general public as evidenced in tourism and the migration of labour across borders, are often assumed to increase the general 'sense of community' of those involved. These phenomena, besides being researchable, are also susceptible to influence (for or against integration) by governments and other interested parties. The same is true of personal and mass communications, integration being enhanced to the extent that capabilities for

[1] Merritt, *op. cit.*, Ch. 9.

[2] H. Teune, 'The Learning of Integrative Habits', in P. E. Jacob & J. V. Toscano, *op. cit.*, pp. 259–60.

[3] See H. N. Bull, 'International Theory: The Case for a Classical Approach', *World Politics* 18:3 1966, p. 372; Young, *op. cit.*, pp. 489–92.

communication and transaction increase to accommodate increased loads. Deutsch and his colleagues have often stressed the importance of mail, telephone calls and other forms of personal communications both as sources and as indicators of integrative habits of mind.[1] The uses of mass media, finally, as propaganda agents and as more subtle socializing influences, are well known, as the policies of European states and organizations are beginning to make clear.[2] Despite the efforts of the EEC and the Council of Europe, however, the states retain a monopoly of those uses of communications by which community can be created or maintained. Until this is changed, it seems unlikely that the sorts of massive 'social learning' needed to create a common European political culture and a 'community of states' on a broad scale, will be forthcoming.

Pluralistic Integration in Europe

In the first two parts of this chapter, we have examined the pluralists' concept of integration and the values and assumptions from which it derives, and then analysed their explanation of the integrative process on three different levels. In this final section, we shall assess the place of the pluralist approach in postwar European integration, attempting to judge the accuracy and usefulness of its explanations and strategies.

The influence of the pluralist approach has been consistently strong in the recent history of attempts to unify Europe, and can be seen in a number of the organizations which have formed part of this effort. From the pluralist perspective, as we have noted an international organization has no real will of its own and no power to create a new political entity apart from the wishes of its members. It is merely the structural manifestation of more or less concerted national policies and interests where cooperation for certain specified

---

[1] Examples of studies of these phenomena in the Deutschian mould are A. Lijphart, 'Tourist Traffic and Integration Potential', *Journal of Common Market Studies*, 2: 3, 1964, pp. 251–62; and H. S. Feldstein, 'A Study of Transactions and Political Integration: Transnational Labour Flow Within the European Economic Community', *ibid.*, 6: 1, 1967, pp. 24–55. See also Russett, *Community and Contention*; and Merritt, *Symbols of American Community*. An important theoretical and methodological exposition is K. W. Deutsch, 'Shifts in the Balance of Communication Flows', *Public Opinion Quarterly*, 20: 1, 1956, pp. 143–60.

[2] Instructive in this connection is the reluctance of governments to see instituted in the EEC, outside their control, a 'Direction Générale' of information. See R. Lemaignen, *L'Europe au Berceau* (Paris: 1964) p. 64.

purposes has seemed desirable. Nevertheless, as such it may serve to enhance international communication and thus lay the ground-work for more supranational forms of integration in future.

In postwar European history, there have been four main points at which explicitly pluralistic types of organization have had the strongest support. At each of these stages a time of crisis seemed to coincide with the adoption or strong expression, by at least one important European state, of pluralist ideas concerning integration. Pluralist ideas have been a persistent option when other, more ambitious schemes have faltered.

The first stage, of course was the formative period of European organization in the immediate postwar years. Even if hope of a broad European economic organization, under the auspices of the UN Economic Commission and covering East and West, was gradually receding, most plans for European cooperation at least envisaged an organization including most of the states not directly under Soviet control. But, despite the speeches of Churchill, it had become evident that as long as Britain was a member of this broad grouping, pluralistic forms of cooperation were the most that could be expected.

This became clear first in the events leading up to the formation of the OEEC. While General Marshall's speech at Harvard in June 1947 insisted only on prior agreement and cooperation among the European recipients of economic aid as to its amount and distribu-tion, many American policy-makers hoped to link this aid to progress in European political unification both to meet a perceived Soviet threat and to resolve the general economic crisis. France and some of the smaller states pressed for some supranational power to be given to the OEEC – which was to institutionalize this cooperation – but as the British in particular were firmly opposed to the supra-national idea, the result of the deliberations took the form of a classic international organization.[1]

From the pluralist perspective, then, the OEEC was an archetypal international organization, designed primarily to facilitate com-munications and cooperation between states over certain problems without jeopardizing their political independence. Moreover, it turned out to be influential in setting in motion other forms of co-operation and other integrative influences. For example, the pro-posals for a free trade area in Europe and for a payments union

[1] Political and Economic Planning, *European Unity*, London, 1968, Ch. 3, esp. pp. 75–82.

originated in the Secretariat of the OEEC under M. Marjolin, and both these ideas subsequently flowered into institutional form. More important perhaps for the pluralist approach, habits of intimate consultation were developed among political leaders and civil servants of the European states, and a pattern of decision-making emerged which, further refined, found employment in the European Communities of later vintage. And finally, the contribution of the OEEC to the economic recovery of the Western European states ensured the rapid expansion of trade ties and other forms of economic and social interdependence between them. The circular integrative process is evident in all these three cases: the organization, produced by communications needs and a rudimentary sense of community, enhanced in turn further forms of cooperation.[1]

At this early stage in postwar European history, another pluralistic organization was formed in response to a perceived military threat to Western Europe's security. Like the OEEC, NATO was seen by some of its members as having a promising potential for integration, perhaps eventually going beyond the initial purely intergovernmental and purely military forms. Article Two of the Treaty set out a number of tasks – economic collaboration, harmonization of economic and social policies, promotion of stability and greater understanding of one another's institutions – which implied a degree and scope of integration well beyond that involved in military planning and rationalization of the alliance's technical and administrative infrastructure. These objectives were reaffirmed in 1956 by the Committee on Nonmilitary Cooperation. But the aspiration for an 'Atlantic Community', expressed in the Committee's report and reasserted periodically throughout the next decade, has not been realized in any more than the minimal (but not negligible) Deutschean sense that the North Atlantic area has remained a war-free zone.

In the Atlantic area, many of the tasks set out by the Article Two and by the Committee have been undertaken by the OECD, the successor to the OEEC. But the thrust of economic integration has been in the narrower context of the Six, and in a manner scarcely compatible with the objective of an Atlantic Community. This subregional tendency has of course reinforced existent tensions – over the sharing of nuclear capabilities and conventional defence costs,

[1] It is equally clear that the OEEC did not seriously reduce the autonomy of those states whose cooperation it advanced. If anything, it served as the major forum in which the nations of Western Europe were rebuilt. See L. N. Lindberg and S. Scheingold, *Europe's Would-Be Polity* (Englewood Cliffs, N.J.: 1970) pp. 11–13.

and over the hegemonic role of the United States in the Alliance's decision-making structure – and thus made it most unlikely that NATO will transcend the form of a classic alliance. Indeed, the recurrent questioning of the strategic rationale for NATO by some of its members, and the tensions produced by differences in domestic political systems, make even the persistence of the bare forms of alliance somewhat doubtful, especially in a period of cautious East-West détente.[1]

The third major European organization which emerged from this first period was the Council of Europe. This body, too, followed the British rather than the French prescription and became a classic type of international organization with a Committee of Ministers representing each member (and requiring unanimity in its decisions) and an Assembly which, far from becoming a European Parliament with supranational powers, developed into a gathering of national parliamentarians. In spite of some early, federalist-inspired efforts to make it the political framework for all European organizations and to create 'a European political authority with limited functions but real powers'[2], the Council has not evolved far from this basic pluralist form. Nonetheless, it has emerged as an important forum for debate over such issues as the Schuman Plan, the EDC–EPC complex, the proposals for a Free Trade Area and the French plans for 'political union'. Despite the efforts and aspirations of ardent European federalists, it could hardly be claimed that the Council's role as a clearing-house for ideas and proposals concerning integration derives from an incipient political authority or any legitimacy as an embryonic European government. But the Council is important because in terms of membership it is the only purely European organization which is strategically placed to link the major growth-point of European integration – the Six – with the broader Europe on which federalists focused their attention in the early postwar years. Thus even if the Council has disappointed its federalist founders by evolving into a pluralistic organization, it has not been without value to them in the latter form.

[1] See Political and Economic Planning, *op. cit.*, Ch. 11. Also K. W. Deutsch, L. J. Edinger, R. C. Macridis and R. L. Merritt, *France, Germany and the Western Alliance*, Chs. 5, 11, 18, and J. Freymond, *Western Europe Since the War* (New York: 1964) esp. pp. 92–6, 138–43.

[2] Political and Economic Planning, *op. cit.*, p. 134–41. Chapter 4 as a whole is a useful description of the Council and its work. See also A. H. Robertson, *The Council of Europe* (London: 1962) and K. Lindsay, *European Assemblies: The Experimental Period* 1949–59 (London: 1960).

In addition to this pure communications role, the Council has of course been active in creating the social and cultural infrastructure of European unity. In working on problems of education, human rights, population-migration, welfare, mass communications, local government and cultural cooperation – most of which lack both the dramatic appeal and political controversy of the EEC's activities – the Council is in a real sense making a tactical application of Deutsch's theories about the linking role of attitudes and social custom in the process of integration. It is clear in this case that there is a close relation between Deutsch's ideas and those of the functionalists. The difference is that whereas the functionalists would concentrate on how the 'social learning' resulting from the Council's programmes would lead to more such programmes, requiring coordination and thus producing new organizations bypassing the states, the pluralists would merely assume these new cooperative habits to feed back into states' foreign policies and lessen the likelihood of war.

The second stage at which pluralist models of European integration came to the fore was immediately following the collapse in 1954 of the attempt to set up the 'supranational triptych' of the Six (i.e., adding a Defence and a Political Community to the Coal and Steel Community). France having at last, after four years of agonizing indecision and strife, joined Britain in the lobby of those opposed to supranationality in vital political areas, the crisis of German re-armament which had precipitated the whole scheme remained unresolved. On British and French initiative largely, the Brussels Treaty of 1948 was revised and West Germany and Italy became members.

The resulting Western European Union was again in the classic pluralist mould of organizations.[1] It had two main functions: a military one, dealing with arms control and problems of Western European defence in relation to NATO, and a political one, in providing a regular meeting place for Britain and the Six. In its former capacity, WEU is the consultative, cooperative body dear to pluralist theory, aiding military security without apparently compromising its members' autonomy. In its latter capacity, the organization has served primarily as a channel of 'elite communication' for its seven members. Nevertheless, recurrent suggestions that its framework be strengthened to provide a forum for continuous evaluation

---

[1] For details on WEU, see Political and Economic Planning, *op. cit.*, Ch. 9. The WEU's main decision-making body, the Council, does take many binding decisions by majority vote, but the significance of this procedure is lessened by the organization's position in relation to NATO. *Ibid.*, p. 329.

of political and economic problems in Europe have met little success. The French consistently opposed the idea, suspecting, not entirely without reason, that its main purpose was to aid Britain's access to the EEC.[1]

Confrontations between pluralist and other concepts of European integration have often been submerged in what seemed at the time to be more urgent or important issues. At the first stage, the major issues were European security and economic recovery; at the second, German rearmament, At the third stage the confrontation was perhaps more stark, but even here it was overlaid by the issue of free trade and the scope of European economic organizations. In 1956–7, as negotiation and signing of the Rome Treaties progressed, the states outside the Six, invoking the successful record of the OEEC in economic collaboration and voicing fears about trade discrimination, proposed a free trade area. Their argument was, as Freymond writes, that 'in view of the evident progress made by a method of collaboration that took account of diverse national conditions, it was difficult, outside the group of the Six, to see the need for hastening the development by confining oneself to the more rigid structures of the Common Market.' The debate over the free trade area, then, encompassed a debate about the degree to which national autonomy ought to be relinquished in the process of European integration. On the one side were the 'partisans of "United Europe" – that is, of a politically and economically integrated Europe whose component states would progressively abdicate their sovereignty for the benefit of a truly European government'; on the other were 'the partisans of "European cooperation", who, valuing the strength and importance of national differences, strove to reconcile unity and diversity.'[2] The negotiations broke down in a British-French impasse; in 1959–60 the economic division in Western Europe became formalized with the emergence of EFTA.

The pluralist approach made its fourth strong appearance in the French challenge to the supranationalist logic of the EEC, at a time when some European disillusionment was beginning to be felt over the prospects of the 'community method'. The French plans for 'political union' (i.e., intergovernmental cooperation among the Six in defence and foreign policy), upon which the Fouchet and Cattani

---

[1] For one such suggestion, see the speech by the then German Foreign Minister, Herr Brandt, to WEU, reported in *The Times*, 9 July 1968.

[2] See Freymond, *op. cit.*, pp. 135–8, and Political & Economic Planning, *op. cit.*, Ch. 10.

committees deliberated with some heat in the early sixties, were presented by the French as a natural sequel or complement to economic cooperation. The institutions proposed for 'political union' included a Council of Heads of State or Government whose decisions would require unanimity, a Political Commission of senior foreign ministry officials to prepare policy proposals and agenda for the Council, and an Assembly with negligible powers of control. The other governments, however – notably the Dutch – tended to see these proposals as an ill-disguised attempt to cripple the 'community method' and draw the increasingly supranational economic organization of the EEC back into the conventional realm of intergovernmental politics.[1]

The idea of 'political union' has remained a cornerstone of French European policy. In his Press Conference of February 1966, de Gaulle proposed regular governmental meetings of the Six to consider 'political subjects' of common interest. This theme, which the General reiterated later that year, was further developed by Couve de Murville in 1967: 'It is obvious that the economic union which is being established among the Six and which operates satisfactorily must be followed by progress toward political union, that is, toward a *rapprochement* among the Six in the political field, not to be too ambitious.'[2]

Not being 'too ambitious' in this case clearly means understanding 'political union', not in the Monnet-Hallstein sense as the culmination of economic integration in a United States of Europe, but in the pluralist sense of a 'community of states' cooperating over the 'inherently political' subjects of defence and foreign policy. Arguing from two premises – the sanctity of the nation-state and the distinction between economic and 'political' matters – the French government has insisted that it is both fallacious and dangerous to assume an inexorable dynamic flow from economic to political integration. The will to cooperate in political matters may be both a prerequisite and a product of economic integration, in other words, but it does not follow that political integration in the federalist sense of the term is either inevitable or necessary at present. In the French view, then, European international organizations exist for the purpose of cooperation in their specified fields, and for no higher political

[1] See Bodenheimer, *op. cit.*, esp. Chs. 3 and 4.

[2] Ambassade de France à Londres, Service de Presse et d'Information, *Excerpt from the Press Conference given by General de Gaulle* (Paris: 21 February 1966), p. 1. See also *Press Conference* of 28 October 1966 and television *Interview* of M. Couve de Murville, 12 November 1967, p. 5.

purposes.[1] Among nations they are the manifestation of friendship and mutual aid, not the prelude to marriage.

It has often been argued by Gaullists, under fire from their critics, that this position, which they have expressed so forcefully and skilfully, is not wholly uncongenial to the other European governments, whose pieties about supranationality would speedily be exposed as hypocrisy if French opposition did not permit them the luxury of supporting it. It is certainly evident that the pluralist position has had wide backing outside France. Adenauer, for example, saw the problem of European unity primarily as one of Franco-German rapprochement; the Schuman Plan which he supported so strongly was not, therefore, so much an end in itself, as a means to a more traditional goal. In this sense its culmination must be seen, not in the EEC or in any political union emerging from it, but in the Franco-German Treaty of 1963.[2] In the post-Adenauer era, West Germany's European policy has often been described as having a Gaullist flavour, in the sense that cooperation in Europe is perceived by some policy-makers primarily as a means to the long-standing and more fundamental national goal of reunification.[3] It has become increasingly clear in the early 1970s that the West German government, especially since the Hague 'summit' of December 1969, shares the French view on the importance of cooperation and harmonization in foreign policy, although it is careful to place this in the long-run perspective of gradual elimination of 'sovereign elements.'[4]

In Britain, the third major Western European state on which the future of integration rests, there is perhaps the strongest pluralist tradition. The positions of the Attlee, Churchill, Eden and Macmillan governments – despite the presence of voices calling for supranational forms of integration – were consistent in their encouragement of

[1] That President Pompidou continues to pursue his predecessor's goals in this respect is clear from a number of his recent statements. In a speech in Strasbourg on 28 June 1970, he spoke of 'a Europe grouping sovereign states that freely agree to lower the barriers that separate them.' In a press conference in Paris on 21 January 1971, he described his vision as a confederation of states which had decided to harmonize policies and integrate their economies, making all decisions unanimously.

[2] See F. R. Willis, *France, Germany and the New Europe 1945–1967* (New York: 1968) Chs. 4, 5, 10.

[3] On this element in Germany's European policy, see H. Kuby, 'German Foreign, Defence and European Policy', *Journal of Common Market Studies*, 6: 2, 1967, esp. pp. 172–78; cf. N. Heathcote, 'Western Integration and German Reunification', *ibid*, 7: 2, 1968, pp. 102–18.

[4] For a recent statement, see W. Brandt, 'Germany's European Policy', *European Community*, January 1971, pp. 7–8.

European political and economic cooperation only so long as it took the form of classic intergovernmental organizations. Churchill's calls for a Council of Europe or a United States of Europe, it soon became evident, were not intended to imply any surrenders of British autonomy. Eden's reaction to the collapse of the EDC project was in a similar tradition: a purely intergovernmental body was given new life and transformed into the Western European Union. Even the Prime Minister whose government made the first attempt to join the EEC had earlier recorded a judgement about the inadmissability of Europeans deciding the fate of British coal-pits or steel-works.[1] Among many committed British 'Europeans' the desire for access to the European markets coexists remarkably easily with a rejection of supranationality as a principle or as a fear. One recent commentator wrote: 'If the Labour Party and many British people are now being converted to the European idea, it is partly because the idea itself is no longer what it seemed in 1963. General de Gaulle has shown that the Eurocrats in Brussels are not supreme, and that national sovereignty can be defended within the community. The prospect of a complete loss of identity in a federal Europe now seems increasingly remote.'[2] Such references to the defence of sovereignty and national identity indicate that the implicit model of integration even among 'Marketeers' is very often a pluralistic one little distinguished from that expounded by the French Government. This can hardly have hurt the chances of Britain's application with the French.

Attempts to organize Europe on pluralistic lines, then, have been a consistent feature of the postwar integration movement, not least because the policies of the major European powers and the outlooks of most of the men formulating them, have been dominated by pluralist assumptions. 'European' policy has not yet transcended the atmosphere of 'political realism' which emphasizes the primacy of security and high politics, the irreducibility of the nation-state and the importance of traditional diplomatic goals and methods. Moreover, judged by the same criteria, Europe might well be described as already 'integrated' as a result of such policies. The touchstone,

[1] Kitzinger, *op. cit.*, p. 11.
[2] Special Correspondent, 'Big Changes in Opinion', in *The Times* with *Die Welt*, Special Report: Britain on Her Way to Europe, 28 October 1966. Advocates of British entry – including Prime Minister Heath – have made this argument increasingly strongly in recent months. See, for example, *The Economist*, 16 May 1970, pp. 11–14; 2 January 1971, pp. 10–11; 20 February 1971, pp. 11–12; and 24 April 1971, pp. 12–13.

after all, is the perceived probability of warfare. Whether one takes institutionalized European groupings such as the Nordic Council, the Six, the members of the Council of Europe, or any other 'Western' European body, one can of course make the plausible *post facto* judgement that a security community of sorts has existed since the last war. (The same cannot be said of Europe on a broader scale, as the various features of the 'German question' well illustrate.)

But if we are to do more than judge in comfortable retrospect, we are bound also to examine socio-economic trends, communications and transactions, cultural changes and political attitudes in Europe. According to the pluralists, it is changes on this level which ultimately guarantee or threaten the existence of a 'community of states'.

On the basis of aggregated data on social communications, public and elite opinion, and content analysis of leading newspapers, Deutsch and his colleagues have come to the general conclusion that the process of Western European integration – in the sense of the growth of a supranational state – is grinding to a halt. What emerges instead is a pluralist's picture of the European future: 'The next decade of European politics is likely to be dominated by the politics of nation-states, and not by any supranational European institutions. In this regard and for this period, the views of President de Gaulle, that only nation-states will be obeyed and supported by the population, and the view of Raymond Aron that there will be no European federation – even for the next twenty years – seems to be borne out by the great preponderance of all the data that we have examined.'[1]

To Deutsch, then, it is clear that the chances of federation through the EEC are steadily receding. In fact, 'European integration has slowed since the mid-1950s and it has stopped or reached a plateau since 1957–8. In the 1957–8 period Europe reached the highest level of structural integration that it has ever had.'[2] But if the prospects of any kind of institutionalized, supranational integration are slim, it is by no means clear that even the minimal pluralist form of integration is any more assured. Deutsch's indices of social communications showed little growth, since 1958, of transactions between the European states, beyond what could be accounted for by the general

---

[1] Deutsch et al., *France, Germany and the Western Alliance*, p. 298. For other data on European attitudes and trends, see R. L. Merritt and D. Puchala, *Western European Perspectives on International Affairs* (New York: 1968), esp. Part II, section 3, pp. 281–317.

[2] Deutsch et al., *France, Germany and the Western Alliance*, p. 218.

increase of world trade and prosperity.[1] Analyses of political attitudes produced evidence which correlated strongly with that based on social communications. Between 1953 and 1963, the elite newspapers showed progressively less interest in the legal and political design of a united Europe and no growth, relative to national consciousness, of a European consciousness. Similar conclusions emerged from public opinion surveys taken between 1952 to 1962. Here there was some evidence of friendly feelings and a decline in the expectations of war between France and Germany; but there was still little expression of mutual trust or similarity of values. And finally, interviews with French and German elites demonstrated that 'the various elite groups generally are closer in their attitudes to each other and to the mass opinion of their own country, than they are to the opinions of their counterparts in the other country.'[2]

The overall impression from these various sources is thus by no means one of an emergent community transcending national boundaries. Rather, Europeans appear to be hesitating on the brink of integration. The most that Deutsch is able to claim is that in European mass opinion – and indeed the elite interviews, policy-statements, institutional changes and social communications bear this out – there is now 'a latent clash between the continuing acceptance of the reality of the nation-state and the newly-accepted image of some vague sort of European unity.'[3] For the European idea to have reached only this level of acceptance and political weight after twenty years which have witnessed unprecedented social and economic expansion and interdependence, a succession of govern-ments and movements pledged to further integration of one kind or another, and the emergence of a host of common organizations, would seem to mean that nationalism is a good deal more durable or adaptable, and the growth of community a good deal slower, than ever Deutsch at his most pessimistic would claim.

One critic of Deutsch's work, using in part the same sources of evidence, has suggested that a much more optimistic interpretation can be given of the present patterns in Europe. Inglehart argues that such influences as the postwar movements for European unity, the general increase of most forms of social communications in Europe,

[1] On this point, Deutsch's argument has been strongly contested. See Inglehart, *op. cit.*, p. 103.

[2] Deutsch *et. al.*, *France, Germany and the Western Alliance*, p. 299. For some recent evidence largely supporting these pessimistic findings, see Reader's Digest Association, *A Survey of Europe Today* (London: 1970).

[3] Deutsch *et al.*, *op. cit.*, pp. 250–1.

and the growth of new institutions, have all served to implant deep-rooted, stable attitudes in European youth which, as this generation moves into influential roles in coming years, will be expressed in a resurgence of national support for integration.[1] The experience of a peaceful postwar era may, in short, have socialized the next generation of European leaders so as to make a high degree of integration a realistic aspiration for the near future. In his concern to demonstrate the continuing relevance of the pluralist thesis about the political force of nationalism, Deutsch may have omitted to apply his own theories of generational change to predicting the emergence of European community. Inglehart shows that the application of Deutsch's approach can produce more than one interpretation of Europe's political prospects.

Thus despite the precision of the methods and indices used, Deutsch's approach to the assessment of integration in a group of states still relies on a great deal of personal judgement and selectiveness.[2] For this, the methodological sophistication cannot be a substitute. Deutsch provides a useful, detailed description of the manifold social and political processes out of which integration might emerge, but the explanations and predictions drawn from this description rely on several assumptions which may not always hold true.

Moreover, the patterns of social communication and attitudes upon which both Deutsch and Inglehart focus as the source of community tend to be seen in isolation. That is, they contain no indication that either the stability of national patterns or the slow growth of a European community might be reinforced or disrupted by such extraneous factors as technological change or shifts in the power-structure of the global international system. The 'other things' that are assumed to remain equal in this sort of analysis are likely in fact to prove the decisive forces for change.

Theorists of foreign policy might also question Deutsch's implicit assumption that the tendencies of states to integrate or conflict with their neighbours are based on public attitudes and patterns of behaviour.[3] On the contrary, the fact that the patterns of public opinion and behaviour are similar to those of the elites may not

[1] Inglehart, *op. cit.*, esp. pp. 91–5.

[2] It should be noted, however, that Deutsch has always recognized and stressed the need to combine quantitative approaches with 'the equally important and indispensable contributions of intuitive, qualitative and humanistic thinking' in studying politics. See 'Toward an Inventory', *op. cit.*, pp. 34–7.

[3] Deutsch *et al.*, *France, Germany and the Western Alliance*, pp. 217, 229.

imply any two-way influence; it may only mean that the public is dutifully following the cues and channels laid out by the government. Public involvement and influence in matters of external policy are traditionally low, and opinion usually formed from above. Hence it could be misleading to rely heavily on the measurement of mass social and political behaviour and attitudes in predicting the course of integration. It may also be inconsistent with another tenet of pluralist theory: if governments are to engage in the continuous, delicate processes of diplomatic adjustment required in a 'community of states', they must not be prey to uncontrolled shifts of popular behaviour and attitudes.

This difficulty – found throughout pluralist thinking on integration – may stem from a subtle confusion of historical perspective. On the one hand, it is true in the long run, if also rather a truism, that the integrative behaviour of states stems ultimately from the social, cultural and political characteristics of their populations; on the other hand, their short-term behaviour seems remarkably free from decisive popular influence. Hence the academic or the statesman who espouses the pluralist view would no doubt agree that supra-nationality might well emerge from long-term social changes. In such a case, however, the governments having necessarily evolved as well, it would remain misleading to speak of popular influence as over-coming governmental intransigence. In fact, the government would be at the forefront of these new patterns of opinion and behaviour as well. In the absence of this sort of long-term change, the committed pluralist is secure in the knowledge that no European government is likely to put itself in a position of being swept out of power by a surge of popular internationalist feeling.

In the chapters which follow, many other limitations of the pluralist position will become apparent. For those, like the functional-ists or neofunctionalists, to whom integration means more than the preservation of peace among nations, the pluralists' minimal defini-tion will seem inadequate. If the causes of war are traced beyond diplomatic spheres to deeper social and economic sources, or if welfare or social justice are held to be more important values than peace and security, then more demanding and dramatic forms of integration may be required. To this the pluralist would no doubt respond that if such 'cures' were politically possible, they could still be carried out in the framework of the existing international system; since they are not, no amount of functionalist logic or federalist rhetoric will make any difference.

63

3 Functionalism: The Technological and Economic Imperatives of Political Change

Functions, Structures and Community

The relationship between social, economic and technological change on the one hand, and political change on the other, has long been a major concern of political theorists. Some have argued that political forms and practices are strictly determined by the economic or technological character of societies; others have suggested that while we cannot infer the political structure of any society from its 'non-political' features, these latter do exert continuous pressure on leaders to reconsider and adapt the political system. The approach to international integration to be discussed in this chapter is founded on this distinction between the political and the non-political aspects of societies, and postulates an increasing tension between the particularistic nature of the former and the internationalizing implications of the latter in the modern era.

Since the 1930s, this position has been argued most forcefully and widely by a small and varied group of theorists usually described as 'functionalists' and best represented by David Mitrany.[1] The functionalists constitute the most explicit and articulate section of a large body of conventional wisdom about international organization. Briefly these ideas reflect a near-consensus that the modern technology of communications, industry and warfare, as well as the growth of economic, ecological and social problems on a regional or global scale, present irresistible pressures toward international cooperation and ultimate political unity.[2] This consensus supplies the chief

[1] The germ of Mitrany's functionalism is in *The Progress of International Government* (New Haven: 1933); his best-known work, first published in 1943, is now available, together with several other essays in D. Mitrany, *A Working Peace System* (Chicago: 1966). For other examples of the functionalist perspective on international order, see P. S. Reinsch, *Public International Unions* (Boston: 1911); and works by L. S. Woolf, such as *International Government* (London: 1916).

[2] Cf. the speculations of Q. Wright, *A Study of War*, abridged edition (Chicago: 1964), pp. 99–100; and of A. Wolfers on the emergence of a 'new medievalism' to replace the multi-state system, *Discord and Collaboration* (Baltimore: 1962) p. 242.

rationale for a large number of international organizations such as the Specialized Agencies and Regional Commissions of the United Nations and the proliferation of technical and economic organizations in Western Europe.

That these technological, economic and social forces can transform the world is by now a truism; whether they can be said to determine the course of history, and more particularly, to lead to global political unity, is much more questionable. To be fair to the proponents of this outlook, not all of them accept the sort of rigorous historical determinism found in Comte or Marx.[1] Some argue that the relationship between the various forms of change is itself a changing one, and that it has become increasingly difficult to describe and evaluate in the modern era. An American theorist, John Herz, has argued that since the basic political unit has always been that which provides military security, its form is dependent on the state of weapons technology. Alfred Weber's theory of history, he notes, suggested that the processes of cultural change and sociopolitical change were cyclical or indeterminate, while technological change was unilinear and progressive. Herz contends that Weber's distinction no longer applies and that 'for the first time in history we can speak meaningfully of 'world politics', based on universality of information and discourse, universalization of concern, and ubiquitousness of power and weapons'.[2]

There is, however, a difference between this process of 'world politics' and the existence of a global political structure. As Mitrany observes, 'The number of problems which take on a world character is growing apace, partly because we have a better understanding of them . . . but also because of their technical peculiarities. . . . These new contacts which crowd upon us from all directions can be as much a source of conflict as of cooperation. . . .'[3] In short, whether international cooperation develops depends on what men choose to make of their new social and technological environment. It is a general theme of these writers that it is unnatural, irrational and

[1] Not all functionalists, for example, would share R. Lemaignen's apparent conviction that European integration is the next stage of the 'irreversible' process whereby province has absorbed tribe, and nation, province: *L' Europe au Berceau* (Paris: 1964) pp. 209–10.

[2] J. H. Herz, 'The Impact of the Technological-Scientific Process on the International System', in A. A. Said (ed.), *Theory of International Relations* (Englewood Cliffs, N.J.: 1968) pp. 107–9; see also his *International Politics in the Atomic Age* (New York: 1959).

[3] Mitrany, *A Working Peace System*, pp. 92–3.

politically suicidal to allow political change to get out of phase with
(or to lag behind) economic and technical changes. In Quincy
Wright's words 'there appears to be a general tendency for change in
procedures of political and legal adjustment to lag behind economic
and cultural changes arising from technological progress. The
violent consequences of this lag can be observed in primitive and
historic societies, but its importance has increased in modern times.'[1]
Technology, it is often argued, is at the leading edge of the process
of historical development. 'L'histoire du monde est dominée par
l'évolution des techniques,' write Armand and Drancourt. 'La
poussée de la technique a pour conséquence de tisser entre les peuples
des liens de plus en plus nombreux, de plus en plus complexes.
Elle débouche sur la planétisation et la solidarité de fait des hommes
et des pays. . . . Les grandes causes de l'humanité a l'aube de l'ère
planétaire dépassent les personnes et les nations. Elles finiront, qu'on
le veuille ou non, par s'imposer à tous. Autant donc se préoccuper
sans plus attendre de construire la société de l'ère planétaire, en
tenant compte des réalités du temps actuel.'[2] Elsewhere these writers
note the contrast between 'le rapprochement "physique" des individus
sous l'effet des progrès techniques . . . et l'écart qui sépare les men-
talités de nos contemporains devenus proches sans être, toutefois,
devenus des prochains.'[3]

In this view of history, then, there is a continuous tension between
technological progress and political structure, the former representing
man at his rational, adaptable and fraternal best, the latter showing
him at his particularistic, conservative and obscurantist worst. Some
technological developments, particularly in communications and
transport, as well as the spread of scientific and managerial outlooks,
can be said to act as agents of political change largely independent
of human choice. At the very least they remove obstacles to integra-

[1] Wright, *op. cit.*, pp. 351–2.

[2] See L. Armand and M. Drancourt, *Le Pari Européen* (Paris: 1968), pp. 161–3:
'The history of the world is dominated by the evolution of technology. The thrust
of technology has as a consequence the weaving of more and more numerous and
complex ties between peoples. It leads to "planetization" and the *de facto*
solidarity of men and countries . . .. The great human issues at the dawn of the
planetary era transcend individuals and nations. They will ultimately, whether
we wish it or not, impose themselves on us all. Accordingly we ought to engross
ourselves in constructing a society for the planetary era, while taking account of
present realities.'

[3] *Ibid.*, p. 58: 'the "physical" drawing-together of individuals under the influence
of technological progress . . . and the split mentality of our contemporaries who
have become near without, however, becoming neighbours.'

tion and suggest the direction of change. But most of the techno-logical changes and most of the economic, social and ecological problems are what the Sprouts refer to as environmental factors that can only be said to influence, condition or otherwise affect 'human values and preferences, moods and attitudes, choices and decisions' to the extent that they are 'perceived, reacted to and taken into account' by individuals.[1]

It is in this light that we must understand the links between this general perspective on international integration and the body of social-scientific thinking known as functionalism. Semantic affinities between this and Mitrany's approach to international organization have led several contemporary theorists to some useful insights, if occasionally to some oversystematized and thus slightly strained conclusions.[2] Functionalism in social science has two main branches, each of which has had influential representatives in anthropology, sociology and latterly, political science. In its most rigorous form, it derives from the literal organicism of the social theories of Spencer and the metaphorical organicism of Radcliffe-Brown and Durkheim, who suggested that all social structures exist for the purpose of satisfying the functional needs of the social system as a whole.[3] Recently this 'requisite analysis' or 'structure-functionalism' has found its most systematic expression in the writings of Parsons, Levy, Almond and Apter.[4] The other form, developed by the anthropologist Malinowski and the sociologist Merton, takes individual needs rather than system-requisites as the 'functions' which are performed by structures. Whereas structure-functionalism is a rigorous conceptual framework oriented toward a general theory of society, the second type is a more flexible, empirical approach which starts from the premise that functions are being performed when individual demands are met by some activity in the system. It is an actor-

[1] H. and M. Sprout, *The Ecological Perspective on Human Affairs* (Princeton: 1965) p. 11.

[2] See, for example, E. B. Haas, *Beyond the Nation-State* (Stanford: 1964) esp. Chs. 1 and 2; and J. P. Sewell, *Functionalism and World Politics* (Princeton: 1966) Part 1.

[3] See H. Spencer, *The Principles of Sociology*, Vol. I (New York: 1897); E. Durkheim, *The Rules of Sociological Method* (Glencoe, Illinois: 1938) esp. pp. 89–97; A. R. Radcliffe-Brown, *Structure and Function in Primitive Society* (New York: 1952).

[4] See T. Parsons, *The Social System* (New York: 1951); M. J. Levy, Jr. *The Structure of Society* (Princeton: 1952); G. A. Almond, 'Introduction', in G. A. Almond and J. S. Coleman (eds.), *The Politics of the Developing Areas* (Princeton: 1960); D. E. Apter, *The Politics of Modernization* (Chicago: 1965).

oriented microcosmic approach to society, while the other approach is system-oriented and macrocosmic.[1]

It is important to keep this distinction in mind when examining the relation between functionalism in social science and theories of integration. The obvious link is in the notion of 'need' and its satisfaction by structural adaptation. Haas has demonstrated the weakness of system-oriented functional approaches, such as those of Kaplan and Modelski, which take 'needs' as pertaining to the international system as a whole and thereby run the risk of making teleological explanations of change.[2] Apart from the occasional hint of technological determinism and a certain implicit organicism, however, the Mitranian functionalists and most of the other writers with a similar outlook are far from the rigours of this kind of 'requisite analysis.' 'The essential principle.' writes Mitrany, 'is that activities would be selected specifically and organized separately – each according to its nature, to the conditions under which it has to operate, and to the needs of the moment.'[3] Such a pragmatic, flexible doctrine seems difficult to reconcile with a teleological or macrocosmic theory claiming that all social systems have the same functional requisites. The notion that the objective community of human needs and the universalizing effects of technology provide an environment which individuals may perceive and react to by integrating their political structures, is a far cry from the holism or determinism attributable to requisite analysis and often attributed to functionalism in general.

Just as in sociological functionalist theories structures are said to evolve according to the demands or needs of individuals or society, so, in this approach to integration, changes in the structure of the international system are said ideally to follow closely on technological and economic changes. International society is conceived, like Le Corbusier's house, as 'une machine à habiter' – it is shaped by what it does. Like Hobhouse's community, it is 'the sum of the functions performed by its members.'[4] Thus any time it deviates from the ideal one-to-one correspondence between needs and structures, 'dysfunctional' tensions set in which may lead to serious breakdown. If for most social scientists this is an empirical statement to be tested, for Mitrany and many of the other theorists who share

[1] See B. Malinowski, 'Functionalism in Anthropology', in L. A. Coser and B. Rosenberg (eds.), *Sociological Theory* (New York: 1964) pp. 637–50; R. K. Merton, *Social Theory and Social Structure*, revised edition (New York: 1957).

[2] Haas, *op. cit.*, Ch. 3, esp. pp. 56–9.

[3] Mitrany, *A Working Peace System*, p. 70.

[4] Mitrany, quoted in Sewell, *op. cit.*, p. 17.

his perspective, the problem is both empirical and urgently practical.

As Claude observes, although many traditional functionalists, particularly those involved with international agencies, see functional forms of integration as working toward solving problems of human welfare – thus elevating functional activities to the rank of ends in themselves – at bottom the theory is 'an assertion and defense of the proposition that the development of international economic and social cooperation is a major prerequisite for the ultimate solution of political conflicts and the elimination of war. . . .'[1] From a slightly different perspective, Armand and Drancourt argue: 'Les effets inéluctables de la technique sont généraux, mondiaux; les structures de gouvernement et d'organisation de la société demeurent incertaines, limitées, nationales. Elles ne permettront pas de faire face à certains dangers, que l'opinion, accaparée par le risque de guerre atomique, ne retient pas assez, mais qui ne s'infiltrent pas moins insidieusement dans la société moderne.'[2] Other theorists, such as Mitrany and Myrdal, emphasize the universality of the concern for welfare, and tend to see the elimination of war as almost an incidental byproduct of global socio-economic reorganization.[3] All these writers stress the dangerous gap between man's technical capacities and his social structures, between the universalism of the former and the particularism of the latter.

From this critique of the present structure of the international political system the prescription is clear enough. Out of an increasing recognition of the imperatives of technological change and the global scale of problems of welfare must develop a network of organizations performing specific functional tasks and transcending national boundaries. In Mitrany's words, 'The nature of each function tells precisely the range of jurisdiction and the powers needed for its effective performance. And for the same reason, unlike rigid political arrangements, functional arrangements can be adjusted, without political friction, when the conditions of the function are seen to have changed.'[4] What is elsewhere called 'fédéralisme à la carte' is very similar to this open, flexible pattern of organization:

[1] I. L. Claude, Jr., *Swords into Plowshares*, 3rd edition (New York: 1964) p. 345.

[2] Armand and Drancourt, *op. cit.*, p. 176: 'The inevitable effects of technology are general and world-wide; the structures for the government and organization of society remain uncertain, limited and national. They will not enable us to meet certain dangers which public opinion, monopolized by the risk of atomic war, is hardly aware of but which infiltrate modern society no less insidiously.'

[3] Cf. G. Myrdal, *Beyond the Welfare State* (New Haven: 1960).

[4] Mitrany, quoted in Sewell, *op. cit.*, p. 62.

'. . . procédons, sans attendre une hypothétique unification, à une série d'accords qui associeront des groupes de collectivités conscientes pour accomplir les tâches imposées par l'évolution.'[1]

Beyond this rudimentary level, however, it is difficult to say what the end-product of the process of integration thus conceived might look like. Many functionalists, notably from Britain and Scandinavia, rarely see the process as developing much beyond intergovernmental cooperation in certain technical areas. Others see functional cooperation as leading to a form of federal union. But most representative of the traditional functionalists is Mitrany, for whom the ultimate goal seems to be a complex, interwoven network of cross-national organizations performing all the traditional welfare-functions of the nation-state while at the same time rendering war impossible. In this community there is perfect elasticity of structures: they develop, as in Lamarck's Third Law, according to 'felt need' and die out with that need.[2]

The basis of the integrated system, then, is a web of organizations meeting all human needs and responding to technological change. A host of technical bodies, on the model of the Allied Cooperative Boards in each World War, the various United Nations technical organizations, the Tennessee Valley Authority or the Danube Commission, would deal with such problems as economic production and distribution, communications and transport, social welfare, education and innovation. To coordinate these organizations, there would then be a second tier, whose form and competence would not be laid down in advance, but rather would be allowed to develop naturally from needs arising in the first stage. A third stage would be coordination of the functional agencies with international planning agencies.[3]

Up to this point the functionalist's ideal system looks fairly straightforward: the divisive and self-perpetuating jealousies of the nation-state system will have been superseded by a smooth-running rational technocracy.[4] The government of men, as in the old phrase, will have become the administration of things. Of course, a number

[1] Armand and Drancourt, op. cit., p. 195: 'Let us proceed, without awaiting any hypothetical unification, to a series of agreements which will link groups of informed collectivities to accomplish the tasks set by evolution.'

[2] Sewell, op. cit., p. 68.

[3] Mitrany, A Working Peace System, pp. 72–5.

[4] See also the notion of 'fédéralisme à la carte', based on an organic network of cross-national firms, in Armand and Drancourt, op. cit., pp. 196, 198, 204. This use of the term 'federalism' recalls the nonterritorial notions of federalism developed in the work of Althusius, Proudhon, Laski and others. See infra, Ch. 5.

of accompanying assumptions may be questioned by those sceptical of the technocratic ideal. The first assumption is that the jealousies of sovereignty are to be found only in territorial units, and not in functional ones, and that therefore the coordination of proliferating and overlapping agencies will not be as difficult as the conciliation of states.[1] Another assumption is that men are able to recognize, design and agree upon appropriate structures for each functional need, so that form follows as closely as possible the exigencies of the functionalist doctrine. This assumption clearly makes enormous demands on human reason. And finally there is the optimistic assumption that organizations designed for a specific need or problem will disappear as the need is met. If Foreign Offices flourish when, in Mitrany's view, they are increasingly irrelevant, what is to prevent international agencies from developing similar inclinations?

Even if we accept these assumptions, the functionalist cannot always go on unambiguously to explain the political aspects of his ideal system. In this school of thought about integration, there are two, often contradictory, strains of attitudes toward the problem of politics. According to one, 'our social interdependence is all-pervasive and all-embracing, and if it be so organized the political side will also grow as part of it. The elements of a functional system could begin to work without a general political authority, but a political authority without active social functions would remain an empty temple. Society will develop by our living it, not by policing it.'[2] Not only is the political authority a secondary consideration; it may also be both unnecessary and dangerous unless subjected to 'checks and balances' and democratic control.[3] Mitrany's notion of world community thus gives a minimal role to 'government' in the sense of the imposition of order on society, and takes 'world law' to be, not an essential requirement for peace, but 'a formal embellishment upon the global community – an index of the efficacy of a functional approach, after the fact.'[4]

In Sewell's view the technocratic and the utilitarian threads in Mitrany's thinking predispose him to see his integrated community

---

[1] Claude, *op. cit.*, pp. 360–1, has sobering observations on these problems in the United Nations system.

[2] Mitrany, *A Working Peace System*, p. 97.

[3] *Ibid.*, pp. 75–6. On problems of representation in international administration, see *ibid.*, pp. 120–8. Cf. W. N. Hogan, *Representative Government and European Integration* (Lincoln, Nebraska: 1967).

[4] Sewell, *op. cit.*, pp. 17–18.

as a rationalist administrative and economic *Gesellschaft*.[1] Another critic of the functionalists observes that 'They would concentrate on commonly experienced needs initially, expecting the circle of the noncontroversial to expand at the expense of the political, as practical cooperation became coterminous with the totality of interstate relations. At this point a true world community will have arisen.'[2] From this it would appear that the functionalist model is a global institutional structure based on an informed calculation of objective common interests and eliminating 'nonrational' political loyalties extraneous to these interests.

The other strain of attitudes toward, and definitions of, politics is somewhat at variance with this outlook. Rather than eliminating the political aspects of modern life, functionalists here seek to build them into the new society. Sometimes this involves capping the reorganization of the system with a form of representative, democratic political control. Paul-Henri Spaak has argued with respect to the European Community that 'it is difficult to believe that six countries can combine their resources, opportunities and capabilities to a greater and greater degree, can integrate and dovetail their interests more and more, without one day setting up a political authority to crown this economic organization.'[3] Mitrany, in places, would seem to agree, while stressing that the forms of democratic control may have to be altered to suit an increasingly technical age.[4] In addition, he argues on occasion that functional areas (he calls them, characteristically, 'negative' functions) of a particularly governmental or political nature, such as 'law and order' or 'security', can be treated, perhaps with 'a certain degree of fixity',[5] but essentially in the same manner as any other functions. Security, he says, is 'a separate function like the others, not something that stands in stern isolation, overriding all the others.'[6]

By themselves, these observations would not suggest that the functionalist model is anything but the *Gesellschaft* suggested earlier. Haas, however, has gone on to argue that for Mitrany 'community is imminent in the evolutionary logic of his action process and hence a notion of integration (that is, in the sense of Toennies' *Gemeinschaft*)

[1] *Ibid.*, pp. 49–50.

[2] Haas, *op. cit.*, p. 6.

[3] Speech to the Council of Europe, 12 January 1964, quoted in M. Camps, *What Kind of Europe?* (London: 1965) p. 128 n.

[4] Mitrany, *A Working Peace System*, pp. 75–6, 124–5.

[5] *Ibid.*, p. 71.

[6] *Ibid.*, p. 76.

is implicitly part of his theory.'[1] As Haas nowhere develops this rather cloudy assertion, except by reformulating the functionalist doctrine himself, we must speculate as to how a sense of community can be said to develop alongside the functionalist restructuring of international society. Perhaps the answer is in the 'public relations' aspect of functionalist theory and the process of 'social learning', whereby men develop habits of cooperation and evolve, with the progress of functionalist organization, to a deeper awareness of their 'real' mutual interests.[2] But this would seem only to suggest that 'community' is the subjective counterpart of an objective reality, a complex of perceptions and expressions relating to concrete common interests. It is hard to see that, however the theorist might separate conceptually the perceived and the objective common interests, the former can be viewed as transcending the latter and indicating a sense of the 'whole' or a *Gemeinschaft*. The case that the traditional functionalist has in mind something more than a *Gesellschaft* would seem, in this light, to remain undemonstrated.

Indeed, starting from his assumptions about the nature of politics, it is hard to see how the functionalist could come to any other conclusion about the desirable form of community. As we have seen, he associates politics with 'political authority' (i.e., government), law and order, the state, security and sovereignty. Political activity thus centres around the instruments of coercion, governmental institutions and diplomatic practices of the nation-state system. Most often it involves debilitating and irrational conflicts for the power to make decisions in a society, decisions which, if men were freed from this political framework and totally informed about their material interests, would usually reduce to utilitarian computations. Hence the functionalist sees the process of integration as an ongoing indirect attack by the rational welfare-oriented side of man against outmoded and inflexible institutions and practices invested with the sanctity of age and reinforced by their use in satisfying his non-rational, competitive and often destructive urges.[3]

---

[1] Haas, *op. cit.*, p. 26. On the *Gemeinschaft-Gesellschaft* problem in international theory, cf. C. A. W. Manning, *The Nature of International Society* (London: 1962) pp. 176–7.

[2] See P. G. Taylor, 'The Concept of Community and the European Integration Process', *Journal of Common Market Studies*, 7: 2, 1968, pp. 83–101. Also 'The Functionalist Approach to the Problem of International Order: A Defence', *Political Studies*, 16: 3, 1968, pp. 393–410.

[3] A good expression of this outlook is in the assertion of Lemaignen that, 'Les entraînements affectifs ont causé aux peuples plus de misère que le respect des durs impératifs de la raison.' *Op. cit.*, p. 11, 'Emotional impulses have caused

At bottom the functionalist shares the technocrat's belief that there is a concrete distinction to be made between activities that are inherently controversial (and hence 'political') and those that are noncontroversial or technical. Activities concerned with national security in the broadest sense – diplomacy, policing, administration of the armed forces – or with competition for control of the governmental machine – the operations of political parties and pressure groups – are self-evidently political because they involve conflict over basic values. On the other hand, such areas as public health, transport or agricultural reform are essentially nonpolitical: if people were aware of the 'facts' they would agree that certain developments in these fields were beneficial to all. It is in these latter areas, where technical information stands a chance of changing attitudes, that the functionalists concentrate their efforts.

The assumption that technical decisions are less controversial than political ones can, of course, be questioned. It is not unknown for scientists and technicians, armed with data from 'objective' researches, to argue long hours over what are ostensibly nonpolitical, factual questions. In the face of this, the functionalist must argue either that in such cases political influences have intruded and biased the use of data, or that any issue over which there is prolonged controversy is *ipso facto* 'political'.[1] In either case he is forced to discard the concrete distinction between political and technical activities. Claude's objection to what he calls the 'separability-priority' thesis of functionalism is somewhat similar. The provisional separation of political and nonpolitical (i.e., economic and social) problems and the intention to concentrate on the latter 'in an international workshop where the nations shed their conflicts at the door and busy themselves only with the cooperative use of the tools of mutual interest' may, he says, be thwarted by the increasing tendency to politicize all international issues.[2] The end of the international 'state of war' may therefore be not a result but a precondition of the 'working peace system'.[3]

The Integrative Process

The end-product of the integrative process as envisaged by these theorists thus differs considerably from that of the 'pluralists',

more misery to men than a respect for the tough commands of reason.' Such might be the functionalist creed.

[1] On this issue, see Haas, *op. cit.*, pp. 14–19, for two case studies.
[2] Claude, *op. cit.*, pp. 350–3.   [3] *Ibid.*, p. 354.

discussed in the previous chapter. As we have seen, it derives from values and assumptions – about the international system, historical processes, relations between social structures and functions, human behaviour and the nature of politics – which are greatly at variance with those of the pluralists. If we turn now to look at the functionalist concept of the integrative process itself, the contrast should become even more apparent.

i) System Change and Technical Self-Determination

On the first level of analysis, that of the international system, integration is taken to be the transition from an 'international' society strictly defined (that is, in terms of relationships between territorially-based sovereign states) to a world society whose units are defined by function. In Kaplan's systems theory there are three types of actor – national, bloc and universal – but he nowhere conceives of a system without reference to national units. The 'bloc actors' in his polar systems are made up of national actors; in his hierarchical system, one national actor dominates the others; and even the international organization dominating his universal system is mainly an arbiter for national subsystems.[1] Integration as seen by the functionalists, on the other hand, means a gradual shift from a balance-of-power, bloc or unit veto system, by way of international organizations to a system whose units are nonterritorial organizations performing functions irrespective of national divisions.

The functionalist clearly starts from a more or less holistic conception of the international system. As we have seen, Mitrany and others insist in talking in terms of global needs and world society. The contrast is drawn between the rigid political-juridical pattern of order in the international system, i.e., the multi-state system, and the functional pattern, which cuts across and overlays territorial boundaries and which looks to 'needs' and to criteria of rational organization for definition of its administrative boundaries. Integration based on traditional national units or geographically defined regions is held merely to perpetuate dangerous political divisions. This is the basis for the functionalist critique of federal and confederal models, as well as of regional forms of integration, which may create, globally, deeper rifts than those they heal locally.[2] If, therefore, we are to

[1] M. Kaplan, *System and Process in International Politics* (New York: 1957) pp. 45–8, 85.
[2] Mitrany, *A Working Peace System*, pp. 174–213.

have regionalism at all, it must be functional, not territorial.[1] In such terms, 'regions' are not entities like Western Europe or the Caribbean, but functional areas like railway transport or epidemic-control. For such fields the geographical scope of cooperation would be defined purely by their technological and human implications: railways, for example, might be planned on a continental scale, epidemic-control globally.

Integration occurs as international organizations – entirely dependent at first on national support – gradually establish their competence to perform functional tasks on their own with reference to a global social system. In postulating the existence – present or potential – of such a system, the functionalist is like the theorist of political development who takes the national framework as given (no matter how frail) and then seeks to determine how certain organizations – notably the bureaucracy – develop their roles in the system.[2] Development is often seen as improvement in the performance of governmental functions by such structures measured against implicit norms of rationality. In the same way, functionalists tend to see integration as system-transformation led by a flexible international bureaucracy responsive to functional needs; success is measured by ability to develop structural support and capacity to solve further functional problems.[3] Just as national development involves the gradual ascendancy of the national bureaucracy and political system over regional ones, so international integration would involve the gradual assumption, by international organizations, of hitherto national functions. Just as the national government can rarely afford, in the early stages of development, a direct clash with sectional interests, and does better to harness and exploit them, so the international agencies, while seeking ultimately to overcome the nation-states, are at first dependent on them.

But the nation-state system today seems firmly entrenched, and the functionalist's starting assumption of an incipient world society seems a hopeless presumption. On what resources, then, does the functionalist analysis and strategy rely? As mentioned earlier, functionalists

[1] *Ibid.*, pp. 53 n, 70–1, 180–7.

[2] In this respect, J. LaPalombara (ed.), *Bureaucracy and Political Development* (Princeton: 1963), offers some useful insights into the problems with which functionalists are concerned. See esp. Chs. 1–7.

[3] See, for example, J. Siotis, 'Some Problems of European Secretariats', *Journal of Common Market Studies*, 2: 3, 1964, pp. 222–50, and 'The Secretariat of the UN Economic Commission and European Economic Integration', *International Organization*, 19: 2, 1965, pp. 177–202. Cf. Sewell, *op. cit.*, pp. 53–6, on problems in operationalizing such measures of integration.

argue that perception of an increasing number of problems, needs and trends outstripping national capacities is bound to result in pressure toward international cooperation. One such problem is that of security. The advent of the nuclear age, the developments in satellites and electronic surveillance, and new techniques of espionage, subversion and guerrilla warfare, have challenged the belief that the nation-state can still perform the basic function of protecting its members.[1] Just as gunpowder spelled the end of the walled city, so, the argument goes, nuclear weapons and airpower spell the end of the nation-state.

Another set of problems, of particular relevance to Europe, is broadly economic. The need for economies of scale for technologically based industries such as aeronautics or electronics, or in order to develop corporations on a scale competitive with American firms, is one example.[2] Related to this is the increasing need to create structures which acknowledge long-existing interdependence. The old remark about the unity of the Pas de Calais-Saar-Ruhr industrial complexes being 'always prescribed by geography, always prevented by history' illustrates the sort of interdependence for which transnational structures, in this case the ECSC, are deemed appropriate.[3] Other forms of interdependence are those in the monetary field where, for example, recurrent European payments crises have created renewed pressure for a European currency or central banking system. Then there are the problems of ecology which are gradually being recognized as international in scope – the most dramatic being pollution. As two French authors comment, 'On ne voit pas comment séparer la pollution du Rhin français et celle du Rhin allemand . . .'[4] Finally, there is increasing recognition that purely national planning of social welfare and economic development is becoming more and more difficult in an age when workers migrate across boundaries and the costs of research and development accelerate daily. 'Les hommes, les marchandises, les idées, les structures industrielles et commerciales franchissent de plus en plus, et de plus en plus vite, les frontières. Les monnaies sont solidaires. L'interdépendence des

[1] Herz, *International Politics in the Atomic Age*; Cf. A. M. Scott, *The Functioning of the International Political System* (New York: 1967) esp. Chs. 13 and 16.

[2] See J. J. Servan-Schreiber, *Le Défi Américain* (Paris: 1967). Cf. C. Layton, *European Advanced Technology: A Programme for Integration* (London: 1969).

[3] U. W. Kitzinger, *The Politics and Economics of European Integration* (New York: 1963) p. 10.

[4] Armand and Drancourt, *op. cit.*, p. 220: 'It is hard to see how one might separate the pollution of the French Rhine from that of the German Rhine.'

collectivités s'accentue, mais la politique n'évolue pas en con-séquence.'[1] Interdependence, in short, is a fact which, if acknow-ledged politically, would dissolve the nation-state system, organising the world not by what divides it but by what unites it.[2]

Another set of factors discussed by such theorists are those technological developments which, whether perceived or not, set in motion a process of 'planétisation'.[3] These include electronic media and their creation of a 'global village'; the revolution in data-processing; the new speed and scale of transport in all media. Accompanying these has been the spread of scientific, managerial and predominantly western 'elite culture', and what Armand and Drancourt call 'la noosphère du savoir'.[4] It is true that 'shrinking world' theorists often overestimate these effects, and underestimate the extent to which they have been harnessed by national govern-ments. Moreover, these developments do not in themselves suggest any alternative political form to the multi-state system. Nonetheless, their pressure on that system and the consequent blurring of its structure and the patterns of behaviour and attitudes underlying it must be acknowledged.

The functionalist asserts that the lag between these changes and changes in the structure of the international political system cannot be allowed to persist. The sociological, economic and technological base of national sovereignty is swiftly eroding, and the future global pattern becoming daily more evident and more necessary.

The dynamic of change upon which the functionalist relies has been referred to as 'technical self-determination'.[5] As problems of a technical (i.e., 'nonpolitical') nature arise, it is argued, they spawn organizations whose sole purpose is to solve them and whose limits of competence are defined by the nature of the problem itself. There is no blueprint or predetermined pattern to this process. As Mitrany says, 'the functional dimensions . . . determine themselves. In a like manner the function determines its appropriate organs. It also reveals through practice the nature of the action required under the given conditions, and in that way the powers needed by the respective

[1] *Ibid.*, p. 187. 'Men, goods, ideas, industrial and commercial structures are increasingly and ever more rapidly overcoming frontiers. Currencies are solidary. The interdependence of collectivities is becoming evident, but politics is not evolving accordingly.'

[2] Cf. Mitrany, *A Working Peace System*, p. 51.

[3] See Armand and Drancourt, *op. cit.*, Ch. 1; cf. C. A. McClelland, *Theory and the International System* (New York: 1966) Ch. 2; Wright, *op. cit.*, pp. 229–36.

[4] Armand and Drancourt, *op. cit.*, pp. 39–60.

[5] Sewell, *op. cit.*, pp. 12, 39, 250.

authority.'[1] Describing Roosevelt's New Deal as a model for this procedure, Mitrany observes that 'every function was left to generate others gradually, like the functional subdivision of organic cells; and in every case the appropriate authority was left to grow and develop out of actual performance.'[2] Similar themes are found in *Le Pari Européen*: 'le fédéralisme à la carte repose sur la nécessité de nouer organiquement les relations entre les hommes à partir de la base au lieu de les imposer du sommet.'[3] The equivalent of the functional unit for these writers is the 'entreprise transnationale'; for them, 'l'entreprise est aujourd'hui la cellule du tissu social de toutes les sociétés modernes et le type de structure le plus adapté au siècle.'[4]

Left at this, the concept of 'technical self determination' appears a rather dubious, deterministic social organicism. In fact, however, it is not difficult to demonstrate the dependence of this impersonal-seeming dynamic on human values and perceptions. 'Whereas the material aspect made its auspicious début through such concepts as "technical self determination"', writes Sewell, 'the human element enters in the guise of the "felt common need".'[5] Even the 'functional autonomy' of international agencies derives ultimately from a moral or political judgement as to the desirability of their activities.[6] Moreover, the process of transfer of functional methods from one context to the next ('ramification', or the 'ever-widening circles' image) depends on the system-wide spreading of a 'new conscience' or set of cooperative habits bred by functional experience.[7] In explaining the dynamics of change, functionalists tend to shift back and forth between faith in an inexorable, impersonal 'technical self determination', and exhortations about the need for new attitudes and political will. They seem torn between the fear of determinism and the desire for a potent theoretical tool.

Following from this are some major criticisms of the whole approach under discussion in this chapter. If a theorist postulates a rudimentary global society and a 'common index of need' and shifts

---

[1] Mitrany, *A Working Peace System*, pp. 72–3.

[2] *Ibid.*, p. 56.

[3] Armand and Drancourt, *op. cit.*, p. 196. 'Federalism *à la carte* is based on the need to tie the relations between men organically, working upward from the base rather than imposing them from the top.'

[4] *Ibid.*, p. 198. '. . . the firm is today the cell of the social tissue of all modern societies and the type of structure best adapted to the times.'

[5] Sewell, *op. cit.*, p. 39.

[6] *Ibid.*, p. 251.

[7] *Ibid.*, p. 56; cf. Claude, *op. cit.*, p. 350.

his perspective from the concrete subsystems (states) to the abstract (functions), he may be assuming a large part of what he sets out to prove. In thus moving away from Merton's actor-oriented notion of function and toward Parsons' system-oriented notion, the theorist runs the risk of accepting a lot of the latter's teleological and tautological baggage. It is, after all, likely to be more powerful theoretically to suggest that the expression of political demands by individuals, groups and states – as opposed to the generalized 'requisites' of an assumed global whole – are the 'functional needs' to which the nascent institutions are a response. The more the functionalist stresses these as the stimuli for integration and the less he relies on systemic requisites, the less tautological his explanations are likely to be.

In the second place, there are certain difficulties with the notion of organization at the system-level. At what point, for example, do the functional agencies take over the initiative from the states? Is it not conceivable that every functional need could be provided for in a framework of strictly intergovernmental cooperation on the pluralist model? Another alternative might be that these functional agencies, far from being the embryo of world society, develop their own vested interests and hinder the 'natural' integrative process with bureau-cratic particularism and resistance to coordination or abolition. In short, the link between functional performance and structural change in the multi-state system might not operate as the functionalists expect, because functional agencies prove either compatible with the existing political arrangement or incompatible with each other.

Finally, it is far from certain that the technological, economic and social conditions described earlier necessarily imply the demise of the multi-state system. As long as problems such as welfare are perceived as national, presumably that is how they will be treated. Moreover, the assumption that an increase in shared problems produces cooperation rather than conflict may be questioned. It surely depends very much on how each group perceives the problems; this is likely to be a function of national culture and political priorities more than anything else. In the same connection, the nation has hardly proved a passive observer of the process of 'planétisation': national control of communications media and technological development, as well as the near-monopoly of primal loyalties, has done much to counteract any inevitability in the integration of the global system.

ii) The Nation-State Under Pressure

Turning now to the second level of analysis, we must examine the functionalist treatment of the role of nation-states in integration. As a structural fossil from an era of limited economic and social problems and rudimentary technology, the nation-state is seen by these theorists as the chief barrier to rational organization for human welfare. Obsolete but obstinate, 'too weak to secure us equality and too strong to allow us liberty' the nation-state symbolizes the ascendancy of politics and power over the common interest.[1] Nations remain the focus of men's irrational, dysfunctional and often destructive emotions. As such they cannot be attacked directly, but can be rendered harmless gradually if welfare needs are organized and frontiers made meaningless 'through the continuous development of common activities and interests across them.'[2] The integration of mankind will thus come about not through, above or beyond, but despite, the nation-state.

In asserting both the political reality and the functional inadequacy of the nation-state, the functionalist draws an explicit contrast between society – natural, beneficial and flexible, with its 'widening circle of communal action' – and the state, the former servant of society now 'turned to prey on its own artificer'.[3] War and totalitarianism, the two related scourges of this century, are seen from this perspective as arising from the overdevelopment of the state as a political form. In this argument, there is an echo of the socialist tradition, which contrasts the internationalist tendencies of societies, 'the people', the proletariat, human needs or technology, with the bellicose and parochial tendencies of such state-dominating minorities as the capitalist classes or the munitions-makers.[4] Besides being irrational and inherently warlike, the state, with its supporting doctrines of sovereignty and nonintervention, is seen as a hindrance to the collective solution of many of the social and economic problems which are at the bottom of war and conflict. Both directly and indirectly, then, the nation-state, as a way of organising man's social and political life, has become a serious liability.

The functionalist remedy for this situation depends greatly upon

---

[1] Mitrany, *The Progress of International Government*, p. 141; *A Working Peace System*, p. 62.

[2] *Loc. cit.*

[3] Sewell, *op. cit.*, p. 31.

[4] See K. Waltz, *Man, the State and War* (New York: 1959) Ch. 5; Claude, *op. cit.*, p. 347.

the force of public opinion and, initially at least, on the temptation of national leaders to reap the domestic political benefits of international cooperation. Thus it will be more effective in states where channels exist for the free expression of political opinion, so that demands and support for further functional cooperation can be made articulate. In addition, the level of economic and technological development may be important: problems of a specialized and 'non-political' nature can be expected to arise most frequently in developed areas. Once several international organizations have grown up on this basis, the theory suggests, there will have developed a common interest in challenging further the competence and power of national administrations and trying to move to supranational forms. At the very least this new 'vested interest' will resist national retrenchment. Functionalist theory, then, sees the state in international cooperation as the insect in a carnivorous plant. Attracted ever inward by the benefits, it finds that behind it the avenues of retreat are progressively blocked.

As in many other theories of integration, there is something of a paradox embedded in this reasoning. At any juncture in the functionalist process, it is argued, the political elites of a state will choose the cooperative option, increasing the probability of their having to do so again and of their losing their jobs in the long run. As such behaviour does not square with what we – functionalists in particular – normally expect of national leaders, this cumulative process requires some explanation. Is it simply that leaders 'muddle through' blindly as decision after decision is thrust upon them from an environment of increasing interdependence, and that they are thus oblivious to where things are leading? Or are the leaders conducting a conscious rearguard action under the illusion that they can reap the political benefits of international cooperation without witnessing the erosion of their own roles and their state's competence? Both of these explanations rely more on economic and technological determinism and less on rational choice and free will than many functionalists would like. A more usual explanation would therefore be that, faced with unprecedented demands and limited capabilities, governments in a context of interdependence make rational choices about delegating these tasks to international agencies where not only authority but also costs are shared. If these choices are perceived, by all who make them, as delegations and not as partial abdications of sovereignty, the results are likely to be viewed with equanimity. But again, functionalists do not normally attribute such a state of mind to national governments. If governments are naturally co-operative, the problem of world order does not arise; if they are not, they can hardly be expected to dissolve themselves rationally and incrementally.[1]

The major criticism of the theory at this level of analysis, however, has to do with the functionalists' reading of world trends. Far from being under inexorable pressure from economic, social and techno-logical forces, the nation-state seems to be moulding these to its own ends. On the basis of statistical data, Deutsch has argued that the trend is away from military, technological, economic and cultural interdependance, and towards a new particularistic, national pre-occupation. In 1900 Britain, France and Germany each spent around ten per cent of GNP through government budgets; now the figure is thirty per cent, a great proportion of which is not on defence but welfare, i.e. just that field held by functionalists to have inter-nationalizing implications.[2] Similarly, international interdependence has declined and remains 'spectacularly lower than that within countries'.[3] In most states, foreign trade as a percentage of GNP has dropped steadily since about 1900; there is less migration and 'wage-interdependence' and increased national concern with infra-structures, services and education; and all international organizations taken together spend less than one per cent of world income (1/30 the percentage of national income spent by government in any developed state).[4] If political loyalty and authority require a socio-logical base – as the functionalists argue quite soundly – and these are the socio-economic trends, then it would appear that their re-sources in the struggle against the nation-state are ebbing away.

To conclude, then, in this approach to integration the states are viewed as playing a passive or restraining role in the process of political change. While the pluralists see integration as compatible with national autonomy and as requiring the development of the decision-making and diplomatic capacities of the states, the function-alists see it as the gradual overlaying and eventual elimination of the state-system by an administrative network which better serves human needs in what is assumed to be an emergent global community.

---

[1] For further observations on this issue, see *ibid.*, p. 349. Cf. Taylor, 'The Functionalist Approach', *op. cit.*, p. 407.

[2] K. W. Deutsch, 'The Impact of Communications on International Relations Theory', in Said, *op. cit.*, pp. 84, 87. This complements J. K. Galbraith's thesis, in *The New Industrial State* (London: 1968) on the unprecedented involvement of national governments in all stages and at all levels of the economic process.

[3] Deutsch, *op. cit.*, p. 89.   [4] *Ibid.*, pp. 84–5, 88–91.

iii) The Individual: Cooperation and Loyalties

It should be clear from the foregoing that the functionalist will be unlikely to cast much of his analysis of the integrative process at the level of the state as actor. In fact, the essence of the functionalist explanation is to be found in a complex set of assumptions about the linkages between international collaboration and the political attitudes of individuals. The mechanism of technical self-determination, which drives the functionalist process of integration, depends, as we have seen, not merely on objective trends but on collective attitudes toward cooperation. Thus, if people believe or can be persuaded that the world is more interdependent, they will act to make it so.

The core of the argument is that creative association and cooperation in problem-solving provides a learning-situation in which participants are gradually weaned away from their allegedly irrational nationalistic impulses toward a self-reinforcing ethos of cooperation. The institutional effect is important: 'Seules les institutions deviennent plus sages, elles accumulent l'expérience collective et, de cette expérience et de cette sagesse, les hommes soumis aux mêmes règles verront non pas leur nature changer, mais leur comportement graduellement se transformer'.[1] As men's attitudes and behaviour change, new areas open up for functional cooperation. The public gradually turns its loyalties away from the outmoded state to the institutions which more and more satisfy its material needs. But until people become aware of the organizations through their sheer impact on daily life, there is an additional need for public education and indoctrination.[2]

The process of attitude change through international cooperation thus operates in two phases. In the first, the direct experience of cooperation is felt only by individuals involved in specific functional activities – scientists on joint committees, coal producers, train travellers – and for the mass public this experience is distant or vicarious if perceived at all. In the second phase the experience has become diffused throughout society by education and the media, while the scope and number of functional agencies have increased

[1] H. -F. Amiel, quoted in J. Monnet, *Les Etats-Unis de l'Europe Ont Commencé* (Paris: 1955) p. 44. 'Only institutions become wiser; they accumulate collective experience and, through this experience and this wisdom, men obeying the same rules will experience, not a change in their nature, but a gradual transformation of their behaviour.'

[2] Mitrany, *A Working Peace System*, p. 95. Cf. Sewell, *op. cit.*, p. 49.

so as to make it likely that every individual has had some personal contact with some activity involving international cooperation. Underpinning this process is the emergence of what has been called 'mondiovision' – an ecumenical sharing of images, emotions and information through the pervasive immediacy of electronic communications.[1]

The simple proposition underlying functionalist theories of integration is that men's loyalties focus naturally on those institutions which gratify their basic material and social needs. Linked to this are two further assumptions. One is that political loyalties can be 'fractionated': just as a community is the sum of its functions, so loyalty to that community is the sum of particular loyalties to agencies in the community which satisfy functional needs. It follows that changes of loyalties can be incremental, function by function, and that there is – or ought to be – no political loyalty *per se* which transcends the sum of functional loyalties.

The second assumption, closely related to the first, is that since political attitudes are primarily rational and instrumental, to change men's loyalties really means to change their expectations as to where material satisfaction is to be found. Political attitudes, then, are almost entirely cognitive; the emotional components are taken to be small, secondary and atavistic. The fact that nation-states are vested with such supports is seen as a sign of their functional inadequacy and political dangerousness. The strategy of public education is an attempt to counteract such unthinking loyalties through an 'appeal to reason'.

Many of these propositions are clearly open to serious challenge. How are the functional needs – on which the community's administrative edifice will be built – to be identified? These problems can only be self-evident or 'objectively' determined within a society whose scale of values is settled, i.e. where people agree on which problems are the most important. The same need for prior consensus arises if one makes the less demanding assumption that a functional need is simply a demand expressed by a group within a society. Unless this natural or prior consensus is assumed, functionalist theory runs the danger of arguing that functional needs are best determined by social scientists, experts or, indeed, political leaders – for who else is in a position to create the consensus on which community must be built?

Similarly, the functionalist view of political attitudes points to ambiguities and inadequacies in the concept of 'function' itself. It is

[1] Armand and Drancourt, *op. cit.*, pp. 50–5.

not clear, for example, whether the sum of all functions is finite or whether community can grow as more and more human needs are 'discovered' and met through administrative agencies on various levels. To the extent that the former proposition holds, the process of political change becomes a competition between national and international administrations for the loyalties of individuals; to the extent that the latter holds (and the welfare orientation of functionalists suggests this as more likely), the process is less one of competition between levels than of structural differentiation, in which significant degrees of loyalty are likely to remain focused on national and subnational agencies where these prove the appropriate solution to functional needs.

The concept of 'function' also serves to illustrate the weakness of this approach in the face of the less rational aspects of political life. Functional needs are usually assumed to be the concrete, material ones of the Benthamite calculus. Inherent in this is a technocratic distaste for political conflict over basic values. By arguing that the objective, material outputs of government are more influential than the subjective or symbolic ones in determining the direction of individual loyalties, functionalists run the risk of being trapped in their own rationalism.[1] Like the pluralists, they find it difficult – indeed paradoxical – to conceive of integration proceeding through conflict.

For the functionalists, the growth of community is primarily a rational, incremental process of learning by association. As their functional needs are met, people discover the source of their welfare and direct their expectations and loyalties to the international agencies rather than to their states. Here again the tactical flaws in this pure learning model become evident. Is it likely that the states, which, at the initial stages at least, are the links between the public and international agencies, will cooperate in this transfer of loyalties? It is more to be expected – and the functionalist demonology would support this – that political leaders will exploit their position as the communications link and claim the gratitude of their citizens for whatever benefits the international agencies have produced.[2] The only way for these agencies to outflank the states would be to seek to make a dramatic impact on the popular imagination – a method not recommended in the cautious pages of the functionalist handbook.

---

[1] On the effective and symbolic aspects of political attitudes, see esp. G. A. Almond and S. Verba, *The Civic Culture* (Boston: 1965) pp. 45 ff; cf. M. Edelman, *The Symbolic Uses of Politics* (Urbana, Illinois: 1964).

[2] On these points, see Claude, *op. cit.*, pp. 349, 355.

The existence of these difficulties does no necessarily invalidate the notion of a psycho-social community underlying the development of functional cooperation.[1] It merely suggests that the functionalists' notion of attitude-change and supportive consensus should be broadened to account for the impact of the symbolic and non-rational side of politics. In the last analysis, for the functionalists' purposes it may be more important that people believe functional cooperation to be beneficial, than for it actually to be so.

Functionalism in Europe

Having examined in some detail the functionalists' concept of the goal of integration and their explanation of the dynamics of the process of structural change, we shall turn now to asses the applicability of these ideas to postwar Europe. Where has the functionalist strategy been successful, and how useful have its explanatory notions proved?

There would seem to be two areas in which to test the applicability of the theory we have been discussing. In the first place, the general assumption about structural responses to the internationalizing pressures of technological and economic change can be examined with reference to the growth of European corporations and trans-national organizations concerned with research, investment and development. In the second place, the more specific functionalist thesis can be tested with reference to various international organizations – both intergovernmental and supranational – set up explicitly to develop functional cooperation.

Some theorists place much hope on the transnational corporation. According to Armand and Drancourt, 'La création et le développement d'entreprises transnationales donneraient à l'Europe plus de cohérence. . . . L'existence et le bon fonctionnement d'entreprises transnationales à base européenne sont la condition pour donner au pari européen un support économique et technique de dimension mondiale. . . .'[2] An observer writing ten years ago remarked on the 'host of new industrial and business associations' which had grown up in Europe, largely under the auspices of the EEC. These included,

[1] See, for example, the model developed by Taylor in 'The Concept of Community', *op. cit.*, pp. 93–4.

[2] Armand and Drancourt, *op. cit.*, pp. 204–5. 'The creation and development of transnational firms would give Europe more cohesiveness. . . . The existence and successful operation of transnational firms on a European basis are the conditions for giving the European wager economic and technological support of world-wide dimensions.'

besides pressure groups, measures of 'business integration' such as industrial and commercial agreements over patents, licensing, marketing cooperation and joint manufacture.[1] The EEC, encouraging cooperation between small and medium-sized firms and seemingly moving toward a supranationally-developed company law for the Six, appeared to be the needed stimulus to form larger industrial operations competitive with the Americans. More recently, however, it has become less certain that this is the trend. If anything, the reciprocal relations between national states and industries have been growing, even in the less 'dirigiste' countries like Germany and Belgium. Governments have encouraged concentration, to be sure, but this has come about slowly, and largely on a national basis. In the era of 'growthmanship' the largest corporations in Europe have been nationally or trans-Atlantically controlled. Despite the renewed efforts of the Six to formulate a Community industrial policy – dealing with such problems as technical barriers to a single market, harmonization of taxation, and a European company law – the anticipated cross-national mergers and 'Eurocompanies' have been slow to form.[2]

In the absence of a comprehensive European industrial policy and in the uncertain economic and political atmosphere of the Six, there are numerous psychological and political disincentives to the formation of multinational corporations. Counteracting the 'Europeanization' of management, the perceived threat of American size and skill and the temptations of scale are the political scepticism and caution of businessmen and the traditional national affinities of the corporations. National governments reflect and support these doubts and affinities in the positions they take in Community discussions of the form of European companies and the administration of the proposed company law. And frequently running counter to what 'European' tendencies exist, there are often thinly disguised governmental intentions of consolidating particularly valued industries on a national basis. This, for instance, was the rationale given by the French government for its 'veto' of the Fiat–Citroen merger[3] and by the German government for its resistance to the French takeover of

[1] Kitzinger, op. cit., p. 132.
[2] M. M. Postan, An Economic History of Western Europe, 1945–1964 (London: 1967) Ch. 2 and pp. 214ff; cf. A. Sampson, The New Europeans (London: 1968) pp. 91–108. On the Colonna memorandum of March, 1970 for a European industrial policy, see European Community, April 1970, pp. 4–5.
[3] The Times, 27 September 1968 and 6 October 1968. There was talk of forming a large national corporation, 'Automobile de France', of which nothing materialized.

a German petroleum company.[1] It seems a fair judgement that many European companies seem to be becoming 'more, not less, national in their character, and to reveal the old rivalries in a new shape.'[2]

Quite apart from political influences, there are economic and technological reasons for this trend. In the first place, the logic whereby technological development would require rationalization of production, which in turn could force concentration of industries and lead to cross-national linkages, has proved less compelling than it seemed. Many of the large European firms appear to have grown much more rapidly before the war than after. Moreover, in order to lessen the effects of market fluctuations, taxation and competition, firms have often chosen to diversify their operations within national economies rather than consolidate with similar firms within or beyond these bounds. It appears, too, that innovation has had the paradoxical consequence of increasing the number of small, specialized establishments in Europe.[3] It can therefore hardly be claimed that technological change has increased the pressure for economies of scale or for European rather than national structures. The industries experiencing the greatest infusion of investment capital in the post-war period and thus having – one might have expected – the greatest tendency to expand into 'Eurocompanies', have been those, like the petrochemical and electronics industries, which are based on modern technology.[4] But such industries have not proved to be the leading edge of integration: national economic policies and the availability of American capital have provided them with viable alternatives.

With some modifications, similar observations apply to the various European organizations for research and development. 'Mettre en commun ce qui est neuf'[5] is a flawlessly functionalist prescription, and such organizations, whatever the degree of direct government support or participation, ought to provide many examples of the integrative process at work under the pressure of technological imperatives.

It is instructive in this respect to look at two fields – the peaceful uses of nuclear energy and the aerospace industry – where a proliferation of transnational collaborative efforts has taken place in Europe. In the nuclear field the multiplication of research and development organizations of various kinds has been swift, but never in a form

---

[1] *The Times*, 13 and 15 January 1969.　　[2] Sampson, *op. cit.*, p. 115.
[3] On these points, see Postan, *op. cit.*, pp. 192–6, 205.
[4] Postan, *op. cit.*, p. 128.　　[5] Armand and Drancourt, *op. cit.*, pp. 143–5.

which suggested that government policies were becoming the tail wagged by the technological dog. The pure research organization, CERN, has been able to function unmolested by governments, clearly because its work is far removed from political relevance. Other forms of cooperation with more likelihood of political impact – because of their implications for national energy policies or military capabilities – have been little more than temporary delegations of certain aspects of national research and development onto the international level by governments carefully calculating costs and benefits (both economic and political). Such has proved the case with programmes developed under the auspices of the European Nuclear Energy Agency (an OECD body) and of Euratom, whose founders, as we shall see shortly, had their sights set much higher. Even collaborative efforts on a narrower scale, such as the British-German-Dutch consortium for the development of the gas centrifuge enrichment process, have not shown the kind of growth the functionalist would expect if technology were in fact the main determinant.[1]

Nor is the principle of 'technical self-determination' particularly evident in the aerospace sector. Like the nuclear energy field, this new technology has seen the hesitant and scattered emergence of collaborative programmes which have been stunted or cut back by government withdrawals or reductions of finances. Here again the temptations of nationally based programmes or of cooperation with the United States have damaged European initiatives. In the areas of space research, satellites and launcher development, the ambivalent attractions of cooperation with the American post-Apollo programme and the inability of the European states to implement the proposed European Space Organization (to incorporate ESRO, ELDO and several other separate bodies)[2] suggest a number of important weaknesses in the functionalist thesis. Considerations of cost have led different countries to divergent conclusions about appropriate partners for, and levels of, technical cooperation; moreover, the 'evident' need for coordination among the resulting proliferation of programmes may be read by governments as a cue to change or withdraw from some of these activities. In the same way the ex-

[1] For a more optimistic appraisal of Europe's nuclear potential, see Layton, op. cit.

[2] For a concise assessment of the current state of European space cooperation, see M. Donne, 'Space Cooperation – But How?', European Community, January 1971, pp. 9–11. Cf. R. L. Pfaltzgraff and J. L. Deghand, 'European Technological Collaboration: The Experience of the European Launcher Development Organization', Journal of Common Market Studies, 7: 1, 1968, pp. 22–34.

perience of various European projects for the development of aircraft, such as the Concorde and the A–300 B Airbus, suggests that governments are not as impressed as they once were with the possibility of 'economies of scale' and are quite willing to opt for the absolute (if short-run) economy of non-participation or the costly pursuit of 'juste retour'.[1] Indeed it would seem that the only motives which keep national governments involved in many of these collaborative efforts are not those the functionalists would suggest, but the less 'rational' and technical ones of prestige and political influence.

The general issue of the state of research and development in Europe, like the concern over the formation of European companies, is of course only partly one of functional integration as such. Of greater concern to Europeans in recent years has been the outstripping of their technology and the penetration of their markets by the United States.[2] Comparisons between European states and the United States in terms of turnover and expenditure on research and development in crucial industries have been adduced as arguments, at the very least, for expansion of national programmes. More usually, however, the response to the 'American challenge' is assumed to be a coordinated programme on a broad European scale which would necessarily, as a prerequisite or a byproduct, increase the level of integration between the states involved. At the moment, however, the prospects for this seem slim; at the last report the contributions of countries in the European Community to multilateral and bilateral research activities stood at eleven per cent of the total public research money, and were declining.[3]

The second context in which to test the applicability of functionalist theory is that of intergovernmental and supranational organizations. Intergovernmental organizations, such as OEEC–OECD and the Council of Europe, seem at first unlikely homes for the functionalist spirit; they resemble either those vague, general international bodies it scorns, or the structurally rigid 'political' bodies it abhors. But a closer look at their concrete activities reveals a surprising amount that fits the functionalist prescription.

The OEEC developed as a framework for a range of specific functional activities arising out of Europe's immediate postwar

[1] For a critical look at such projects as forerunners of a European technological community, see *The Economist*, 16 May 1970, p. 38.

[2] The best-known exposition of this issue is J. J. Servan-Schreiber, *Le Défi Américain* (Paris: 1967).

[3] For full details, see *Le financement public de la recherche et du développement dans les pays de la Communauté*. Etudes et enquêtes statistiques, No. 2, 1970.

problems. These needs were defined by the Committee for European Economic Cooperation in 1947: (a) increased production in specified areas, (b) the elimination of inflation, (c) the promotion of economic cooperation, (d) solution of the dollar payments problem.[1] For these general purposes, there was set up the classic organizational structure – intergovernmental Council, Executive Committee, Secretariat. But this structure was underpinned by technical committees corresponding to specific functional tasks into which the four problem-areas were broken down. These committees were either 'horizontal' (concerning questions of fiscal policy, economic policy, trade, payments, manpower and overseas territories) or 'vertical' (concerning more specialized economic and technical areas).[2] This represents a flexible structural response to a series of needs or demands. Not only were communal decisions reached and executed as to Marshall Aid; further structures were evolved as further needs arose, as in the area of payments (EPU) and, perhaps most important, a new procedure of governmental interaction and negotiation known as the 'confrontation method', was developed. To be sure, the OEEC owed its success in part to the special circumstances states found themselves in after the war and their consequent political will to cooperate. But the type of shared need differed only in intensity, not in kind, from that described by functional theory. With its transmutation into the OECD in 1961, the organization retained many of its functionalist characteristics, but became increasingly oriented towards problems of trade and aid among its members and between them and the developing countries. The change of focus and membership would appear to place limits on the growth functionalists might expect in the organization.

The importance of the political context is well illustrated by comparisons between the OEEC and the United Nations Economic Commission for Europe (ECE). Despite the efforts of its Secretary-General, the ECE proved unable to develop intra-European trade and economic cooperation across Cold War boundaries. In the early years some technical cooperation was possible, and the less controversial committees have persisted. Latterly it is only the prospect of East-West *détente* that has revived speculation about a role for the ECE in a broader European integration.[3]

[1] Political and Economic Planning, *European Unity* (London: 1968) p. 79.
[2] *Ibid.*, pp. 85–6.
[3] *Ibid.*, Ch. 2. Cf. D. Wightman, *Economic Cooperation in Europe* (London: 1956); Siotis, 'The Secretariat of the UN Economic Commission and European Economic Integration', *op. cit.*

The Council of Europe, despite its classic political structure (Committee of Ministers, Consultative Assembly, Secretariat) and its early federalist intentions has, like the OEEC–OECD, become primarily a framework for a large variety of functional activities. The Council has stimulated the creation of structures to deal with technical cooperation in agriculture, transport and communications, energy and other fields. In addition it has operated in the areas of human rights, technical aspects of law, education, cultural cooperation and social welfare (i.e. public health, refugees, worker migration). In this there is a variation on the pattern described by Mitrany: the 'coordinating' level, instead of arising out of needs emerging from the first tier of organizations, has either already been present or has evolved out of an organization originally created for other purposes. This aspect of the Council's development has escaped much notice. Almost in the same breath those who assert the unifying effects of education, welfare, and cultural cooperation dismiss the Council of Europe as irrelevant or ineffectual because it is not operating in the intended political field. Whether the Council's quiet, uncontroversial work can bring about the sort of consensus which might support bolder functional cooperation at a later date is still in doubt. Like the Nordic Council, it has not challenged national governments. This is impeccable functionalist tactics, even if at this stage the outcome remains an article of faith.[1]

The two European organizations of a supranational kind to which the functionalist analysis applies in its strict sense are the Coal and Steel Community (ECSC) and Euratom.[2] The aim of the ECSC was to set up among the Six a single coal, iron and steel market, planning for productivity and redeployment of resources, abolishing trade barriers and encouraging fair competition so that the coal and steel sectors of the European economy might modernize and grow. Accompanying this economic interpretation of the inherently transnational nature of the industry was a political interpretation – that tying up the French and German economies in this way would preclude the two states' going to war again. Schuman's announcement of 9 May 1950 was recognized as a landmark in international

[1] See Taylor, 'The Concept of Community', *op. cit.*, pp. 97–8, for a suggestion that the Commission adopt similar tactics.

[2] The EEC, although it clearly embodied aspects of functionalist theory at the outset, has evolved a notably different philosophy and method of decision-making, and will therefore be discussed in the next chapter. On the differences between the EEC's and the Coal and Steel Community's methods, see Camps, *op. cit.*, pp. 129–30.

organization, proposing the transfer, to a common organization, of real powers (legal and financial) over a limited field. Schuman talked of building Europe 'through concrete achievements, which first create a *de facto* solidarity'.[1] Inasmuch as he, Monnet and the other supporters of the scheme saw it as the means to a European federation, or as a 'partial federation'[2] itself, it might be difficult to take the ECSC as a pure example of functionalism. On the other hand, as a method of integration and, more important, in the European context as it developed in the 1950s and after, the ECSC gradually assumed an unambiguous functionalist character.[3]

Nevertheless, it is clear that the ECSC has, in its successes, taken the functionalist method beyond its original scope. Willis has described in detail the political processes operating during the national debates over signing and ratifying the Treaty, and Haas has argued that the Community's working methods represented a practical reformulation of functionalist logic.[4] For example, the political argument that the ECSC would rid Germany of Allied control of the Ruhr and perhaps hasten the end of the occupation was undoubtedly more important in gaining German support for the Treaty than were the pure economic arguments.[5] At almost every stage, too, the decisions of the Community involved not just technicians and bureaucrats, but political parties and interest groups. Moreover, as economic conditions changed, flaws were revealed in the Treaty which gave the national governments renewed opportunities to intervene.[6] Thus it would clearly be an oversimplification to interpret the changing fortunes of the ECSC as a reflection of economic and technological imperatives. Political dynamics entered into the picture in a way functionalist theory was not always equipped to perceive.

Of course constant, often unpredicted, shifts in the economic and technical base lay at the root of many of the organization's troubles. Many of the problems initially expected to be central to the ECSC's work, such as price-fixing, the 'dirigisme-laissez-faire' issue,

[1] Political and Economic Planning, *op. cit.*, p. 257; Willis, *op. cit.*, p. 87.

[2] See Kitzinger, *op. cit.*, pp. 63–4; W. Diebold, 'The Relevance of Federalism to Western European Economic Integration', in A. W. Macmahon (ed.), *Federalism: Mature and Emergent* (New York: 1955) p. 440.

[3] Mitrany himself certainly argues this. See *A Working Peace System*, pp. 110–11, 207.

[4] Willis, *op. cit.*, pp. 94–103, 120–9; E. B. Haas, *The Uniting of Europe* (Stanford: 1958); see also W. Diebold, *The Schuman Plan* (New York: 1959).

[5] Willis, *op. cit.*, pp. 104–5, 109.

[6] Political and Economic Planning, *op. cit.*, p. 290.

or even the expansion of coal and steel production, have proved less difficult than predicted or have declined in importance as different and unforeseen problems have arisen. On the other hand, initial difficulties in treating the coal and steel sectors in isolation from other economic sectors, and in deciding the powers of the High Authority reappeared during the market crises of the mid- and late fifties. In years of excess steel-supply, governments have resisted the closure of less efficient mills or the cutting back of their national production. But perhaps the most significant shift of this kind has been the major change in Europe's energy-pattern: the share of coal in total energy consumption dropped from seventy-three per cent (1950) to fifty-three per cent (1960) to thirty-four per cent (1966), and will fall further.[1] This necessitates further cutbacks which, combined with the rationalization of production and improvement of *per capita* output, has meant undertaking a vast programme of welfare and retraining for redundant coal workers. While ECSC steel production doubled in fifteen years (to eighty-five million tons in 1966), steel trade increased one hundred and fifty-seven per cent until the end of the transition period in 1958, and much important technological advance was made, it has become clear subsequently that much of this success was based on a temporary solidification of the economic and technological base and on the political abstinence of governments. General economic expansion, the coal glut of the late fifties and recurrent shortages of petroleum in Europe masked the secular downward trend in the coal industry and the now apparent fact that much of the ECSC's authority was inadequate and in the wrong areas; moreover governments were less inclined subsequently to equip it any better. As Servan-Schreiber notes, 'les faillesses de la CECA viennent de ce qu' on lui a denié les pouvoirs qu'on lui reproche maintenant de ne pas exercer'.[2] If, however, the decline of coal and the increasing difficulties of treating economic sectors in artificial isolation prove the stimuli to a common European energy policy, the ECSC may yet be claimed by some functionalists to have vindicated their thesis. It is unlikely, however, that such a policy will emerge without a

[1] European Community Information Service, *The Facts* (London: 1967) p. 11; ECSC High Authority and European Community Information Service, *Europe and Energy* (Luxembourg: 1967) pp. 46–7. Estimates for 1970 place coal consumption (not including lignite) at less than twenty-five per cent.

[2] See Servan-Schreiber, *op. cit.*, p. 120. 'The weaknesses of the ECSC derive from the fact that it has been denied the powers which it is now attacked for not exercising.' For a penetrating analysis of the Community's response to the coal crisis, see Lindberg and Scheingold, *op. cit.*, pp. 198–216.

dramatic political push of the kind the ECSC's own history sensitizes us to.

The Schuman Plan stimulated ideas for a number of similar 'pools', notably in agriculture (Mansholt), transport (Bonnefous), energy (Monnet) and health, but the atomic energy community (Euratom) was the only one to be realized on a similar pattern as the ECSC. As a new field where there were few established economic and political interests, nuclear energy seemed a clean slate on which to design a common civil industry and undertake common research. Moreover, the economic incentive was present: a rise in European energy demand was predicted, of which it was expected nuclear power would assume a greater proportion. Up to 1965, this proportion was negligible, but by 1970 it was supposed to be around one per cent and by 1980, between eight and eleven per cent.[1] Thus there seemed to be a solid, technically sound future for cooperation and integration in this field.

Why, then, is the consensus today that 'Euratom bears the indelible imprint of failure'?[2] Euratom has not only failed in the broader context of expectations about the enhancement of political co-operation and integration; it is even questionable whether it has fulfilled the narrower technical and industrial role assigned to it. In Christopher Layton's words 'all the lessons of European integration so far are that pooling research has limited value, if it is not followed by steps to apply the results in a common industrial operation.'[3] Yet Euratom has in recent years moved more and more into pure research and away from the promotion of a common industry. At the same time, it has assumed the position of adjunct or complement to separate national nuclear programmes rather than director or coordinator of a unified European programme.

The difficulties of Euratom, like those of the ECSC, can be accounted for not only by the evident political constraints on the organization, but by changes in its economic and technological rationale. The post-Suez petroleum shortage, which was a major stimulus to the idea of a European nuclear energy industry, proved shortlived, and the five to ten per cent annual increases in Europe's energy needs have so far been met by commensurate rises in petroleum and natural

---

[1] ECSC and European Community, *Europe and Energy*, pp. 46–7. In fact, even the modest 1970 figure has not been reached.

[2] L. Scheinman, 'Euratom: Nuclear Integration in Europe', *International Conciliation*, 563, 1967, p. 54.

[3] *The Times*, 4 March 1968.

gas supplies.[1] But almost all of the Community's petroleum, which provides over sixty per cent of its total energy, is imported, and the recent dramatic confrontation with the supplying countries (led by Libya, which alone supplies one-third of the Community's oil) has underlined the need for other sources of energy and for a common fuel policy. It does not, of course, necessarily follow that Euratom will experience a revitalization; the range of alternatives for European energy has increased markedly since 1956, and nuclear sources are a less evident option.

The structure of the existing nuclear industry has also evolved in a way which works at cross-purposes to the growth of Euratom. The United States now supplies a growing number of Europe's reactors. Even within Europe, new forms of production are being developed outside the jurisdiction of Euratom, either on a national basis (the French gas-diffusion programme) or on a multilateral basis (the proposed British-German-Dutch project). Euratom is reduced to assisting in the flow of technical information among such projects (when possible) and to seeking reassurances that they do not conflict with the aims of the Rome Treaty (which they often do). Even the functionalist who optimistically sees Euratom as the emergent co-ordinating body between all these projects is brought up sharply by the persistent disputes between it and the International Atomic Energy Agency on the one hand, and the European Nuclear Energy Agency on the other, as to who should coordinate what.

Most fundamentally perhaps, Euratom has suffered from political changes since its establishment. It has tended to become caught up in the struggle between the French government and the Commission of the EEC, and tarred with the same broad Gaullist brush. Since M. Hirsch was replaced by M. Châtenet in 1961, the emphasis in Euratom has moved perceptibly from the development of a 'powerful nuclear industry within the Community' to the 'coordination and supplementing of national programmes' – a move very much in keeping with French desires.[2] This has been accompanied by budgetary cuts, by strict application of the principle of 'juste retour' and by national pre-empting of new areas of research such as plutonium production. Underlying all these changes are a number of political problems relating to possible military applications and the issue of proliferation, particularly with respect to West Germany.

[1] For summaries of recent figures, see *European Community*, March 1970, p. 26 and April 1971, p. 16.
[2] See A. Spinelli, *The Eurocrats* (Baltimore: 1966) pp. 39–43.

These have aided the crumbling of the consensus on which Euratom was founded. As a result, nuclear energy deserves the remark by Sampson that, 'So far from being a basis of European unity, energy has become "a pocket of resistance to integration"'.[1]

On the basis of European postwar experience, then, we must draw some unhappy conclusions about the possibilities of integration through functional cooperation. First, the 'shrinking world' outlook of which functional theory partakes must be treated very sceptically. European experience suggests there is nothing inherently integrative in technology or economic growth *per se*. The relation between functional need and structural adaptation, central to the theory, is 'necessary' only in the sense of being an ideal or norm, not in the sense of predetermining the direction of change.

Secondly, even the purest and most self-conscious application of Mitrany's functional strategy, the ECSC, has not proved immune to political influence. On the contrary, structures have generally seemed more responsive to political than to economic imperatives. Pressure groups, parties and changes of regime have mattered greatly, and shifts in the technological and economic foundations have allowed governmental reassessments of policy and reassertions of will. Again what appeared in 1950 or 1956 to be an objective 'community of need' (as evidenced in energy patterns) came subsequently to be recognized as a rough governmental estimate. For the most part, then, functionalist endeavours like ECSC and Euratom were not, like OEEC, at the level of 'felt need' but were largely bureaucratic manifestations of technological projections relevant only to business and governmental elites. Popular support was thus a missing link.

Finally, and more optimistically, the functionalist process *has* operated, and continues to do so, but in unexpected areas and with unpredictable effects. It has been suggested that the OEEC and the Council of Europe were two organizations where such cooperation in basic and undramatic undertakings may be subtly transforming European society. As Jean Monnet has said, 'The history of European unification shows that when people become convinced a change is taking place that creates a new situation, they act on their revised estimate before that situation is established.'[2] Perception and expectation are thus all-important, and the kind of social learning that takes place on these basic levels of economic and social activity may encourage a gradual anticipatory shift in popular political conscious-

[1] Sampson, *op. cit.*, p. 82.   [2] Quoted in *ibid.*, p. 10.

ness, towards support of greater integration. This blending with Deutsch's notion of community is not a denial but a readjustment of functionalist theory, to where it can benefit from other social-psychological approaches to political integration.

In general, then, functionalists find the European experience disappointing because they have placed their expectations on organizations and activities which were not as 'non-political' or as close to public needs as they assumed. Paradoxically, considering their welfare-orientation, they have not been sufficiently struck by the deep involvement of the modern state in most of the economic and technical activities which they rely on as integrating forces. Awareness of this fact would have the effect of reorienting functionalism in one of two ways. Either the theory could begin to account for governments, not merely as 'passive' or 'negative' actors in the integrative process, but as actors which can both push for integration and lessen its effects on popular perceptions and on structural change in the system. Or functionalists could focus more on truly technical activities with a much lower potential for controversy and a closer relationship to the daily life of the mass public. As we shall see in the next chapter, the first option has, to some extent, already been taken; the second option offers an important new direction for functionalism as a theory of integration.

4 Neofunctionalism and the European Community Method of Integration

Political Community: The Search for a Concept

Both pluralism and functionalism represent long-standing traditions of theory about international order. In recent years, however, the study of international political integration has been dominated by a relatively new approach, which has come to be called 'neofunctionalism'. This approach has its origins in a sympathetic critique of the older functionalism discussed in the previous chapter; it has derived much of its dynamism and support from the success of the European Economic Community; and it owes much of its conceptual and explanatory apparatus to the development of American political science in the past two decades. These three major influences have blended to form a distinctive, if not always coherent, body of concepts, hypotheses, assumptions and beliefs pertaining to political integration on the regional and global levels.

The essence of the neofunctionalist argument is that political integration comes about less through pressures from functional needs or technological change as such, and more through the interaction of political forces – interest groups, parties, governments, international agencies – which seek to exploit these pressures in pursuit of their own interests. In certain kinds of conditions, it is argued, the conflicts inherent in such a process are resolved so as to give greater powers and competence to common organizations, and increase the range and importance of decisions taken jointly rather than separately by national governments.

In their pursuit of rigorous explanations of political integration, neofunctionalists have been highly sensitive to conceptual and methodological issues. In particular they have been concerned with the elusiveness of what they are trying to explain. Neofunctionalists, it is true, share the view that political integration is not a condition but a process of change which leads to some sort of political community. The difficulty comes in establishing the characteristics of this community. In fact many of the basic values and assumptions behind this approach will become apparent if we examine how various representative theorists have wrestled with the problem of defining the goal or end-product of the integrative process.

In the writings of Ernst Haas, where neofunctionalism has its foundations, the concept of the integrated political community has undergone a continuous, subtle evolution. Professor Haas' *The Uniting of Europe* (1958), the first major expression of the neofunctionalist viewpoint, is a study of the political dynamics in the development of the Coal and Steel Community, and contains a crucial definition of integration: 'Political integration is the process whereby political actors in several distinct national settings are persuaded to shift their loyalties, expectations and political activities toward a new centre, whose institutions possess or demand jurisdiction over the pre-existing national states. The end result of a process of political integration is a new political community, superimposed over the pre-existing ones.'[1] This is a rigorous, demanding definition of political community, difficult to distinguish from that espoused by the federalists. A new centre of authority gradually supersedes the states, building up its competence in sector after sector of public life. The shift of loyalties, expectations and activities, then, describes the development of a new, supranational state. At the very least, this will be a weak state, little more than a pluralistic system with minimal machinery for common decisions; more likely, however, under the pressures from economic and social interdependence, is evolution toward a more centralized, amalgamated system resembling the Western nation-state.[2]

In a later article (1961), Haas repeats his definition of the integrative process, but the concept of 'political community' as the terminal condition seems to have become broader and more ambiguous. He suggests that 'a variety of constitutional and structural factors are compatible with this notion (of political community); political community exists when there is likelihood of internal peaceful change in a setting of contending groups with mutually antagonistic aims.'[3] It is clear from this that Haas would consider Deutsch's minimal, pluralistic form of integration quite acceptable. By these criteria, the existence of political community is indicated simply by the prevalence

[1] E. B. Haas, *The Uniting of Europe* (Stanford: 1958) p. 16.

[2] *Ibid.*, pp. 4–11.

[3] E. B. Haas, 'International Integration: The European and the Universal Process', in *International Political Communities: An Anthology* (New York: 1966) p. 94.

of peaceful conflict-resolution among independent units. Yet the working definition implicit in Haas' analysis of the integrative process refers us to the emergence of an institutionalized supranational system of some kind. There is, therefore, some ambiguity as to where the threshold of political community has been placed.

This ambiguity emerges again in an article published three years later, where Haas and a colleague write that political union 'implies any arrangement under which existing nation-states cease to act as autonomous decision-making units with respect to an important range of policies', where 'the actors have already transcended their earlier exclusive identification with the pre-existing national state', and where 'the politicized decision-making process has acquired legitimacy and authority.'[1] The constitutional expression of this condition could be (a) a unitary state, (b) 'the principle of shared but not sharply divided powers which is typical of the European supranational approach', or (c) even a confederal arrangement.[2] In apparently trying to avoid adopting the restrictive, institutional model of the nation-state writ large, Haas risks making his definition of 'political community' so broad and flexible as to lose all analytical force. Much depends, for instance, on how literally we are to take the terms 'autonomous' and 'exclusive'. It is questionable whether any nation-states today act as 'autonomous decision-making units' with which actors identify 'exclusively'. In the same way, it can be argued that decision-making processes in the UN have acquired some 'legitimacy and authority'.[3] To conclude from such analyses that the global international system is a 'political community' does not seem to get us very far.

By the mid-sixties, however, Haas' concept of political community crystallizes around the idea of supranationality as a distinct political form, 'a unique style of making international decisions, unique because of the nature of the participants, the context in which decisions are made, and the quality of the decisions produced. . . . Supranationality, not federation, confederation or intergovernmental organization, seems to be the appropriate regional counter-

[1] E. B. Haas and P. C. Schmitter, 'Economics and Differential Patterns of Political Integration', in *ibid.*, pp. 265–6.

[2] Haas argues that the last form would qualify only if an 'actual delegation of national power to a central agency' had taken place: *ibid.*, p. 265. It is, however, debatable whether in such cases the system could still, strictly speaking, be described as 'confederal'.

[3] On this point, see I. L. Claude, Jr., *The Changing United Nations* (New York: 1967).

part to the national state which no longer feels capable of realizing welfare aims within its own narrow borders, which has made its peace with the fact of interdependence in an industrial and egalitarian age.'[1]

Underpinning this concept of supranationality is a critique of the distinction usually made between 'the nation-state as a warm and self-contained community' and 'the colder and more calculating world of nation-states labelled "international society"'.[2] On the one hand, modern political communities tend to 'lack the warmth and devotion we associate with ascriptive ties and communities based on primary contacts or loyalties'; they are communities based on 'abstract symbols and vicarious identification', and on an underlying procedural consensus.[3] On the other hand, the interdependence of these national communities tends to reproduce these same characteristics on the international level and thus to decrease the mechanistic, instrumental qualities of regional or global systems. The typical modern political community, according to Haas, is a 'multi-group competitive national society' where there is 'agreement on the means of resolving internal conflicts by peaceful methods, . . . a *Gemeinschaft* that looks and acts like the *Gesellschaft* we associate with our modern international system.' It is to this type of community, a conceptual compromise between the traditional 'ideal types' of international society and national community, to which integration at the supranational level is directed.[4]

The difficulties in rendering this sort of concept operational are illustrated in a recent article by Haas, in which he remarks on the compelling need of integration theorists to establish their 'dependent variable', and on the inability of neofunctionalists in particular to agree on what it might be.[5] Integration, he argues now, is concerned with 'how and why states cease to be wholly sovereign, how and why they voluntarily mingle, merge, and mix with their neighbours so as to lose the factual attributes of sovereignty while acquiring new techniques for resolving conflict between themselves.'[6] The terminal

---

[1] E. B. Haas, 'Technocracy, Pluralism and the New Europe' in S. Graubard (ed.), *A New Europe?* (Boston: 1964), reprinted in J. S. Nye, Jr., (ed.), *International Regionalism* (Boston: 1968) p. 151, 159.

[2] *Ibid.*, p. 161.

[3] E. B. Haas, *Beyond the Nation-State* (Stanford: 1964) p. 39. For his analysis of earlier functionalist concepts of community, see also pp. 22 and 26.

[4] *Ibid.*, pp. 39–40.

[5] E. B. Haas, 'The Study of Regional Integration: Reflections on the Joy and Anguish of Pretheorizing', *International Organization*, 24: 4, 1970, pp. 622 and 628.

[6] *Ibid.*, p. 610.

condition to which this process may lead ought to be visualized, not in terms of 'ideal types reconstructed from our historical experience at the national level', which 'are inadequate because they foreclose real-life developmental possibilities', but in terms of the master concept 'authority-legitimacy transfer', which suggests such possible outcomes as a 'regional state', a 'regional commune' or 'asymmetrical overlapping'.[1]

A number of Haas' colleagues and former students, having done detailed case-studies in the neofunctionalist vein, have gone on to develop concepts of the end-product of integration which constitute slight but significant variations on the original. Of these scholars, perhaps Lindberg has gone farthest in exploring the implications of the neofunctionalist model. In his first study of the European Economic Community (1963), he adopts a 'more cautious' conception of political integration than that of Haas, 'limited to the development of devices and processes for arriving at collective decisions by means other than autonomous action by national governments.' It is logically and empirically possible, he suggests, that 'collective decision-making procedures involving a substantial amount of political integration can be achieved without moving toward a political community as defined by Haas'.[2] Lindberg's political community is simply 'a legitimate system for the resolution of conflict, for the making of authoritative decisions for the group as a whole.'[3] He suggests it is not necessary, and perhaps even misleading, to postulate an end-point in analysing the emergence of this type of system.[4] In thus abstracting the process variables and playing down the structural goal and the policy-content of integration, Lindberg seems to be trying to avoid imputing a teleological quality to the integrative process.

And yet, as successful as he may appear in these efforts, Lindberg does not prevent a notion of the end-product from creeping into his analysis. The implication of his two-part definition of the integrative process is a federal system, if not in terms of constitutional structure then certainly in terms of political processes. Nations 'forgo the desire and ability to conduct foreign and key domestic policies independently of each other, seeking instead to make joint decisions or to delegate the decision-making process to new central organs'.

---

[1] *Ibid.*, pp. 630–6.

[2] L. N. Lindberg, *The Political Dynamics of European Economic Integration* (Stanford: 1963) p. 5.

[3] *Ibid.*, preface, p. vii.   [4] *Ibid.*, pp. 5–6.

In addition, 'political actors are persuaded to shift their expectations and political loyalties' to this new centre. The model implied here would seem to differ from Haas' supranational decision-making system only by requiring less of a shift of fundamental values.[1]

Following up this attempt to abstract the political variables in integration, Lindberg has been drawn toward systems-theory.[2] He argues that because systems-theory identifies the essential political processes, offers a comprehensive and functionally interrelated set of categories for analysing any political system, and is based on a study of a wide variety of systems (primitive, democratic, totalitarian and international), 'it is thus free of many of the kinds of assumptions involved when the nation-state is the sole empirical example from which a model of the political process in general or the integrative process in particular is derived.'[3] Thus, through a shift of perspective, integration theorists can avoid the conceptual limitations of the nation-state analogy. Unhappily, however, Lindberg feels obliged to add a footnote to the effect that since the existing political form from which the systems-model is derived is pre-eminently the nation-state, there is bound to be some distortion or bias in it. To the last Lindberg is, quite justifiably, unwilling to accept the easily-conceived model of the supranational state as the goal of integration. And yet all his invocations of systems theory seem unable to rid his analytical framework of its presence.

Nevertheless, the concept of the integrated system which Lindberg employs in his most recent work is remarkably consistent with his early ideas. 'The essence of political integration is the emergence or creation over time of collective decision-making processes, i.e. political institutions to which governments delegate decision-making authority and/or through which they decide jointly via more familiar intergovernmental negotiation.'[4] Integration, as the growth in scope and institutional capacity of such a collective decision-making system, may be susceptible of analysis with reference to some more or less explicit, but distant, terminal point such as a federal state. But this need not preclude our asking about the stability of collective

[1] *Ibid.*, p. 6. See, esp. the note on the problem of measuring shifts of values.

[2] L. N. Lindberg, 'Integration as a Source of Stress on the European Community System', *International Organization*, 20: 2, 1966, pp. 233–65; and 'The European Community as a Political System', *Journal of Common Market Studies*, 5: 4, 1967, pp. 344–87.

[3] *Ibid.*, p. 350.

[4] L. N. Lindberg, 'Political Integration as a Multidimensional Phenomenon Requiring Multivariate Measurement', *International Organization*, 24: 4, 1970, p. 652. See also pp. 649–50, 663.

decision-making systems which fall short of such goals and for which assumptions of equilibrium look more plausible.[1] The end-product of integration – as the case of Western Europe suggests at present – may well turn out to be a mixed system in which the Community's institutions and the national governments, rather than competing for a fixed amount of political support and a finite set of jurisdictional areas, gradually form a symbiotic relationship.[2]

It is clear from other neofunctionalist writings that Lindberg's definition of the dependent variable as a collective decision-making system of this kind is close to the present consensus on the issue.[3] In the early optimistic years of the European Community, it was generally assumed that the terminal point of the integrative process would be some sort of federal state in Western Europe. Those involved in the Community often described themselves as working toward a European federation by functional means. This self-image, combined with the early successes of the Community, tended to reinforce neofunctionalist practice and theory alike in its assumption about continuous growth toward a supranational federation. Nonetheless, as doubts and qualifications emerged among the academics, so cautionary notes were sounded by a few activists and analysts of the day-to-day activities of the Community. Walter Hallstein, while accepting the usefulness of the federal analogy in analysing the EEC, warned that since the Community was '*sui generis*, a new kind of political animal, the analogy should not . . . be pressed too far. . . . Just as language precedes grammar, so politics precedes political theory. . . .'[4] Similarly, Roy Pryce observed that events in Europe were outstripping theory, so that the goal of integration was largely unformulated except in federalist terms which might prove totally unsuited to the European situation.[5]

It is fair to conclude, then, that the neofunctionalist concept of the goal of political integration remains somewhat undefined. On the

[1] L. N. Lindberg and S. Scheingold, *Europe's Would-Be Polity* (Englewood Cliffs: 1970) pp. 24–5, 99, 183–4.

[2] *Ibid.*, pp. 32, 37, 94–5, 261–2 and 306–10.

[3] See also the articles by J. S. Nye, Jr., P. Schmitter and S. Scheingold in the valuable symposium on regional integration in *International Organization*, 24: 4, 1970, esp. pp. 798–9, 836 and 1001.

[4] W. Hallstein, *United Europe: Challenge and Opportunity* (London: 1962) pp. 25–9.

[5] R. Pryce, *The Political Future of the European Community* (London: 1962) pp. 22–4, 56–9. See also M. Camps, *What Kind of Europe?* (London: 1965) pp. 124–131; and 'Interview' with Jean Rey, *European Community*, February, 1969, p. 6.

one hand, there is a reluctance to adopt the model of the supra-national federal state, which derives partly from fears about teleo-logical implications, partly from a sense that it forecloses conceptual options, and partly from an awareness of the less ambitious but equally interesting alternative suggested by the present stability of the European Community. On the other hand, the model of the emergent federation still provides most of the standards by which the success or failure of integration is measured; the use of scales of centralization of decision-making suggests that this model remains a working assumption of many neofunctionalists.

The neofunctionalists' acceptance and analysis of the concept of a mixed national-supranational decision-making system does not mean that their challenge to the nation-state as a political unit is no longer potentially total. Any function performed by the existing nation-states is grist to the mill of the collective decision-making system. Pluralist theorists, on the other hand, do not challenge the nation-states, but rather reaffirm them in their basic functions and simply seek to regulate their diplomatic relationships; functionalists chal-lenge them, but only in the areas of material welfare. But the neo-functionalist supranational system could, in theory, not only in-fluence or perform the allocation of material things but also provide internal and external physical security and become the prime focus of political loyalties and expectations. This wealth of roles is reflected in the rich diversity of reasons adduced by every shade of political opinion supporting European supranational integration. For some it is a matter of security, either against future internecine wars or against some outside power such as the Soviet Union; to others it is a matter of preserving economic, political and cultural autonomy or enhancing global influence, *vis-à-vis* the United States in particular. For many such purposes, the minimal 'pluralist' model or the narrowly administrative functionalist model might well seem in-sufficient. For the neofunctionalist, then, the whole range of activities, purposes and meanings of the nation-state as a concept of political organization is under scrutiny.

The explanation for the potential breadth of this scrutiny lies largely in the neofunctionalist view of politics and, hence, of 'political' integration. Whereas the older functionalists and the pluralists tend to see the political as a concrete type of activity (usually associated with defence, foreign affairs or the acquisition of power), the neo-functionalists see it in the abstract. Essentially, politics is viewed as the process of conflict and decision-making involved in the allocation of basic values in a community. For Haas 'all political action is purposively linked with individual or group perception of interest'[1] and the political process is primarily one in which a variety of interest groups, political parties, individuals and, on the international level, states, seek access and direct their expectations to some centre which regulates the allocation of values. Political processes in international organizations, he suggests, can be compared most fruitfully with the classic liberal image of domestic politics as unregulated competition for a limited supply of welfare and security.[2] Essentially, then, politics is involved whenever values are scarce; it is not, as the older functionalists tend to argue, inherent in some activities (such as defence) and absent from others (such as health). Thus, for the neofunctionalists, it is only proper to argue that some matters are inherently more 'political' than others to the extent that they can be said to have more potential for conflict of interests and hence controversiality.[3]

A similar and much more explicit abstraction of the notion of politics occurs in Lindberg's writings. This is evident even in the largely substantive early study of the EEC, where he stresses that 'it is not the policy content, but the method and context, of decision-making that is of greatest interest',[4] and where his definition of the political community foreshadows his espousal of Easton's systems theory.[5] In his later writings he follows Easton in defining the political system, not as a set of institutions or a group of people, but as 'that system of interactions in any society (including pre-national or multi-national societies) through which binding or authoritative allocations are made and implemented.'[6] Its boundaries

[1] Haas, *Beyond the Nation-State*, p. 34.

[2] *Ibid.*, see esp. pp. 32–8.

[3] Cf. Haas and Schmitter, *op. cit.*, p. 262, on the notion of 'politicization'. In many ways the difference between the neofunctionalist approach and the others over the nature of politics comes down to this: to the former, some issues are relatively more associated with political conflict than others, although potentially any issue can be 'politicized'; to the latter, some issues are political, while others are not supposed to be, even if they cannot always remain 'immune'. Cf. S. J. Bodenheimer, *Political Union* (Leyden: 1967) pp. 18, 21–2 on the difficulties, in the face of 'political' obstacles, of maintaining this abstract notion of politics and the accompanying neofunctionalist faith in the likelihood that integration will 'spill over' into more and more issue-areas irrespective of their inherent qualities.

[4] Lindberg, *The Political Dynamics of European Economic Integration*, p. 278. Cf. *Europe's Would-Be Polity*, p. 32: 'For us . . . politics is defined not by substance, but by process.'

[5] *Ibid.*, preface, p. vii.

[6] Lindberg, 'The European Community as a Political System', *op. cit.*, p. 346.

are neither geographical nor institutional nor personal, but behavioural; politics, as a pattern of behaviour, is an essential component of any social system.

'Politics as substance' or 'politics as process' – this debate has tended to range pluralists and classically-minded theorists of international relations with the former notion, and neofunctionalists with the latter.[1] The 'process' definition is clearly congenial, even essential, to a theory of incremental growth, where integration is viewed as spilling from one policy area to the next without encountering resistance of a qualitatively different kind. In fact, the neofunctionalists found this view difficult to defend. Lindberg, in trying to account for the impact of de Gaulle on the Community, acknowledges that he, Haas and other theorists of integration 'have tended to treat reassertions of *purely political goals* such as national grandeur or independence either as atavisms or at best as residual categories.'[2]

In a somewhat agonizing recantation, Haas takes the argument to its logical conclusion. 'The history of the European unity movement,' he writes, 'suggests that the relationship between politics and economics remains somewhat elusive.'[3] Drawing a distinction between 'low' politics – the incremental decision-making processes of the economic and technical spheres – and the 'high' politics of diplomacy, strategy and national ideologies, Haas argues that we can properly expect the neofunctionalists' dynamics of integration to operate in the former context. The extent to which the process of incremental integration, from economic to political unity, can occur, depends on the state of relations in the 'high' political sphere. 'Pragmatic interests, simply because they are pragmatic and not reinforced with deep ideological or philosophical commitment, are ephemeral. Just because they are weakly held they can be readily scrapped. And a political process which is built and projected from pragmatic interests, is bound to be a frail process, susceptible to reversal.'[4] The source of reversal will be deterioration of the consensus among elites, either over the aims and methods of integration itself,

[1] For a strong statement of the former position, see S. Hoffmann, 'Obstinate or Obsolete: The Fate of the Nation-State and the Case of Western Europe', in Nye (ed.), *International Regionalism*, esp. pp. 198–206.

[2] Lindberg, 'Integration as a Source of Stress on the European Community System', *op. cit.*, p. 235. Emphasis added.

[3] E. B. Haas, '"The Uniting of Europe" and the Uniting of Latin America', *Journal of Common Market Studies*, 5: 4, 1967, p. 315.

[4] *Ibid.*, esp. pp. 327–8.

or over some substantive 'high' political issue. By this reformulation, then, the integrative process comes to be seen not as automatic but as contingent.

Such redefinitions of politics clearly place severe constraints on the explanatory power of neofunctionalism. Much of the original appeal of this approach lay in its claim to show how a cumulative integrative process could build sufficient momentum eventually to erode even the most intractable bastions of national particularism, and create, in so doing, a new supranational state. But if this process cannot be said to operate indifferently as to sectors of political life, allocating values over the whole range of issue-areas, if the 'spillover' is effectively choked off, then neofunctionalism becomes considerably less useful for explaining political integration as this problem was originally conceived. In effect, then, neofunctionalism becomes a theory of 'low' political integration and puts aside the relationship of 'low' to 'high' politics as unresearchable. The problem, in short, has been redefined.

Neofunctionalism claims to have reconciled the classic functionalist concern with economics and welfare with a theory of political conflict and choice, and to have shown how integration can develop, not through an economically determined process but through the resolution of political conflicts among elites and interest groups. But the concept of political conflict derives from one of the dominant images of American political science – that of liberal, pluralistic interest-group politics played out against a backdrop of ideological consensus.[1] In the age of the 'end of ideology' the competitive pursuit of individual and group interests according to certain 'rules of the game', is the basic dynamic of economic and political development, whereby the system's institutions allocate values as they enhance their own authority and legitimacy.

The 'end of ideology', despite the severe attack to which it has been subjected of late, is at least a plausible assumption for the political scientist to make in analysing post-industrial societies with a considerable history of formal national unity. It is also plausible to argue that certain areas of political life are imbued with a basic ideological consensus which allows for a competition over scarce resources which can have integrative effects. It is less easy to see how the 'end of ideology' assumption could be transplanted to an international system – even one so seemingly cohesive as Western Europe

[1] For a classic statement of this view, see S. M. Lipset, *Political Man* (New York: 1960) Ch. 13; and Daniel Bell, *The End of Ideology*, rev. ed., (New York: 1962).

– and made into a component of a theory of political integration which laid claims to all sectors of political life.[1]

Far from reformulating functionalism by building into it a liberal vision of political conflict, then, it appears that neofunctionalism makes very similar assumptions about underlying consensus. Politics, therefore, is not about the common good of the political community – these issues are assumed to be settled. It is, rather, the behaviour of individuals and groups competing in pursuit of their own interests in the context of a political system which authoritatively allocates political goods.[2]

An integrated system with interest-politics built into it is thus the functionalist technocracy at one remove. That is, instead of the goal of integration being a 'nonpolitical' system of government distributing values for a society free of all conflict, it is a 'political' system doing exactly the equivalent, free of all conflict save that which provides its circulatory dynamic. The ideal type of political system, in this view, responds to demands with infinite flexibility, aggregates them and ties them to political support so that all interests are to some extent conciliated in the packaged set of values which emerges. Whereas the older functionalists state an unabashed preference for administration over politics, the neofunctionalists create, in their concept of the integrated system, a blend of the two, but a blend in which there remains an administrative flavour to the 'politics'. In short, the neofunctionalists have largely retained the rationalism of their intellectual forebears. At bottom they are, like the functionalists, good Weberians, seeing integration as a gradual increase in stability and rationality through the growth of a bureaucratic polity.

In many respects, neofunctionalism reflects the state and preoccupation of American political science in the late fifties and early sixties. Like few other theorists of integration, neofunctionalists form a selfconscious scholarly community concerned to arrive at a systematic, coherent theory of international political integration. In the past, unceasing toil has gone into the identification, classification

[1] The 'end of ideology' argument is outlined in Haas' 'Technocracy, Pluralism and the New Europe', in Nye, *op. cit.*, pp. 149–76.

[2] For a critique of this concept of politics, see C. Bay, 'Politics and Pseudo-politics: A Critical Evaluation of Some Behavioural Literature', *American Political Science Review*, 59: 1, 1965, pp. 39–51. For an argument that this concept also pervades the 'undemocratic, bureaucratized' European Community, see A. Spinelli, *The Eurocrats* (Baltimore: 1966). The Commission, Spinelli says, has long been a prisoner 'of the illusion that politics consists simply of proposing and applying regulations for the realization of the Common Market' (p. 150). One wonders what Spinelli now thinks, since he himself has become a Commissioner.

and operationalization of numerous independent variables; now, as we have seen, the focus, belatedly, is on the clearer specification of the dependent variable. The drive is always toward the construction and empirical testing of hypotheses and toward the measurement of the extent of integration achieved.

This theoretical energy has been manifested in a breaking away from traditional modes of analysis – seen in the concern for dynamics rather than statics, political sociology rather than law and history – and in the dissolution of such classic dichotomies as those between politics and administration and between domestic and international politics. As in contemporary political science generally, this conceptual and analytical liberation has produced a new and diverse collection of candidates for independent and dependent variables, and a range of more or less testable propositions. Some attempts have been made to draw these together under such macro-structures as group or systems theory, and many collective research efforts are anticipated.[1]

The capacity for self-criticism which marks scholarly communities such as this is likely to be sorely needed as neofunctionalism comes up against stresses and criticisms from the several sources suggested in the foregoing analysis. The apparent stagnancy of European integration has produced a fundamental reappraisal of the assumed terminal point of integration. It has led some neofunctionalists to begin asking about the purposes and consequences of integration.[2] These stresses have led to the clarification of some central concepts and, on occasion, revealed the degree to which some theorists have incorporated, despite their disclaimers to the contrary, many of the biases and assumptions of the older functionalism. To the extent that these latter are retained, and to the extent that the neofunctionalists opt for the minimal concept of the end-product of integration as a mixed decision-making system in equilibrium, this approach may find itself having less and less to say about crucial issues of change in the international system. Such pessimism, however, is probably unwarranted at present, and should not obscure the considerable conceptual and explanatory sophistication which neofunctionalism has already added to the field of integration studies.

[1] For attempts to create macro-analytical frameworks, see Haas, *Beyond the Nation-State*, part I; Lindberg, 'The European Community as a Political System', *op. cit.*, esp. pp. 345–9; and Lindberg and Scheingold, *op. cit.*, esp. Chs. 1–4, 8 and 9.
[2] S. Scheingold, 'Domestic and International Consequences of Regional Integration', *International Organization*, 24: 4, 1970, pp. 978–1002.

The Integrative Process: Political Development Through Interest-Politics

Both their view of the goal of integration and the values and assumptions supporting this view provide neofunctionalists with a distinctive approach to the problem of international order. As suggested, however, neofunctionalism is far more concerned with processes than with goals, conditions or values, and it is in respect to processes that the major distinctions between it and the other approaches become most evident. We have observed that neofunctionalism, historically, was an amalgam of federalism and functionalism. The federalists, initially at least (and still implicitly) supplied a model of the end-product – a supranational state; the functionalists provided the dynamics of change in the idea of a structural evolution based on socio-economic pressures. For both functionalists and neofunctionalists, then, the levers of integration are to be found in international organizations performing those economic, social and technical functions which are putting increasing pressure on the capacities of individual states. For both, too, the effect of international interaction in these organizations is a gradual incremental process of institutional development 'beyond the nation-state'. Within this general framework of agreement, however, there are fundamental differences between functionalism and neofunctionalism as to the process of integration.

i) *System-change as political development*

Of all the approaches to international integration, neofunctionalism has the closest affinities with the field of political development as this has emerged in comparative politics. In general, neofunctionalists have preoccupied themselves with determining the conditions under which a rudimentary political system – usually a regional grouping of states – gradually develops its capacity to make and execute common decisions. Most of the conditions and mechanisms of this process of change are taken to be qualities, not of its constituent states or individuals, but of the system as a whole.

As a theory of systemic growth, neofunctionalism therefore sets out from a quite different perspective on international systems from that held by the pluralists or the older functionalists. Pluralists tend to retain the classic distinctions between national and international political systems – based primarily on differences in the distribution

of legitimate power or sovereignty – and the accompanying separation of foreign and domestic policy. The interdependence in international systems is seen as diplomatic and strategic, foreign policies
being conducted in an austere universe apart from the mundane
matters of domestic politics. Functionalists, while accepting this as
an accurate description of our current unhealthy condition and as an
example of our unhelpful ways of thinking about world politics,
go on to postulate a natural interdependence of technology, economics and welfare which they see as calling for fundamental global
reorganization. In contrast to both of these schools, neofunctionalists,
both empirically and by definition, conclude that in most international systems sufficient *de facto* political interdependence exists
that we can ignore the classical distinctions and simply assume the
functioning of some kind of political system analogous to a primitive
national one.

Neofunctionalists can take this step because, as we have seen, for
them a political system exists wherever there is a pattern of conflict
or decision-making in which values are allocated authoritatively
for the participants. In national systems such political functions may
be performed through party competition and interest-group conflicts
and reflected in legislative, executive and judicial procedures; in
international systems, diplomatic bargaining and war may be more
prevalent modes. But the differences are of structure, style and scale,
not of function. In both cases, a political system is operating, and it is
this common element the neofunctionalists emphasize.

On the obsolescence of the classic national-international distinction, Lindberg is most explicit. He writes of political actors moving
'beyond the nation-state as a basic framework for action', and of
forces at work in Western Europe that may 'alter the nature of international politics'.[1] Elsewhere he notes 'the incipient breakdown of the
differentiation between foreign affairs and domestic affairs.'[2] The
systems approach which he has adopted subsequently makes the old
conceptual distinction even more meaningless. Thus, rather than ask
how a classic diplomatic system might evolve to something like a
supranational state, Lindberg starts from a positive answer to his
question: 'Is the European Community a system of interactions that
constitutes a political system?', finds operational equivalents on the
international level to structures and processes of national politics
(i.e. Easton's various categories and concepts), and then proceeds

---

[1] Lindberg, *The Political Dynamics of European Economic Integraiton*, p. 4.
[2] *Ibid.*, p. 80.

to ask whether this postulated system can persist over time.[1] In his most recent work, for example, the European Community's political system is defined in terms of two characteristics: (a) its functional scope (or the range of decisions it may now make) and (b) its institutional capacities, which are the decision-making structures and the 'decision rules and norms which define the system's existing procedural consensus'. Whether the system develops, stagnates or declines depends not only on these, but on the type and level of demands made on it, the 'systemic support' afforded it by elites and publics, and the leadership resources available to it on the national and supranational levels.[2] Lindberg's use of the systems framework is perhaps the best reflection of how far the neofunctionalists have gone toward abstracting the political variables which produce the underlying similarities of national and international systems and which also, they suggest, represent the crucial dynamics of integration.[3]

In part, then, the removal of the classic national-international distinction in favour of *a priori* assumptions about the existence of a regional political system, is a deliberate strategy of analysis which allows the neofunctionalists to ask new questions about integration and to ignore old and perhaps fruitless ones. In addition, however, neofunctionalists generally argue that the empirical evidence for such a view of interdependence is so compelling – at least in developed areas – that to undertake this shift of perspective is no longer unrealistic. They would agree with the functionalists that conflicts and decisions in one state with respect to almost any field – defence, economics, education, welfare – tend to produce inputs into other states' political systems, even if the issues are by classical definitions 'domestic'. Moreover, one of the consequences both of this informal interdependence and of the growth of formal intergovernmental cooperation is that various political forces such as interest groups,

[1] Lindberg, 'The European Community as a Political System', *op. cit.*, pp. 349–50.
[2] Lindberg and Scheingold, *op. cit.*, Ch. 4, esp. pp. 110–16. For a further elaboration of these five key variables into ten, see Lindberg, 'Political Integration as a Multidimensional Phenomenon', *op. cit.*, pp. 660–717.
[3] Cf. Haas, *Beyond the Nation-State*, p. 39. On the similarities between national and international politics, see C. F. Alger, 'Comparison of Intranational and International Politics', *American Political Science Review*, 57: 2, 1963, pp. 406–19, which draws on anthropological and sociological literature; cf. M. Beloff, 'National Government and International Government', *International Organization*, 13: 4, 1959, pp. 538–49; and R. Aron, *Peace and War* (New York: 1966) pp. 51, 396, 460–2.

parties and public opinion have already begun to operate alongside governments and bureaucracies at the international level, and thus to reproduce many of the environmental conditions of domestic political systems.

But if all this political interdependence constitutes, for the neo-functionalists, evidence of a political system operating on the international level, it is a political system of a particularly primitive kind. Accordingly, political integration is seen as a process of political development whereby this system acquires something like the capacities of a modern state for the formulation and execution of collective decisions. Lindberg originally suggested a 'developmental' approach to the European Community based on the Almond–Coleman systems model;[1] since then he has turned to Easton's type of systems model, which is less directly oriented toward 'developing areas', but from his list of 'specific variables' and indices for measuring integration it is clear that the 'development' analogy pervades.[2]

An integrating international system, for this perspective, can be seen as facing the same problems as an emergent nation. Most of these problems centre around attempts of the central institutions to assert authority and overcome traditional political divisions. According to Pye, a new state must face a series of crises in order to (a) attract allegiances from older political institutions or subsystems, (b) establish the legitimacy of its activities, (c) penetrate popular awareness at all social levels, (d) become a centre of political activity and expectation for groups, parties and individuals, (e) develop a capacity to allocate values efficiently and authoritatively, and (f) draw the whole system together in a web of interactions.[3] From a slightly different perspective, integration (or political development) is the attempt to extend the scope of communal or cooperative decision-making to issue-areas where relations have been traditionally either those of dominance or the strict sovereign equality of actors. From the first perspective, the crucial issues are those of vertical growth, or the accretion of the authority and legitimacy of super-

[1] L. N. Lindberg, 'Decision Making and Integration in the European Community', in *International Political Communities* (New York: 1966) esp. pp. 200–3.

[2] See, for example, Lindberg, 'The European Community as a Political System', *op. cit.*, pp. 356–63, 372. Almost all of what Lindberg calls 'variable properties' or what Nye calls 'process mechanisms' are concepts which could easily be applied in studying a developing nation-state. See Lindberg, 'Political Integration as a Multidimensional Phenomenon', *op. cit.*, pp. 660–1, and Nye, 'Comparing Common Markets', *op. cit.*, pp. 803–12.

[3] See L. Pye, *Aspects of Political Development* (Boston: 1966) Ch. 3, esp. pp. 63–6.

ordinate institutions. From the second perspective, development involves horizontal growth through the diffusion of a particular style of decision-making throughout the system, from one functional sector to the next.

In such a developmental process, the role of central institutions is clearly crucial. The organs set up by the Treaties of Paris and Rome, for example – Commission and bureaucracy, Council, Assembly, Court and various committees – are seen not as instruments of a classic international organization, but as an embryonic supranational state.[1] The neofunctionalist writers judge the prospects and progress of integration very much by the extent to which these central institutions can 'represent the common interests which have brought the Member States together' and 'accommodate such conflicts of interest as will inevitably arise.'[2] In their view, these institutions perform more than a classic mediatory function. They sustain or expand the political system by providing regular information, by forcing members to re-examine their interests and priorities, by supporting and developing a regular international bureaucratic and political elite, by socializing participants to new norms and loyalties, and by providing an ever-present arena for conflict-resolution. In the European Community, of course, this analysis applies particularly to the Commission, which is the archetype of the activist bureaucracy, that is, not simply an administrative-technical body but one which possesses considerable political skills and resources. Among these are capacities for goal articulation, coalition building, recruitment and organization, expansion of scope, and brokerage or the creation of package deals.[3]

[1] Spinelli, *op. cit.*, p. 196, notes the consensus, even among opponents of Monnet's vision, that the EEC must be the core of any future European federation. Whence, presumably, the Commission's regrets that the Council of Ministers, an organ of this future state, sometimes acts like a mere 'international conference' or 'intergovernmental organization': *European Community* (March, 1969) p. 5. See also J. Monnet, *Les Etats Unis de l'Europe ont Commencé* (Paris: 1955) p. 53, where the common institutions of the Six are described as 'les premiers organismes fédéraux de l'Europe'. One scholar suggests parallels between the institutions of the European Community and those of some European states in their formative periods: W. H. Clark, *The Politics of the Common Market* (Englewood Cliffs: 1967) pp. 12–15, 39. Lemaignen has argued that the French antipathy to the Brussels bureaucracy derives in part from their national experience of administrative over-centralization: R. Lemaignen, *L'Europe au Berceau* (Paris: 1964) pp. 107–8.

[2] Lindberg, *The Political Dynamics of European Economic Integration*, pp. 8–9. Cf. Haas, *Beyond the Nation-State*, Ch. 4; and Lindberg and Scheingold, *op. cit.*, pp. 82–98.

[3] *Ibid.*, pp. 92–5.

In the neofunctionalist model, as in most development-theory, the political community is said to be 'engineered' by the central institutions. The idea of state creating nation, prevalent both in contemporary and nineteenth-century national development, has been carried by neofunctionalist writers like Haas and Lindberg, and by statesmen like Monnet and Hallstein onto the international level. And just as development-theory has broken with the traditional view of bureaucracy as a passive, dependent variable in national growth,[1] so neofunctionalism relies on a positive role for bureaucracy on the international level. More than this, indeed, the ultimate political form is taken to be immanent in the existing institutions. The maintenance and growth of these institutions along their present lines are deemed more important than the possibility that at some stage they might prove a hindrance to further integration and, being explicitly 'political', might prove difficult obstacles to remove. Nevertheless, one can easily conceive of a recalcitrant, conservative Commission gradually emerging, overloaded with bureaucratic detail and reluctant to take further political risks in democratizing the Community. M. Pisani may be right that the signatories of the Rome Treaty are 'condamnés a réussir'[2] but their very success may in turn condemn them to an increasingly inappropriate institutional structure for further political change.

It should be clear, then, that the neofunctionalists see integration on the systems level as the process of change from a rudimentary international political interdependence, by means of creative common institutions, to a 'developed' supranational political system characterized by a high degree of common authoritative decision-making. The crucial explanatory hypotheses about this process have usually been constructed around the concept of 'spillover'. This term refers to 'the process whereby members of an integration scheme – agreed on some collective goals for a variety of motives but unequally satisfied with their attainment of these goals – attempt to resolve their dissatisfaction either by resorting to collaboration in another, related sector (expanding the *scope* of the mutual commitment) or by intensifying their commitment to the original sector (increasing the *level* of mutual commitment) or both'.[3] The essence of spillover, according to Lindberg, is that 'the ability of any of the Six to achieve

---

[1] See J. LaPalombara (ed.), *Bureaucracy and Political Development*, Chs. 1–3, esp. pp. 4–5.

[2] Quoted in Lindberg, *The Political Dynamics of European Economic Integration*, p. 269.

[3] Schmitter, 'Three Neofunctional Hypotheses', *op. cit.*, p. 162.

major policy goals is dependent upon the attainment by the others of their policy goals. In such a situation, the role of the central institutions in helping to define the terms of the final agreement is crucial'. As integration progresses, 'the initial task and grant of powers to the central institutions creates a situation or series of situations that can be dealt with only by further expanding the task and the grant of power.'[1]

Initially, as developed by Haas in *The Uniting of Europe*, spillover purported to link the socio-economic variables stressed by the older functionalists with the political variables they so often ignored. While denying the automaticity of 'technical self determination', Haas came close to asserting the inevitability of spillover.[2] Partly in conceptual refinement, and partly under pressure of events, neofunctionalists have now generally retreated from any universal and deterministic claims for this process, and concentrate instead on the socio-economic and political conditions producing varying *probabilities* of spillover.[3] Spillover, it is now argued, need not imply a smoothness, linearity or inevitability in the integrative process; it is merely an organizing concept or hypothesis about the likelihood of integration when certain specified conditions are present.

Perhaps more important than this dilution of spillover itself is the neofunctionalists' recent recognition that it may be only one of a number of dynamic processes involved in integrating (or disintegrating, or stagnant) systems. Lindberg and Scheingold now delineate five alternative 'process models', of which only one, 'forward linkage' resembles the old notion of spillover. Other alternatives are 'output failure' (or failure of spillover), 'equilibrium', 'spill-back' (a retraction of the scope or level of integration) and 'systems transformation', a qualitatively different process in which the original commitments are transcended through an 'entirely new constitutive bargaining process'.[4] These terms, then, describe the broad patterns of systems change, which themselves may result from the success or failure of a

[1] Lindberg, *The Political Dynamics of European Economic Integration*, p. 288, 10. Cf. Haas, *The Uniting of Europe*, Ch. 8, and *Beyond the Nation-State*, p. 111: '. . . policies made in carrying out an initial task and grant of power can be made real only if the task itself is expanded.' See also A. Etzioni, *Political Unification* (New York: 1965) pp. 53–4: U. W. Kitzinger, *The Politics and Economics of European Integration*, p. 63.
[2] Haas, '"The Uniting of Europe" and the Uniting of Latin America', *op. cit.*, p. 315.
[3] See Haas, *op. cit.*, pp. 327–31; Schmitter, *op. cit.*, p. 164.
[4] Lindberg and Scheingold, *op. cit.*, pp. 134–9.

number of 'process mechanisms', separately or in combination, or, in a slightly different conception, a number of 'actor strategies'.[1] The task then becomes to discover the conditions under which each of these processes and strategies is likely to emerge.

Neofunctionalists have traditionally, of course, been most concerned with the conditions favouring incremental political development in the system, via spillover or forward linkage. They are generally agreed that spillover will most likely occur in an international system with a strong system-wide political and bureaucratic elite, with complex, interdependent socio-economic structures, with a stable ideological and cultural consensus, and with some commitment on the part of its members to common long-term goals. But there is little agreement on which of these sets of conditions is the most important, nor on how to operationalize the variables subsumed in them.[2]

For example, several conditions are suggested by the idea of a strong system-wide elite. Some writers stress the creative political capacities and adaptability of national governments and of 'supranational' elites such as the Commission.[3] In other places the emphasis is more on such notions as bureaucratic interpenetration, 'elite complementarity' or the role of system-wide interest groups and political parties. Whatever the emphasis, it is clear from neofunctionalist writings that a prime requisite of any integrative process is some sort of established pattern of elite interaction, usually formalized in system-wide institutions. This has two important corollaries. One is that as conceived and analyzed by neofunctionalists, the integrative process begins, not in a condition of classic international anarchy, but from a previously established structural base, however minimal. The other corollary is that integration is perceived as exclusively the business of elites operating in a community system whose 'technocratic orientation and indirect institutions imply

[1] On the seven process mechanisms, see Nye 'Comparing Common Markets', *op. cit.*, p. 803. Note that only numbers one and three refer to the idea of spillover. On actor strategies, see Schmitter, 'A Revised Theory of Regional Integration', *op. cit.*, pp. 844–6.

[2] For a useful critique of Haas' list of variables, see Nye, 'Patterns and Catalysts', *op. cit.*, esp. pp. 870–3. Cf. M. Barrera and E. B. Haas, 'The Operationalization of Some Variables Related to Regional Integration', *International Organization*, 23: 1, 1969, pp. 150–60. For a recent revised list of variables, see Nye, 'Comparing Common Markets', *op. cit.*, pp. 812–22.

[3] Lindberg, *The Political Dynamics of European Economic Integration*, pp. 7–12, 202–3; Haas and Schmitter, *op. cit.*, p. 272; and, esp., Lindberg and Scheingold, *op. cit.*, pp. 128–33; and Lindberg, 'Political Integration as a Multidimensional Phenomenon', *op. cit.*, pp. 682–702.

limited participation'.[1] Such conditions, even in this general formulation, would seem to place severe limitations on the applicability and
on the growth potential of the neofunctionalist strategy.

Similar observations apply to neofunctionalist discussions of the
requisite socio-economic structure. The differentiation and complexity of a modern industrial society is generally held to be advantageous for integration, since it is likely to encourage a high rate
of transactions, to provide many sectors where cooperation is
possible on specific functional tasks and with which the 'package
deals' and 'tie-ins' essential to the bargaining process can be made,
and to sustain a pluralistic interest group structure in which temporary
coalitions can be formed to advance integration. In a regional
system composed of several such societies, it is almost inevitable that
some cross-national linkages will have developed between functional
sectors. The neofunctionalist process of spillover in fact presupposes
considerable political and economic interdependence – in short,
something approaching a modern western social system – on the
international level. Nonetheless, some theorists have speculated
about possible 'functional equivalents' which would make the
approach applicable in areas less developed than Western Europe.[2]
Others have debated the problem of tactics – which functional area
is best to start the process, so as to maximize spillover and overcome
the 'autonomy of functional contexts'.[3] The consensus seems to be
that the most 'inherently expansive' tasks are to be found among
economic sectors (rather than military, social or cultural). The
economic system, affording particular scope for rational calculation
of interests, seems to allow maximum play for the strategy of the
'planned anomaly' on which spillover thrives.[4]

On the final two sets of conditions – consensus and commitment –
there is perhaps less debate. Neofunctionalism, as we have seen,
assumes the existence of a regional political culture which permits
'non-ideological' politics to be practised, at least in certain tacitly

[1] On the problem of elitism and participation, see Scheingold, 'Domestic and
International Consequences of Regional Integration', op. cit., pp. 993–4.

[2] See esp. Haas and Schmitter, op. cit., p. 274; Nye, 'Patterns and Catalysts',
op. cit., pp. 877–80, and 'Comparing Common Markets', op. cit., passim.

[3] Etzioni, op. cit., p. 55; Haas, 'International Integration: The European and
the Universal Process', op. cit., 101–4; Lindberg and Scheingold, op. cit., pp.
117–21.

[4] Kitzinger, op. cit., pp. 229–30; Haas, 'The Study of Regional Integration',
op. cit., p. 616; cf. A. O. Hirschman, The Strategy of Economic Development
(New Haven: 1958) Chs. 4 and 6, on the strategy of 'unbalanced growth' induced
through the 'backward and forward linkages' of a new economic project.

agreed sectors of social life. It also assumes a degree of procedural consensus, and a general, usually vague, commitment by governments to some distant goals.[1] These conditions, which Haas likens to those present in 'the modern pluralistic-industrial democratic polity',[2] allow for assumptions of long-term compatibility of interests and create the atmosphere of bargaining which permits states to accept occasionally unfavourable outcomes in the short run. Particularly important is the constitutional expression of this consensus in such documents as the Treaty of Rome, which, by its very scope, allows for and encourages the short-term bargaining out of which increased supranational authority gradually emerges.[3]

To sum up, then, on the systemic level neofunctionalists, interpreting international integration as a process akin to national political development, have set about listing and rendering operational a set of conditions likely to enhance that process, and linking these conditions to visible political change by means of 'process mechanisms' such as spillover. As Haas points out, the degree of consensus among neofunctionalists on the important conditions and mechanisms is very low, and what empirical generalizations we can derive are of doubtful theoretical status.[4]

ii) Nation-states: Governments and other actors

Both the pluralist and the functionalist approaches treat the national actors in integrating systems as undifferentiated wholes. Pluralists see integration as the enhancement of the capacities of these sovereign units while, conversely, functionalists take the persistence of national autonomy and power to be the major obstacle to international community. The great contribution of neofunctionalism has been to break with the monolithic view of the nation-state and to perceive it as a complex of interests and issue-areas, some of which have more integrative implications than others. Rather than refer to states in the holistic sense, then, neofunctionalists prefer to identify them with governments or political elites. These elites – consisting of political leaders and bureaucratic officials – interact at the national

[1] Lindberg, *The Political Dynamics of European Economic Integration*, pp. 7–12, 290–5; Haas, *Beyond the Nation-State*, pp. 48, 457.

[2] Haas, 'The Study of Regional Integration', *op. cit.*, pp. 627–8.

[3] Political and Economic Planning, *European Unity* (London: 1968) pp. 473–4.

[4] Haas, 'The Study of Regional Integration', *op. cit.*, p. 614. Perhaps the best summary of the current consensus on conditions and mechanisms is in Nye, 'Comparing Common Markets', *op. cit.*, p. 821.

and international levels not only among themselves but with the representatives of interest groups and parties and with influential individuals. National governments, then, are both the foci of political activity (group conflict and decision-making) at one level, and actors in political processes, alongside other types of actors, at the international level.

When Haas describes integration as resulting from 'an institutionalized pattern of interest politics, played out within existing international organizations',[1] he is therefore talking of a political process involving states as one type of actor among several. Lindberg's analysis of the EEC, similarly, so fragments the states into parties, interest groups and committees, both subnational and crossnational, that it becomes difficult to conceive of a purely 'intergovernmental' process at all. By taking part in an organization like the EEC, government officials, like other political actors, become caught up in a continuous mixed-motive game. Conflicting perceptions of interests by governments and other political actors co-exist, in the unique atmosphere of the 'community method' with a sense of shared purpose that creates a sort of corporate, 'conspiratorial' outlook.[2]

Integration, then, is said to occur on the basis of shifting coalitions of convergent (not identical) interests represented by government officials, interest groups, parties and committees. Any time such a constellation of interests forms that results in a greater role for the central institutions, integration can advance. In this process 'certain kinds of organizational tasks most intimately related to group and national aspirations can be expected to result in integration even though the actors may not deliberately work toward such an end'.[3]

There is a strong flavour in all this of the liberal theory of the state, especially in its modern guise as group theory. Haas acknowledges this intellectual debt, which can be traced in most neofunctionalist writing.[4] According to this creed, the common interest can best be served, not so much by self-conscious cooperation (which may be less productive) but through the ruthless pursuit of individual and group interests within a generally accepted set of norms. In the classic liberal view, central institutions (governments or international

---

[1] Haas, *Beyond the Nation-State*, p. 35.

[2] Lindberg, 'Decision Making and Integration in the European Community', *op. cit.*, p. 206.

[3] Haas, *Beyond the Nation-State*, p. 35. Cf. Haas, 'The Study of Regional Integration', *op. cit.*, pp. 627–8: 'A new central authority may emerge as an unintended consequence of incremental earlier steps'.

[4] Haas, *Beyond the Nation-State*, pp. 32–5.

organizations) were sometimes arbiters, sometimes merely passive registrars of the results of the conflicts inevitably arising in such a system. In its contemporary versions pluralist liberalism tends, first, to stress the importance of the normative order underlying this group-struggle: just as a revolutionary group not sharing the constitutional ethos can break up the domestic political system, so a government not sharing the underlying consensus of the international organization can put an end to integration. In the second place, the theory now relies less on the 'hidden hand' as an assurance that conflict will be resolved to the common benefit. In its place there is more emphasis on the capacities of central institutions to manage and direct conflict and, in the process, to enhance their own power and legitimacy *vis-à-vis* that of other actors. In thus exploiting political opportunities derived from socio-economic interests, the state or the international organization moves far from being the 'night watchman' of classic liberalism.

Despite these changes, neofunctionalists would still claim two of the virtues of classic liberalism: first, a reconciliation of the principle of autonomy for interest groups and other actors with that of the 'common good' for the members of a system as a whole; secondly, continued resistance to holistic or metaphysical notions of the state, less out of moral or utilitarian disapproval (although that is present) than out of sheer exasperation at the theoretical difficulties involved in explaining processes of integration on that basis. To replace un-differentiated 'national interests' with a complex of group and individual interests is to dissolve the paradox which threatens pluralists and functionalists when they try to account for the apparent self-abnegation of states in integrating systems.

The neofunctionalist view of international integration at the analytic level of the state derives, in essence, from a predominantly liberal political philosophy stressing a theory of interest and a theory of conflict and decision in a pluralistic society. The theory of interest is the first major departure from the older functionalism since it stresses perceived rather than objective interests. That is, mere functional interdependence, 'technical self-determination' or the presumed 'common interest', are judged of little importance in themselves as pressures toward integration. They only matter to the extent that they are perceived by different elites and groups as relevant to their particular interests, and thus pass into the political system, that is, the process of interest group conflict and accommodation. In the neofunctionalist view, then, the nature of the functional tasks is less important than the patterns by which they are transformed into political demands and outputs.[1] For the older functionalists, a task or a need is something like a cell or unit of a social whole, observable to participant and analyst alike. While the sum of these needs is presumably a variable quantity, its variations can be discerned and agreed upon by all. For the neofunctionalists, however, such a notion of consensus and common interest is replaced by the equation of functional tasks or needs with demands. The range of functions performed in a community is thus determined by the range of interests perceived and articulated by groups and the issue-areas into which these coalesce.

Such a formulation of the links between functional tasks, interests and the political process clearly assumes an instrumental, rational outlook on the part of political actors. In particular, it relies on their instincts for seeking access to the most promising source of material satisfaction.[2] No matter what his sentiments or his actions, then, a French farmer who demonstrates in Brussels rather than Paris is acting in line with neofunctionalist assumptions of instrumental rationality.

A number of criticisms can be made of these components of neo-functionalism. An obvious one is that it infers interest from behaviour (i.e. the making of demands), and, in effect, assumes all political behaviour to be 'interested' in this sense. It thus leaves little room for judgements about non-rational or ideological behaviour, where it might be argued that individuals or groups are acting contrary to what observers perceive as their 'real' interests.

A more serious flaw, perhaps, is that this theory fails to distinguish between different types of interests according to the groups holding them. In particular, it underestimates the difference between national governments and other 'interested' actors. What is unusual about governments is not that they act on the international level very much like interest groups; rather it is that the interests they pursue are usually aggregates or syntheses of interests expressed in their own societies which they have the unique and authoritative capacity to minister to by allocating political goods. This amounts to a qualita-tive difference of political skills and resources, and a difference in

---

[1] The systems-model used by Lindberg and Scheingold incorporates a concept of interest along these lines. See *Europe's Would-Be Polity*, Ch. 4. For the origins of this model, see D. Easton, *A Framework for Political Analysis* (Englewood Cliffs: 1965).

[2] See Clark, *op. cit.*, p. 97; W. Feld, 'National Economic Interest Groups and Policy Formation in the EEC', *Political Science Quarterly*, 81: 3, 1966, p. 395.

function. Increasing recognition of this has led some neofunctionalists to attribute to governments a greater role – still often positive in its effects – in the integrative process.[1]

Another major departure from the older functionalists is in the apparently paradoxical assertion that integration advances by means of conflict and crisis. As long as conflicts are resolved so as to 'upgrade the common interest',[2] and not simply by more traditional diplomatic methods, the central institutions increase in power and scope (rather by definition, since they are assumed to *represent* the common interest!). But this notion that conflict-resolution in some sense secretes additional authority on the central institutions and so increases integration, is not without difficulties.[3] At the early stages of integration, the central institutions relied upon to settle conflicts can, by definition, have few resources to do so, and are thus faced with the Archimedean problem of finding a basis of support so as to 'move the world'. Either one attributes sufficient resources to them, in which case it is legitimate to ask how these were acquired; or one credits the settlement to the actions of the states, in working out the conflict themselves by classic means of accommodation or perhaps by performing a Hobbesian act of delegation to a central authority. In either case, the advances on traditional theories of conflict resolution are not exactly striking. Moreover, when the process is well advanced the increase in capacities of the central institutions is offset by the increase in the degree of conflict (or politicization) over the next steps. The difficulty of conflict-resolution, in short, seems to increase in direct proportion to its integrative consequences. Thus it could well be that 'integration through conflict' is relevant only in certain early phases of the process.

There are, then, some weaknesses in the neofunctionalist analysis of integration on the level of the state as actor. The theories of interest and of integration via conflict resolution, considering their central importance in neofunctionalist logic, have been explored and elaborated surprisingly little. The dissolution of the classic, monolithic nation-state concept into a complex of interests and issue-areas is an

[1] Lindberg and Scheingold, *op. cit.*, pp. 121–33.

[2] Haas, *Beyond the Nation-State*, p. 111. Cf. Lindberg, 'Integration as a Source of Stress in the European Community System', *op. cit.*, passim, for the best statement of this view.

[3] On this theory, see also R. C. North, H. E. Koch and D. A. Zinnes, 'The Integrative Functions of Conflict', *Journal of Conflict Resolution*, 4: 4, 1960, pp. 355–74. Cf. L. A. Coser, *The Functions of Social Conflict* (Glencoe, Ill.: 1956).

important advance in integration theory. Even here, however, experience in Europe suggests that the power of national governments and the evocativeness of 'national interest' were somewhat too casually set aside.

iii) The Individual: Elite images and permissive consensus

As we have seen, many neofunctionalist definitions of integration include references to a shift of political loyalties and expectations to the emergent common decision-making centre. Implicit in this are many assumptions and hypotheses about the way in which individuals develop, maintain and change their political attitudes. Since this is the level of analysis on which neofunctionalism seems to have made the least progress, it is worth examining some of these assumptions and hypotheses and seeing how they fit with the rest of the theory. Important questions concern the neofunctionalists' concept of political attitudes, the individuals whose attitudes and behaviour are considered most important, the timing of attitude change in relation to institutional change, and finally, the mechanisms of change assumed to be involved.

In earlier neofunctionalist writings, much of the theory about individual attitudes is implicit. It is clear, however, that a distinction is drawn between the cognitive and affective components which together make up the total complex of attitudes, or the 'image'. The cognitive components relate to perceptions of the political world, and thus to what Haas describes as 'expectations' concerning the sources of interest-fulfillment. The affective components are, in utilitarian terms, less 'rational' and have to do with loyalties, values and the sense of community. Unlike the older functionalists, the neofunctionalists have generally given some weight to the latter aspects of the individual's political orientation. Nonetheless, they argue that changes in loyalties and values ultimately come about only 'as a result of new patterns of political expectations and activities.'[1]

A useful schema developed by Lindberg and Scheingold makes an explicit distinction between 'utilitarian' and 'affective' components of political attitudes, and draws a further distinction between 'identitive' support (the horizontal interactions among European peoples) and 'systemic' support (or vertical links between the public and the Community system).[2] Their conclusions, admittedly tentative, are

[1] Lindberg, *The Political Dynamics of European Economic Integration*, p. 6 n.
[2] Lindberg and Scheingold, *op. cit.*, pp. 39–41.

certainly congruent with earlier neofunctionalist assumptions. In summary, it appears that among the general European public, utilitarian support for the Community is more positive than the affective support, and systemic more positive than identitive.[1] In short, the leading edge of attitude change seems to lie in individuals' cognitions and expectations about the sources of benefits in the system, rather than in their emotions toward that system or each other.

This is not to say that neofunctionalists do not consider the affective and identitive components important. To the extent that a state-like supranational community is seen as the goal of integration, it will be important to develop a sense of supranational political community or a political culture in which people are capable of responding to symbols in the same ways. Even for less ambitious purposes, integration seems to require a general, passive, 'permissive consensus' where at least few people exhibit violent antipathies to each other and to the community's institutions and practices. But when the neofunctionalists move from discussing requisite conditions to discussing the dynamics of change, it is the utilitarian attitudes which hold their attention.

Because they are so strongly oriented toward utilitarian satisfaction and because in a developed, pluralistic society the sources of such satisfaction will be manifold, an individual's political attitudes – as conceived by the neofunctionalists – will tend to be multiple and internally divided.[2] It follows that shifts of loyalties and expectations will be neither total nor simultaneous, but piecemeal. As in the older functionalism, utilitarian attitudes will tend to shift to the locus of functional performance; but neofunctionalism makes no assumption that affective attitudes will follow automatically.

Turning from the concept of political attitudes to the types of individuals who hold them, we find an elite-centred theory compatible with the foregoing and with many propositions found in development theory. For the neofunctionalists, the political attitudes that matter are those of the national political, administrative and economic elites and the representatives of international organizations. Lindberg, for example, stresses that the second part of his definition of integration ('the process whereby political actors in several distinct settings are persuaded to shift their expectations and political activities to a new centre') applies to the 'perceptions and resulting behaviour' of just these elites, and that 'the relationship between this

[1] *Ibid.*, pp. 45–63, esp. pp. 60–1.
[2] Haas, *Beyond the Nation-State*, pp. 21–2, 49–50.

128

set of indicators and those referring to governmental decision-making is very close'.[1] What is of interest, then, is not so much the generalized process of 'social learning' which pluralists and functionalists rely upon, but a more restricted process of attitude change among those individuals characterized by an instrumentalist, active orientation toward political life and by a high rate of political participation.

Neofunctionalists have, therefore, tended to neglect or to consider secondary the problem of general public attitudes. Only recently have they begun to find a place for questions of this kind, perhaps because the public consensus or apathy which they long took for granted in Europe now seems increasingly problematic.[2] For Inglehart the basic issue now is: 'To what extent do public preferences constitute an effective influence on a given set of national decision-makers, encouraging them to make decisions which increase (or diminish) regional integration?'[3] Among the factors Inglehart examines are (a) the openness and responsiveness of national decision-making structures (the effects of the 'permissive consensus' on elites), (b) the distribution of political skills in society ('cognitive mobilization' producing public attitudes more favourable to integration) and (c) the relation of decisions to deep-seated values among the public (internalization of integrative values, and the relative effects of short and long-term feedback). With these concepts and hypotheses public attitudes should become more researchable.

One of the major issues which Inglehart's work raises, and which has hitherto been rather neglected, is that of the timing or phasing of attitude changes. In the functionalist and neofunctionalist worlds, of course, changes are incremental. Perceptions and expectations about political life are assumed to change as an intrinsic part of the development of common institutions. Growth of attention to these institutions is inseparable from the growth of their capacity to allocate values. The problem of phasing arises, however, with respect to affective attitudes (loyalties, fundamental values) especially as these

[1] Lindberg, *The Political Dynamics of European Economic Integration*, pp. 6–7.

[2] Much of this new interest was sparked by the debate between Deutsch and Inglehart. See K. W. Deutsch, 'Integration and Arms Control in the European Environment: A Summary Report', *American Political Science Review*, 60: 2, 1966, pp. 354–65, and R. Inglehart, 'An End to European Integration?', *American Political Science Review*, 61: 1, 1967, pp. 91–105. The most impressive attempts to develop a systematic analysis of public attitudes in integration are in Lindberg and Scheingold, *op. cit.*, pp. 38–63, and Ch. 8, and in R. Inglehart, 'Public Opinion and Regional Integration', *International Organization*, 24: 4, 1970, pp. 764–95.

[3] Inglehart, 'Public Opinion and Regional Integration', *op. cit.*, p. 764.

are held by the general public. It is not clear what kind of system might emerge if there were a lag between utilitarian and affective attitude change. The developmental assumptions of neofunctionalism suggest that either the lag will be temporary (there being a causal 'pull' between the two types of attitudes) or that the central authorities should undertake to redirect the affections of the public through propaganda and education. Like governments in developing countries, these authorities may have considerable resources for manipulating public attitudes; on the other hand, as 'politicization' sets in in the later stages of integration, the forces of political and psychological resistance to such influences are likely to have increased as well.

The final question to be considered concerns the mechanisms assumed by neofunctionalists to bring about the required shifts of political expectations and loyalties. On the elite level these can be grouped under the notion of socialization, broadly conceived. Neofunctionalist analysis relies on the combined effects of the organizational context of decision-making, the pressures of the crisis situation, the force of habits and procedure, the interaction with other political actors, the awareness of a commitment or need to agree, and similar features of the political setting, to force actors to a redefinition of their situation, interests and methods.

In this analysis there is a noticeable debt to the theory of group dynamics, to social-psychological literature on contextual pressures toward attitude change (communications, interactions, 'cognitive dissonance', time-perception) and, most evidently, to Snyder's formulation of the decision-making process.[1] In this view individuals act, not according to an objective self-interest or situation, but according to how they *perceive* these. Thus the experience of decision-making (and even conflict) in an integrating system is assumed to have important, indeed crucial, effects in socializing elites to a new perception of their interests, from which will derive calculations likely to encourage further integration. Lindberg, for example, remarks on the importance of continuing elite-contacts in Brussels; he and Haas also stress the importance of socially learned commitment among these elites in influencing specific decisions and bringing about a 'creative adaptation' of norms and goals.[2]

Neofunctionalist analysis is clearly still very speculative on the

---

[1] R. C. Snyder, H. W. Bruck and B. Sapin (eds.), *Foreign Policy Decision-Making* (New York: 1962).

[2] See Lindberg, 'Decision Making and Integration in the European Community', *op. cit.*, pp. 218–23, and *The Political Dynamics of European Economic*

elite level; it is even more so at the level of mass public attitudes. Here a variety of mechanisms of change is suggested by the literature. These would include: the old functionalist notion of stimulus-response learning by a public increasingly exposed to new sources of need-satisfaction; the effects of transactions and communications media; the youthful internalization of values which surface in later political life; and many others. There is little indication as yet that neofunctionalists – apart from Inglehart – are really tackling these tangled problems. In the meantime, their approach, like all the others, retains important but only semi-articulate premises about individual attitudes which desperately need examination.

Neofunctionalism and the European Community

In this last section, we shall examine the neofunctionalist approach to integration in the context of Western European experience. How valid are the explanations derived from this approach, and how applicable are its prescriptions about tactics and strategy?

The dominance of the neofunctionalist approach to integration theory has coincided with that of the European Communities as a practical attempt to realize the 'European idea'. It is possible, certainly, to trace neofunctionalist ideas back to such organizations as the OEEC and the ECSC: the 'confrontation' method of inter-governmental decision-making in the former foreshadowed much of the EEC's emphasis on the 'situational' restraints on national autonomy which operate even in such formally intergovernmental bodies as the Council of Ministers; and the ECSC was the laboratory in which Haas first developed and formulated the neofunctionalist emphasis on interest-politics in 'sector integration'. But the OEEC remained a classic international organization, imposing few structural limitations on national sovereignty, while the ECSC, whose High Authority possessed real, but sectorally-confined, supranational powers, is on the whole better interpreted as a model of the older functionalist ideal. Not until the Treaties of Rome setting up the EEC and Euratom came into force in January 1958 did there exist a framework in which the neofunctionalist 'community method' could find extensive application.

Integration, pp. 286–90 on elite contacts. On 'engagement', see *ibid.*, pp. 84–6. Also Haas, 'The Study of Regional Integration', *op. cit.*, pp. 642–4. For a systematic enumeration of such factors as resources for collective decisionmakers, see Lindberg, 'Political Integration as a Multidimensional Phenomenon', *op. cit.*, pp. 682–782.

In many respects the relationship between the European Community and neofunctionalist ideas would make a fascinating study in the sociology of knowledge. Works such as those of Haas and Lindberg, based on interviews and personal contacts in the Community environment, and on massive absorption of Community documents, inevitably imbibe the ethos and assumptions of those organizations and become, in a sense, their academic expression. The reverse relationship is rather more elusive – Monnet, Hallstein, Spaak and their successors being first and foremost pragmatists – but it can be assumed at least that the extensive theorizing carried on about the Community's workings has served to reinforce what rapidly became the 'conventional wisdom' of Brussels.[1]

Now clearly this symbiotic relationship has had both advantages and dangers. The imaginative design, political promise and initial successes of the Communities since 1957 have certainly inspired widespread attempts to provide a more systematic theory of integration; and any resulting self-consciousness, on the part of the 'Europeans' in Brussels, about the implications of methods and tactics is potentially of practical political value. Nevertheless, the almost exclusive identification of the 'European idea' with the EEC in recent years seems also to have closed off many theoretical and practical options. The early successes of the Community, in what retrospectively seem rather special environmental conditions, tended to produce illusions of inevitability among academics, and delusions of grandeur among 'Eurocrats'. As a result, other broader designs for Europe and other views of the integrative process, were either deprecated or ignored by most theorists, while neofunctionalism assumed the status of an unofficial ideology in Brussels.

This accusation of theoretical rigidity has of course often been wielded by opponents of the Brussels enterprise. General de Gaulle talked of the Six 'brandishing afresh absolute theories as to what should ideally be the future European edifice; . . . imposing a rigid framework laid down in advance for such complex and changing realities as those of our continent's life and relations with the outside world . . . (and) being bogged down once again in myths and abstractions. . . .'[2] The traumatic effects of the General's first veto of Britain, and of the crisis in 1965–6, both on the Community and

[1] On this point, see Schmitter, 'A Revised Theory of Regional Integration', *op. cit.*, p. 838: 'Some of us have had the rather unnerving experience of hearing our special jargon spouted back at us by those whom we are studying.'

[2] Ambassade de France à Londres, Service de Presse et d'Information, *Press Conference Given by General de Gaulle*, Paris, 21 February 1966, p. 2.

among neofunctionalist writers, are difficult to explain except in terms of some such rigidity which had narrowed the common perception of what integration was about and had sealed off much information challenging those views. What Lindberg calls the 'Community romanticism'[1] may indeed have evaporated, but it has been replaced by a number of less obvious myths, such as the 'truth by definition' that the Community is in politics, not business and that its institutions are organs of an existing and not merely a potential political community. To the extent that such beliefs closed out new and often cautionary information, the questionable political judgement of the Commission which led to the crisis of 1965–6 might well be seen in Deutsch's terminology as a 'sin of pride'.[2]

In order to explore more fully the relationship between the neofunctionalist approach and the European Community's experience, it would be useful to look briefly at the origins and development of its institutions. This is not the place for a history of the Community, nor for a detailed economic analysis; the purpose is simply to examine some of the important political preconditions and implications of the organization which tend to have been overlooked in recent years.

The Rome Treaties, as Kitzinger observes, 'were drafted in some haste to exploit the political constellation of 1955-7, when M. Mollet was French Prime Minister, before Dr. Adenauer had to face his electorate in the autumn of 1957, and while the economies of Europe were experiencing a boom'. If to the pure economist the results seem strange, he adds, this is because the Treaty's aims are political and thus its methods 'politically conditioned'.[3] What emerged from this period of creative opportunism was a new application of the 'sector' approach to integration first applied in the ECSC. In the Rome Treaties the focus was both on new sectors (Euratom) and on multiple and interrelated sectors (the broad economic scope of the EEC). In any event, it is the combination of economic scope and functional specificity in the EEC Treaty which has proven the principal ally of the Commission in its efforts to develop the Community's political capacities.

[1] Lindberg, 'Decision Making and Integration in the European Community', *op. cit.*, p. 206.

[2] See Deutsch, *op. cit.*, pp. 229–31: '. . . the attitudes indicated by the concept of humility, and by their contrast to the sin of pride, are attitudes favourable to new learning, to maintaining and extending the channels of intake of outside information, and to the readiness for inner rearrangement.'

[3] Kitzinger, *op. cit.*, p. 18. For a particularly good description of the political climate in France and Germany at the founding of the EEC, see F. R. Willis, *France, Germany and the New Europe, 1945–67* (New York: 1968) pp. 242–72.

While the Community's institutional structure embodies or has developed several innovations (the roles of the Commission and the Permanent Representatives, for example), it is, on the whole, of a kind found in many more traditional international organizations. What is unique about the Community is how these institutions have come to operate, or be operated, in the context of tasks and long-term commitments set by the Treaty of Rome. The way the institutions work is often described as the 'Community method' of decision-making, with the clear implication that it is a method indigenous and perhaps exclusive to the EEC. This method has been described many times. It involves, essentially, a continuing dialogue between, on the one hand, a Commission charged not only with the execution of Community policy and the safeguarding of the Treaty's requirements but also with the initiation and proposal of policy, and, on the other hand, a Council of Ministers representing the national viewpoints in which majority voting is to emerge over time, even on major issues.[1] In this framework and in the lesser institutions surrounding it is played out the interaction of interest-groups and parties described in the neofunctionalist analysis.[2] The conclusions of most writers have stressed the uniqueness of this system: Lindberg suggests that while policy-making in the EEC may resemble a kind of inter-governmental negotiating process, 'it is cast in a new framework that transforms its fundamental characteristics'.[3] From another direction Kitzinger stresses that the 'Community method' is 'quite different in its constitutional ideas and objectives from the notion of federalism' and that it has shown a persistent flexibility and a tendency to expand both in intensity and scope.[4]

If the European Community is thus unique in being neither a classic intergovernmental organization nor a monofunctional body nor a federal system, this character, it is often claimed, derives in part from the peculiar communal ethos which presides over its operations. In the Commission, this ethos is manifested in the adoption of a

[1] The Luxembourg agreement of January, 1966 has drawn the teeth of this last feature of the Treaty. This 'compromise', which ended the 1965 crisis, embodies the French view that decisions concerning the 'very important' interests of one or more members must be unanimous.

[2] For extensive descriptions of the 'community method', see Lindberg and Scheingold, *op. cit.*, pp. 82–98, esp. pp. 87–9, 95–7; Political and Economic Planning, *op. cit.*, Ch. 6, esp. pp. 171–92, 254–6; Pryce, *op. cit.*, Ch. 2; Clark, *op. cit.*, Chs. 2 and 3; Kitzinger, *op. cit.*, Ch. 3; Spinelli, *op. cit.*, esp. Ch. 3; and S. Holt, *The Common Market* (London: 1967) Ch. 3.

[3] Lindberg, *The Political Dynamics of European Economic Integration*, p. 46.

[4] Kitzinger, *op. cit.*, p. 232.

quasi-conspiratorial sense of common identity and objectives. In the Council, it is expressed in acceptance of the Commission as legitimate representative of the collective interests of the national governments and as a vital actor in the bargaining process. This process, moreover, assumes a pragmatic tone of reasoning together over agreed common problems. In the short term, then, the 'community spirit' helps create an unusual pattern of negotiation in the EEC. It is well to recall, however, that this spirit itself derives from a deeper and longer-term calculation by each government that the persistence of the Community will be to its benefit politically and economically. In other words, it is based on a fundamental bargain struck at the outset, which constitutes an 'agreement to agree' perhaps even to the extent of specifying deadlines and tasks to be met.

This, of course, is exactly what the Rome Treaty represented, at least in the first five to seven years of the EEC's life. By the Treaty the Six agreed to undertake what amounts to two types of long-term economic and political operations: 'the creation of a "customs union" by the removal of artificial barriers and forms of discrimination which make the member countries into separate economic units, and the more far-reaching creation of an "economic union" by the establishment of common policies or the gradual coordination of national policies'.[1] Beyond this there is the oft-invoked but rather vague reference in the Preamble to an 'ever closer union among the European peoples', and the rather clearer belief among many 'Europeans' that once the economic aims of the Treaty have been achieved, political union will either have come about in the process, or will be inevitable and immediate.

The customs union was clearly a prerequisite for economic union, and it is in this field – where the Treaty lays down detailed commitments and deadlines – that most of the activity and nearly all the success took place in the first ten years of the Community. The elimination of internal tariffs and quantitative restrictions on industrial and agricultural goods (and the acceleration of this process in some areas), the freeing of labour and capital flows between the Six, the alignment of external tariffs – these decisions, involving detailed

[1] Political and Economic Planning, *op. cit.*, p. 193. Economists generally mention three aspects of economic integration, roughly liberalization (free movement of resources), development (scale, capital and competition) and coordination of policies. See B. Balassa, *The Theory of Economic Integration* (Homewood, Illinois: 1961); P. Streeten, *Economic Integration* (Leyden: 1964); T. Scitovsky, *Economic Theory and Western European Integration* (Stanford: 1958). For a detailed economic analysis of the Treaty, see Kitzinger, *op. cit.*, Ch. 2.

and highly intensive negotiations have, for the most part, concerned what John Pinder has called 'negative' integration,[1] or the removal of obstacles to free exchange between the states. It is in the tests of 'negative' integration that the Community's decision-making method has evolved, and it is here that its achievements are most striking.[2]

The political successes of the 'Community method' in these areas – and their subsequent economic impact – have been the subject of much academic analysis and the source of both morale and practical political lore for participants in Brussels. What in retrospect seems to have been absent from these lessons is an awareness of the underlying similarity of the issue-areas in which the method appeared to be working. As the Community began to experience difficulties in the early 1960s, however, its critics began to point out this similarity. If one accepted the 'high politics-low politics' dichotomy, all the successes were in the latter field; if one accepted Pinder's 'positive-negative' distinctions the Community, with a few exceptions, had managed very little in the first kind of integration, which involves the creation of common policies covering whole functional areas.

Neofunctionalist optimism about the prospects of European integration, then, was generated by studies which focused almost entirely on the removal or adjustment of economic barriers, whether in the narrow coal and steel sector as with Haas' first book, or in the Western European economy as a whole. The creation of a common market for coal, iron and steel was rapid indeed. The broader European customs union was achieved on 1 July 1968, a year ahead of the original schedule. The decision in 1960 to accelerate the process of tariff reductions – prompted by the salutary effects of initial reductions, the general expansion of the European economies, pressures from outside the Six, and the growth of a supportive coalition of European business and political interests – was steered through by the Commission in an adroit piece of brokerage politics that seemed to illustrate the great promise of the 'Community method'. The

[1] See J. Pinder, 'Positive Integration and Negative Integration: Some Problems of Economic Union in the EEC', *World Today*, 24: 3, 1968, pp. 90–1.

[2] For summaries of these achievements see various publications of the Community's Information Service, esp. *Uniting Europe* 1950–67 (London: 1967) pp. 17–19, and *The Facts* (London: 1967) pp. 7–10. For more detail, see the Commission's *General Reports on the Activities of the Community*, annually from 1958. See also Political and Economic Planning, *op cit..*, Ch. 6; and Lindberg and Scheingold, *op. cit.*, pp. 62–75.

Commission, France and Belgium in particular were pushing for acceleration. The more reluctant Germans were persuaded to go along by the promise of subsequent redress in other areas, as were the Dutch by the tying in of agricultural issues. The Commission itself drew in the issue of the external tariff. In short, 'the inability of the governments to agree on a precise formula forced them to delegate the task of formulation to the Commission. None was willing to accept the possibility of a deadlock'.[1] In such a context the process of forward linkage could, and did, flourish.

The other aspect of a customs union is the formation of a common external tariff. In the case of the EEC, the principle itself first had to be defended in the Free Trade Area negotiations of 1957–8, where the nascent Community was challenged to remain open to other OEEC countries who saw themselves threatened by the tariff wall. Germany and the Benelux countries were attracted by the free trade idea; France, Italy, the Commission and some groups in the other countries opposed it. Eventually, since the Six were unable to arrive at a common position and unwilling to negotiate without one, the inherent strength of the defensive position prevailed. The Commission increasingly defined the Community's goals and policies for it, and with the demise of the Free Trade Area proposals by the end of 1960, the way was clear to set up the common external tariff.[2]

The pressures to formulate this tariff illustrate well the interdependence of economic issues on which neofunctionalists rely. In particular, these issues included the need for a common Community position in external commercial relations (in GATT) and the impending acceleration of internal tariff reductions. Moreover, the completion of the external tariff would be made easier if a start were made on the complex issue of a Community agricultural policy, since so many of the items on the tariff schedule were agricultural. Within this context of interdependent and often highly technical issue-areas, the Commission was faced with the task of finding a mean – sometimes by mathematical computation and sometimes by political compromise – between the generally low tariffs of Germany and the Benelux countries and the high tariffs of France and Italy. On the commodities requiring political compromise (the 70 items of List G), the Community achieved agreement on the rate of adjustment and eventual level of the external tariffs in 1960, two years

---

[1] Lindberg, *The Political Dynamics of European Economic Integration*, Ch. 9, esp. pp. 192, 200, 202.
[2] *Ibid.*, Chs. 7 and 8, esp. pp. 164–6.

ahead of the deadline in the Rome Treaty. In this process, again, the Commission was instrumental: 'it initiated proceedings, kept them moving ahead, and intervened with procedural and substantive proposals, presenting the dossier from a Community point of view. It is surely not too much to say that agreement would not have been achieved without the Commission's intervention.'[1]

The formation of a common agricultural policy for the Community is held by many to be the premier triumph of the neofunctionalist method. From another perspective, however, what has been achieved demonstrates the severe limitations of this approach. The policy as it emerged in the 1960s is essentially the extension of the customs union into the agricultural area – that is, the removal of barriers to agricultural trade among the Six and the establishment of a Community marketing system involving common levies and price maintenance. The next phase, the setting of common commodity prices, is now well on the way to completion. These are undeniably impressive achievements. Nonetheless, it is arguable that success has been possible only where the interdependence of agricultural issues with those of the customs union was most clear. In the vital areas of 'positive' integration, which in this instance means structural reform and long-term planning, little headway has been made. Until production costs can be lowered by increased specialization and consolidation of farms into larger units, the Community will continue literally to pay an enormous price for the privilege of a common agricultural policy. Ironically, it is the success of the 'Community method' which created this situation. It is not at all clear, the optimism of some observers notwithstanding, that the same method is adequate for completing the task. At present, the Mansholt Plan for structural reform remains in political limbo.[2]

The case of agriculture illustrates a fundamental weakness, not only of the 'Community method', but of neofunctionalist analysis. If one measures the integrative effects of the method by the extent to which the resolution of the tariff and marketing issues of the early 1960s resulted in increased authority and capacity for the Commission and other Community bodies, then it is easy to arrive at positive conclusions. If, however, one is concerned with the content of policy and makes judgements about its quality or, more important from

[1] *Ibid.*, p. 217.

[2] For detailed analysis and optimistic prognoses concerning Community agricultural policy, see *ibid.*, Chs. 11 and 12, and Lindberg and Scheingold, *op. cit.*, Ch. 5. See also *The Common Agriculture Policy* (London: 1967) (Community Topics 28), published by the European Community Information Service.

our perspective, if one is concerned with how integration will proceed from the present stage, then it is legitimate to wonder if the manner in which earlier problems were resolved may not make further progress more difficult.[1]

In any case, it seems fair to say that the Community has now arrived at a critical juncture between the 'negative' and 'positive' phases of integration. The existence of a functional logic and a reservoir of political will whereby success in 'negative' integration would inexorably lead to 'positive' integration is now somewhat problematical. As the specific requisites of the Treaty are met and the more general commitments to common policy-making are brought forward to the table, it is questionable whether the 'Community method' will be able to operate with its accustomed force. It is tempting to suggest that the neofunctionalist generalizations about integration through the 'community method' (emphasizing the initiative of the Commission, the relatedness of issues and the precise requirements of the Treaty) are applicable only to 'negative' integration or to the formulation of general statements of intention, and that 'positive' integration is a qualitatively different undertaking.

The creation of a full economic union involves the construction of common institutions through which common planning can be undertaken, diverse and entrenched national policies harmonized, and fundamental structural change promoted for the benefit of the entire Community. In functional areas such as agriculture, energy and transport, there has been much progress in the removal of discrimination and restrictions on fair competition and free exchange, but in common planning and policy-making and, above all, in the structural change necessary to rationalize these economic sectors, the national positions diverge greatly even where the Commission itself has managed to produce policy proposals.

In some areas, there has been substantial progress toward common policy-making, but again this is not entirely explainable in terms of neofunctionalist methods. In social policy, for instance, there has been considerable success through the Social Fund, in enhancing the mobility of workers and the transferability of their security benefits throughout the Community. These requirements came to the fore, of course, as trade barriers were removed among the Six and industrial growth points (particularly in Germany) began to attract labour from other countries (such as Italy). But social policy is also an

---

[1] See Pinder, *op. cit.*, pp. 97–100, on the built-in obstacles to 'positive' integration in the present EEC system.

area where, unusually, the Treaty lays down obligations in considerable detail as to positive integration.[1]

In other areas where some success in common policy-making has been achieved, it is explainable largely in terms of an external challenge or pressure. This was the case, not only with the Free Trade area proposals, but with the Kennedy Round negotiations under GATT, where the Commission established itself as the representative of the Community and negotiated on the basis of what amounted to a common policy. Although there is an emergent consensus that this is a desirable development, it is clear that little sense of precedent has been established yet. Negotiations over British entry, for example, have been conducted, not between the applicants and the Commission (despite its efforts to establish such a role) but at the ministerial level between Britain and the Six. On future issues of external relations, too (Atlantic and Soviet trade relations; the developing countries; policy over association), it is not at all clear that whatever agreements emerge will do so by other than classic diplomatic bargaining.

Since the Hague summit conference of December 1969, most of the hopes for steps towards 'positive' integration have rested on the governments' commitment, made then, to adopt a schedule for economic and monetary union. In June 1970 the Community adopted the Werner Plan's main proposals for a three-stage, ten-year schedule. In the bargaining over implementation of the proposals, however, the Six nearly came to a deadlock. Germany and Holland, in particular, pressed for greater supranational authority over monetary policies, capital markets and national budgets, which would begin with a tightening of exchange rate margins and move toward a federal reserve system, and eventually, a common currency. France, fearing these supranational implications and long-term commitments, held out for more immediate monetary and credit cooperation to support the franc. Since Germany made it clear that such support would not be forthcoming unless a long-term commitment were made, the agreement finally reached by the Council in February 1971 embodies most of the Werner Plan's objectives. But the concrete commitments are all for the first phase (to the end of 1973) and amount to a trial period for economic and monetary cooperation. At the end of this phase – involving, in the economic field, obligatory consultation on short and medium term planning, coordination of budgeting, harmonization of fiscal policies, and, in

---

[1] On the Social Fund, see Political and Economic Planning, *op. cit.*, pp. 220–2.

the monetary field, cooperation of central banks in narrowing currency fluctuations and moving to a stabilization fund for currency aid – it is assumed the incentive will be strong to move on to fully supranational institutions by 1980.[1]

To some observers, this agreement will appear to be a new long-term commitment of the kind which will reactivate the 'Community method' and permit a whole range of incremental bargaining to take place. It is evident that the tying-in of such issues as short-term currency stability (France's major concern), central banking control (Germany's interest), structural change and regional development (Italy's interest) enhances the possibilities for inter-sectoral exchanges. At the same time, the issue of planning will raise fundamental differences of national economic philosophies, which range from 'dirigisme' to modified 'laissez-faire'. It will also, increasingly, raise questions of economic equity and the redistribution of resources in the Community from richer to poorer areas – questions which will not become any easier to resolve if the economic growth rate begins to taper off. It is, then, somewhat premature to conclude that the 'Community method' is about to move into the area of 'positive' integration in the 1970s.

On the present balance, the Community is moderately to highly integrated in a 'negative' sense in several areas of 'low' politics. It has made tentative inroads into 'positive' integration with respect to certain economic functions. Its role in 'high' politics is as yet negligible.[2] An optimist, faced with these ledgers, might well project past trends ahead, or, at worst, assume that the forces for integration in Europe are gathering strength for a new *'relance'* like that of the mid-fifties. A more prevalent interpretation, however, has been that the current situation is stagnation or stalemate, which marks a crisis not only in the EEC but in neofunctionalist theory.

Have the neofunctionalists and the Brussels 'Europeans', therefore, been deceived about the political implications of economic integration? In the early years of the Community, neofunctionalist writers and Western European statesmen repeatedly expressed the conviction that there would be inevitable, irreversible progress from 'negative' through 'positive' economic integration and on to 'political union'

---

[1] On recent problems of monetary and economic union, see *The Economist*, 19 December 1970, p. 68. For details of the agreement, see *New York Times*, 10 February 1971, and *European Community*, March 1971, pp. 12–15.

[2] See the distribution of high scores for integration among Lindberg and Scheingold's functional categories, *op. cit.*, pp. 70–5.

(both in the sense of democratically controlled European government and in the sense of military and foreign-policy integration).[1] For about five years (1958–63) this conviction seemed justified, but that period is now seen by some as having constituted the apogee of the Eurocrats and of the approach to integration they represented.[2] Now heed is once again paid to the views of more classically-oriented political analysts, who have long argued that 'federalism without tears' is illusory, and that the 'Community method' merely postpones the hard choices. Raymond Aron, for example, argues that the 'hope that the European federation will gradually and irresistibly emerge from the Common Market is based on a great illusion of our times', namely that economics and technology have devalued the fact of 'political sovereignty'.[3] In a similar vein, another observer lumps the neofunctionalists and the older functionalists together, dismissing their claims by asserting that the 'Eurocracy' is essentially an international administration on the sufferance of national powers. Since the political power-base remains firmly national, a so-called potentially supranational administration can only realize this potential, not through its own acts, but through those of states.[4]

Having written in 1961 that 'the established nation-state is in full retreat in Europe',[5] Haas has perhaps had the most difficult theoretical reconsideration to undertake. It is not, he argues, so much that the background conditions prevalent in postwar Europe or, more particularly, the patterns of homogeneity (social structures, elite expectations, bureaucracies) were unique to the 1950s (although absence of these patterns in non-western regions may limit the scope of the theory there). Rather, the crucial factor, no longer present, was a deep political consensus: 'the logic of functional integration could move forward . . . because the key politicians . . . had simply decided to leave the game of high politics and devote themselves to the building of Europe, to achieve more modest aims. And thus the

[1] See Hallstein, *op. cit.*, p. 65, and as quoted in Lindberg, *The Political Dynamics of European Economic Integration*, p. 69; Haas, *The Uniting of Europe*, passim; Kitzinger, *op. cit.*, p. 234; Political and Economic Planning, *op. cit.*, p. 256.

[2] Spinelli, *op, cit.*, pp. 21–3.

[3] Aron, *op. cit.*, p. 108.

[4] F. Rosenstiel, 'Reflections on the Notion of Supranationality', *Journal of Common Market Studies*, 2: 2, 1963, esp. pp. 132, 137–8. This article, written in a powerful, rather dogmatic style, can be construed as support for either a Gaullist or a classic federalist position, depending on how feasible one judges the sorts of national change Rosenstiel sees as necessary for integration.

[5] Haas, 'International Integration: The European and the Universal Process', *op. cit.*, p. 93.

economic technician could play his role within the shelter of the politicians' support.'[1] Since we cannot assume the 'superiority of step-by-step economic decisions over crucial political choices', Europe must await the return of some such political agreement, a consensus among statesmen and non-governmental elites on the need to resume incremental-economic methods.[2]

But why has the underlying consensus on which the EEC flourished now apparently evaporated? Some would argue that the central institutions are simply not powerful enough yet to create the support necessary for further integration; consensus will clearly be more difficult to maintain as the more sensitive areas begin to be touched upon. Others stress the paradox that the very success of the European movement since the war has weakened the incentive for further integration, strengthened the states and induced a new conservatism among its members which is represented by an unwillingness to jeopardize what they have achieved by trying to go further.[3]

In either case, the conclusion would seem to be that a break-through is needed, perhaps in the form of a new constitutive bargain on the pattern of the Rome Treaty. The difficulty with 'negative' integration is that it can lead to a pluralist form of integration where states' needs are met without imposing new central institutions or generating a consensus for further integration. In short, it very quick-ly reaches a stable equiblibrium point. But 'positive' integration, in the absence of such institutions or consensus, requires a dramatic new commitment which itself amounts to a transformation of the system. Thus, both the neofunctionalist who admits to the dis-continuity between low and high politics and the Eurocrat who acknowledges the ebb of the integrative consensus in Europe, find themselves attempting to rescue the theory by means of a classic federalist *deus ex machina* long scorned by gradualists.[4]

Some neofunctionalists, however, in commenting on the condition of European integration, have recalled their functionalist ancestry

[1] Haas, '"The Uniting of Europe" and the Uniting of Latin America', *op. cit.*, p. 323. In this article, Haas appears to accept wholly Hoffmann's distinction between 'high' and 'low' politics and thus to abandon many more valuable aspects of neofunctionalism. In 'The Study of Regional Integration', *op. cit.* however, he is more critical of this distinction and defends his own theory rather better against Hoffman and other critics. See pp. 629–30.

[2] *Ibid.*, p. 327–9.

[3] Lindberg and Scheingold, *op. cit.*, pp. 291–7.

[4] The concept of 'systems transformation' developed by Lindberg and Schein-gold, *op. cit.*, Ch. 7, is a promising attempt to reconcile this idea with neo-functionalist theory.

and pointed to the strength of the less visible infrastructure of the Community and of the vested interests and commitments holding it together and making regression difficult. Others have made the same point – about this curious inattention to low-level incremental change – in discussing neofunctionalism in general.[1] This suggests that the neofunctionalist might pay more attention to what the older functionalists and the Deutschian theorists of social communication have been saying about gradual social change.

According to other critics, however, the crisis of neofunctionalism derives from more fundamental weaknesses related to the way in which the political component of integration is defined. As we have seen, for the neofunctionalist, with his definition of politics as a pattern of decision or conflict-resolution, measurement becomes a matter of qualitative assessment of styles of conflict resolution or more quantitative assessment of the 'locus of decision' in a community on various issues. To an unsympathetic critic, however, these procedures might seem merely sophisticated expressions of the Brussels myth that since the EEC carries out some functions traditionally performed by the states, and operates in a 'political' manner through negotiation and conflict of interests, it is *ipso facto* a supranational polity. The 'realists' therefore set much harder criteria. Aron requires that, before we can call the EEC a supranational system, there be a renunciation of the unanimity principle, a direct relation between the legislative or regulative power of the EEC and the citizens or enterprises of its members, and agreements concluded by the EEC with foreign states. He concludes that while EEC has a strong influence it cannot be said seriously to limit the sovereignty of its members.[2]

The 'realists' (and indeed, the classic federalists) can therefore

---

[1] On Europe, see Lindberg, 'Integration as a Source of Stress on the European Community System', *op. cit.*, pp. 234, 237; also 'Decision Making and Integration in the European Community', *op. cit.*, pp. 218–24; cf. Spinelli, *op. cit.*, p. 112. On neofunctionalism generally, see J. N. Rosenau's critique of Haas' study of the ILO, 'Transforming the International System: Small Increments Along a Vast Periphery', *World Politics*, 18: 3, 1966, esp. p. 544.

[2] Aron, *op. cit.*, pp. 744–6. Cf. D. Sidjanski, 'Federal Aspects of the European Community', in J. D. Montgomery and A. Smithies (eds.), *Public Policy*, 14, 1965, esp. pp. 417–20. On the issue of supranationality, see also M. Beloff, 'International Integration and the Modern State', *Journal of Common Market Studies*, 2: 1, 1963, esp. p. 55. Gaullists and federalists are agreed on this point – that the issue of sovereignty is inescapable. Because, they would argue, the issue has not been faced directly, the EEC's claim to be a new political and corporate entity with a new political method, is something less than sound. See, for example, Rosenstiel, *op. cit.*, passim; Spinelli, *op. cit.*, pp. 133–4.

argue that neofunctionalist indices of political integration mistake style for substance, and that the 'locus of power' has in fact not shifted at all. Essential to any analysis of integration, in their view, is the traditional search for the resting-place of coercive power and wealth. The extent to which these power-bases are shared between members and central institutions gives a clearer measure of the extent of supranationality or federalism. By these measures, the EEC has stopped short of routing the nation-state by some distance.

In conclusion, then, the neofunctionalist approach and its European expression, the 'Community method', are under theoretical attack from a number of directions. Accompanying and enhancing these theoretical criticisms is a growing debate, both within and beyond neofunctionalist ranks, as to whether this approach has much to tell us about the new political problems facing the Community. Among these are institutional development (in particular, completion of the fusion of the three Communities and the development of democratic controls through a directly elected European Parliament with some budgetary powers), new membership and its implications for decision-making processes, external relations (in particular, with a United States increasingly unhappy about the alleged economic closure of Europe) and, above all, of course, the optimum structure and exercise of political power to increase integration beyond the present level. It is also clear that the Community will have to make trade-offs between these various objectives. Is democratic control, for example, compatible with the powerful, technically based Commission which further integration may require if national resistance is to be overcome? Is expansion of membership not likely to preclude rather than stimulate a new rush to supranationality, either because of the outlook of new members or because the decision-making machinery becomes less intimate and more like a classic international conference? These are clearly major issues with which integration theorists ought to be concerned, but, as yet, neofunctionalism offers us little help with them.

Going beyond this is an increasing doubt in some quarters about the relevance of the EEC to the fundamental problems of Western Europe. For trade liberalization the 'Community method' might suffice; but if the real need is for fundamental social transformation the politics of consensus and coalition, it is argued, may not be adequate. What is needed is a true federalist 'revolution'. The implication is that an EEC free to run its full, and largely economic, course would not necessarily lead to a true political community in

Europe, but simply to a technocratic polity which has somewhere 'lost its soul'.[1]

Whatever the merits of these various criticisms, it is clear that despite the potential analytic richness of the new directions in the neofunctionalist approach, events in Europe continue to outpace academic theory. As the 'Community method' seems to have run out of momentum, so the statesmen seem to have run out of ideas.

But to end this analysis on such a pessimistic note would be to underestimate the significance of the neofunctionalist approach. If its limitations are greater than initially expected, so is the complexity of the integrative process in European society. The realization that an approach is not universal in applicability need not blind us to its analytic depth. It is perhaps useful, therefore, to end by balancing two judicious statements by students of European integration who are sympathetic to the neofunctionalist outlook. 'The performance of the EEC institutions', write the authors of the PEP report, 'tends to show that they have approached more closely to the benign circle of mutually reinforcing institutions and political will then the intergovernmental organizations have been able to do.'[2] And yet, as Kitzinger adds: 'The Community dialectic has never worked by historic inevitability but has at each stage required hard effort of intellectual planning and political will.'[3]

[1] On this the populist wing of the European federalist movement would seem to be in uneasy agreement with the 'New Left'. See Spinelli's attacks on 'L'Europe des offices', in *op. cit.*, pp. 24–5 and passim. For a good description of the European radical movement, and its implications for federalism, see A. Sampson, *The New Europeans* (London: 1968), Chs. 21 and 22. See also Scheingold's comment on the journal *Agenor*, which he describes as the 'conscience of European Community': 'Domestic and International Consequences of Regional Integration', *op. cit.*, pp. 991–2.

[2] Political and Economic Planning, *op. cit.*, p. 475.

[3] Kitzinger, *op. cit.*, p. 241.

5 Power and the Supranational State: Varieties of Federalist Theory

Federalist Forms of Supranational Community

Prior to the nineteenth century, the possibilities of international integration were discussed almost exclusively within what might be called the literature of pacifism. In general this literature envisaged two major types of solution to the problem of war. The first of these, from which descended the pluralist approach discussed in Chapter 2, stressed the desirability of moral, political and economic change within states and the need for improved techniques of interaction between them, to ensure that they would resolve their conflicts peacefully and coexist in a stable, harmonious system of sovereign entities. The second type of solution called for the formation of a super-ordinate authority to regulate the behaviour of the states and assume many of their sovereign rights, duties and powers. This latter, federalist approach has often been identified with formal, legalistic attempts to draw up peace plans or constitutions for the international system. But its dominant values and assumptions are also present in a tradition of thought about society and about international order which focuses much more on the sociological conditions, processes and forms of integration. These two streams of federalist theory – the 'classic' and the 'sociological' – have often intermingled in the minds of individual federalist writers. Moreover, they share a characteristic concept of the end-product of integration and an emphasis on the role of power in the process of political change which together have given them a uniqueness and a persistent importance in the literature.

The classic federalist picture of international integration has the same deceptive clarity and simplicity as Hobbes' description of the birth of Leviathan. The essence of the integrative process, according to this view, is the formation, among a group of previously sovereign powers, of a common supranational state. In this new legal and political entity are merged the international identities of the constituent states; internally, jurisdiction is divided so that these states and the federal government possess complementary but independent powers. As we shall see, many of the assumptions involved here – about the need for a 'constitutional conference' and the dramatic emergence of a 'contract' among the states, and about the possibility of maintaining a clear-cut demarcation of powers in any modern state – have come under scrutiny in recent federalist thinking. What is important for the moment is the point that federalists are concerned to direct the integrative process toward a definite, well-articulated ideal – a supranational state with specific characteristics.

A similar specificity about the end-product of the integrative process can be found in the writings of the sociologist Amitai Etzioni. Etzioni's work, while not explicitly federalist, nevertheless represents a remarkable body of federalist assumptions and modes of analysis translated into the language of modern sociology.[1] In his view, the end-product of a process of international integration is a 'political community'. This is a community which possesses 'three kinds of integration: (a) it has an effective control over the use of the means of violence (though it may "delegate" some of this control to member-units); (b) it has a center of decision-making that is able to affect significantly the allocation of resources and rewards throughout the community; and (c) it is the dominant focus of political identification for the large majority of politically aware citizens'. He adds: 'A political community is thus a state, an administrative-economic unit, and a focal point of identification.'[2] This is clearly a far more definite and demanding concept of the end-product than any of those we have discussed in previous chapters. In particular Etzioni shows no hesitation in using the single-state analogy.[3] There is every likelihood that such a state will be formally federal (Etzioni's emphasis on the continuing role of the units suggests this); for this discussion, however, the important similarity with the federal viewpoint is his insistence on the element of supranationality.

As we have seen, although the neofunctionalists tend, in practice, to accept the supranational state as the goal of integration, they are

[1] See especially A. Etzioni, *Political Unification* (New York: 1965). A more recent work, *The Active Society* (New York: 1968) subsumes and develops his earlier ideas on international integration in a general treatment of consensus and control in societies. See especially Part V, 'Beyond Tribalism', for a sophisticated argument in the federalist mode.

[2] Etzioni, *Political Unification*, p. 4.

[3] On the stringent demands of this definition of integration compared to others, see *ibid.*, p. 6, footnote 5.

generally less concerned with the goal than with the process.[1] On pragmatic, empirical or ideological grounds many neofunctionalists are willing to countenance non-federal forms of political system as the end-product (e.g., the notion of the 'mixed system'). The federalists, on the other hand, insist on a supranational state of a specific kind, justified not only in terms of certain political and philosophical values, but in terms of the diversity of the international society from which it emerges. The neofunctionalist is impressed, above all, with not only the economics but also the politics of scale; the federalist is more concerned to balance the advantages of size and uniformity with those of smallness and diversity.

Needless to say, the federalists' stress on political solutions and political institutions finds little sympathy among the older functionalists. While the functionalists are concerned with eliminating the state-system in the process of building a welfare-oriented world society, the federalists see integration as superimposing a new state (either global or regional) to keep order among the old ones and, after some time, perhaps to replace them entirely. In the functionalist's eyes this is no solution at all: federalism retains the old political divisions that are the source of our present discontents, and only compounds the evil by building even larger states on a new level. Nevertheless, federalists and functionalists do share one very important belief, namely that the nation-state cannot meet many of our present needs and that the desirable system is one in which policies are made and executed at the level of society they most directly concern.[2]

Philosophically, the federalists perhaps have most in common with the pluralist approach. Unlike the two groups of functionalists, who espouse an 'indirect' strategy of political integration, working through the economic, social and technical sectors, federalists share with the pluralists the perception of integration as a directly 'political' phenomenon, to do with the behaviour of national political elites and with problems of power, responsiveness and control. In both approaches, too, the nation-state is accepted as a basic political 'given', to be accommodated rather than abolished or circumvented in any scheme to reorganize world politics. It is in the prescriptions drawn from their reading of the international system that the federalists differ from the pluralists: since the classic mechanisms of

[1] Etzioni and many federalist writers, by contrast, see integration primarily as a condition to be achieved or maintained. See Etzioni, *loc. cit.* Federalist theory has been notoriously 'static' in this sense.

[2] For a federalist argument along these lines, see H. Brugmans, *La Pensée Politique du Fédéralisme* (Leyden: 1969) Ch. 5.

international adjustment have proved impermanent or unreliable for maintaining peace and security, real institutional limitations must be placed on the autonomy of states – however difficult this may be. While autonomous states can be influenced by diplomacy and communications, they can only be controlled if they give up some of their autonomous powers. Hence, in the federalist view, the need for a supranational state.

But what precisely are the characteristics of this state? To explore this question it is necessary first to review some of the formulations of leading federalist writers. In this process it should become evident, first, that the classic federalist prescription is neither as clear nor as simple as is sometimes suggested, and, secondly, that the more recent concepts of the federal state owe much to the sort of sociological perspective espoused by Etzioni. The theoretical interplay between these two types of federalism has had, on the whole, rather mixed effects.

Perhaps the most influential of the classic formulations of federalism in recent years has been that of K. C. Wheare: 'By the federal principle I mean the method of dividing powers so that the general and regional government are each, within a sphere, co-ordinate and independent.'[1] This, he makes clear, is a principle of both organization and practice. That it is embodied in a consitution may not be itself mean the state is federal; what matters is how the governmental system operates.[2]

Most classic descriptions of federal systems are variations on this theme of the formal division of powers between levels of government. Federalism, for another writer, requires (a) a distribution of power between central and local governments, not subject to legislative change, (b) 'substantial' rather than 'trivial' local powers, (c) contact between the central government and individual citizens, (d) some freedom for the member-states as to their own internal organization, and (e) legal equality of the member-states.[3] Many other definitions of federalism share this emphasis while stating the basic principle more parsimoniously. Watts, for example, sees the federal concept as entailing 'two coordinate levels of sovereignty within a single country',[4] while Merle describes the 'strict' definition of federalism as a

[1] K. C. Wheare, *Federal Government*, 4th edition (London: 1963) p. 10.

[2] *Ibid.*, p. 33.

[3] A. W. Macmahon, 'The Problems of Federalism: A Survey', in A. W. Macmahon (ed.), *Federalism: Mature and Emergent* (New York: 1955) pp. 4–5.

[4] R. L. Watts, *New Federations: Experiments in the Commonwealth* (London: 1966) p. 10.

technique of 'apportioning jurisdiction among organized col-lectivities'.[1] One of the authors of the *Federalist Papers* is said to have concluded, in effect, that the only essential rule in a federal system was that there must be a 'constitutional distribution of powers between the central establishment and the members of the system'.[2] In perhaps the most concise statement of this classic theme, Riker argues that a system is federal if it has two levels of government, each of which has at least one area of action in which it is autonomous and some guarantee that this autonomy will continue.[3]

As a model for international integration, classic federalism is firmly based on existing archetypes of federal government, particularly the United States and Switzerland. Many of its prescriptions and analyses therefore stress formal institutional requirements such as an explicit constitutional embodiment of the divisions of powers, a bicameral legislature where one house represents the member-states equally, and independent electoral systems for the two levels of government. But since existing federal systems differ greatly even in these respects, international federalists usually rely on minimal criteria such as Riker's. The value of such criteria is, of course, that they provide a sharp, clear measure of the degree of integration in a system. They do so, however, at the cost of some rigidity and an insensitivity to many sociological variables by which it is possible to measure and perhaps predict the gradual emergence or decay of a federal system.

In reaction to the potential legalism and inflexibility of these criteria, a number of theorists have attempted to broaden (or 'deepen') the concept of federalism. The most articulate and forceful exponent of this approach has been C. J. Friedrich. In his view, a federal system is a 'union of groups, united by one or more common objectives, but retaining their distinctive group character for other purposes'.[4] Federalism is 'the process of federalizing a political

[1] M. Merle, 'Federalism and France's Problems with its Former Colonies, 1945–63', in J. D. Montgomery and A. Smithies (eds.), *Public Policy*, 14, 1965, p. 403.

[2] W. H. Bennett, *American Theories of Federalism* (University of Alabama: 1964) p. 72, describing the view of Alexander Hamilton.

[3] W. H. Riker, *Federalism: Origin, Operation, Significance* (Boston: 1964) p. 11. Cf. P. Hay, *Federalism and Supranational Organizations* (London: 1966) p. 98.

[4] C. J. Friedrich, 'New Tendencies in Federal Theory and Practise,' paper presented to the Sixth World Congress of the International Political Science Association, p. 2, quoted in A. H. Birch, 'Approaches to the Study of Federalism', *Political Studies*, 14: 1, 1966, p. 18.

community', either through the differentiation of a hitherto unitary state or through a process of integration where separate political organizations (not necessarily territorial states) come to make joint decisions.[1] Federalism is thus taken to be a general principle of social organization. This implies that sociological rather than legal criteria must be applied in assessing the degree of federalism in a system. In the words of another critic of the classic approach, 'the essential nature of federalism is to be sought for, not in the shadings of legal and constitutional terminology, but in the forces – economic, social, political, cultural – that have made the outward forms of federalism necessary'.[2] It also implies that the 'federalizing process' may be present both in systems which appear, institutionally, to be classic international systems, or confederations (alliances), and, at the other end of the continuum, in unitary or even totalitarian states.

From the contention that the federal idea 'is not confined to the political sphere of the state, but is the general basis of human organization',[3] it is clearly possible to make ambitious claims about the present and future success of federalism. Robert Pelloux, for example, postulating that federalism may take 'consultative' and 'functional' as well as 'political' forms, argues that all three are now operating in Europe.[4] Many writers make no distinction between the federal and functional principles, suggesting that new forms of economic federalism (of large enterprises and of functional organizations such as the Coal and Steel Community) are emerging as conceivable rivals to territorially based organizations.[5] Federal characteristics, it appears, can be discerned in anything from a hierarchical structure to a decentralized administrative system to a loose pattern of intergovernmental cooperation.

Many of those who take this position invoke venerable European

[1] C. J. Friedrich, 'Federal Constitutional Theory and Emergent Proposals', in Macmahon, *op. cit.*, p. 514. See also 'Federalism and Nationalism', *Orbis*, 10: 4, 1967, pp. 1009–10; and *Trends of Federalism in Theory and Practise*, (London: 1968).

[2] W. S. Livingston, *Federalism and Constitutional Change* (Oxford: 1956) p. 1.

[3] S. Mogi, *The Problem of Federalism: A Study in the History of Political Theory*, 2 vols. (London: 1931) p. 1111. Cf. L. Armand and M. Drancourt, *Le Pari Européen* (Paris: 1968) for a similar concept of federalism. See also H. Brugmans and P. Duclos, *Le Fédéralisme Contemporain* (Leyden: 1963) Part II.

[4] R. Pelloux, 'Le Fédéralisme Européen', in G. Berger *et al.*, *Le Fédéralisme* (Paris: 1956) pp. 361–405.

[5] See A. A. Berle, 'Evolving Capitalism and Political Federalism', in Macmahon, *op. cit.*, esp. pp. 70–3; and W. Diebold, 'The Relevance of Federalism to Western European Economic Integration', *ibid.*, pp. 433–5.

doctrines of federalism such as those of Althusius, and juxtapose them to the dominant Anglo-Saxon legalistic tradition. But a similar challenge has been expressed by many working within the latter mode. Some argue that a rigid division of powers is impossible to maintain in modern societies. In the United States and Canada a vast literature has suggested that these divisions are already beyond repair. In the words of one expert: 'Under the heat and pressure generated by social and economic change in the twentieth century, the distinctive strata of the older federalism have begun to melt and flow into one another.'[1] This is not to say that the principle of the formal division of powers is not still central to any federal system. Rather it is to suggest, first, that the allocation of powers must be flexible and, secondly, that we must expect and encourage inter-governmental cooperation across these lines of demarcation if a modern society is to function effectively. Clearly, then, it is possible to retain the precise institutional criteria of federalism while becoming more sensitive to the political and social dynamics of such systems than were many classic theorists.

But it is not clear what purpose is served by broadening the concept of federalism so as to devalue institutional criteria almost entirely. For example, the useful classic distinction between a federation and a confederation – that in the former the powers of defence and foreign policy (the attributes of 'external' sovereignty) are in the hands of the central government[2] – is rendered meaningless by a dynamic perspective which sees a degree of federalism in practically every situation. Quite aside from the problem of finding alternative precise measures, the notion of a 'federalizing process' risks ignoring the possible need for a qualitative break between an international and a federal system – a break that inescapably involves the constitutional redistribution of powers. The federalist goal of integration thus loses its singular clarity and precision.

On the other hand, the devaluation of institutional criteria has itself forced a new appreciation of the political and social forces operating within federal systems. For example, Wheare's strict definition gave him many difficulties in deciding whether Switzerland

---

[1] J. A. Corry, 'Constitutional Trends and Federalism', in A. R. Lower *et al.*, *Evolving Canadian Federalism* (Durham, N.C.; 1958) pp. 121–2. For similar arguments, see Watts, *op. cit.*, pp. 11–12; C. Aikin, 'The Structure of Power in Federal Nations', in Montgomery and Smithies, *op. cit.*, esp. pp. 326, 347–8, 353; and M. Beloff, 'The "Federal Solution" in its Application to Europe, Asia and Africa', *Political Studies*, 1: 2, 1953, pp. 127–8.

[2] R. Aron, *Peace and War* (New York: 1966) p. 758.

and Canada were truly federal states, and in the latter case he was forced to improvise the rather unhelpful category of 'quasi-federal'.[1] Rather than trying to determine at what point the accretion of the powers of the central government makes a system no longer federal in practice (an omnipresent problem in the current age of centralization), it might therefore be more useful to recognize that a variety of relationships can exist simultaneously between the units of a federal state. There can be direct confrontation between some states and the central government over jurisdiction or taxation; there can be un-coordinated, duplicated activities by several governments; there can be cooperation. This does not mean the demise of federalism, but merely requires different kinds of analysis.[2]

The importance of the sociological perspective, then, is not that it necessarily leads to a restatement or a blurring of the basic federal principle (although it can do so) but that it demonstrates both the necessity and the feasibility of measuring the growth and decay of federal systems against more sensitive standards than the classic constitutional ones. The constitutional standard may still be the one by which we discern if integration has been successful or not. But in order more accurately to trace the shifting locus of power in the system, it is useful to have at hand a set of sociological variables such as those laid out in Etzioni's 'paradigm'.[3]

The common analytical and normative theme running from the classic federalists through to Etzioni's writings is that of power. As Neumann remarks, the theoretical argument for federalism revolves around the potential of political power for evil; this argument, he notes, has links both with the anarchism of Proudhon and the liberalism of Acton.[4] Within the integrated state, the fragmentation of power that is the essence of federalism is seen as a safeguard against domination by a single group or against totalitarian centralization. Indeed, classic federalist literature on the state is full of references to 'checks and balances' and the 'separation' or 'balance' of power, and abounds in mechanistic metaphors about the delicate interplay of interests and institutions. Etzioni's perspective is perhaps

[1] Wheare, *op. cit.*, pp. 16–20.

[2] For some, of course, the concept of 'cooperative federalism' with its blurring of traditional jurisdictional demarcations, is merely a euphemism masking the centralization of all modern states.

[3] Etzioni, *op. cit.*, p. 15. The variables are discussed in more detail in his third chapter, and hypotheses developed about some of them in Chapter Four.

[4] F. Neumann, 'Federalism and Freedom: A Critique', in Macmahon, *op. cit.*, pp. 45–7.

less overtly mechanistic (he tries to build in Parsonian functionalism and Deutschian cybernetics as well), but the bulk of his analysis is in terms of the power of the central institutions, the units and the integrating 'elites'. Like the classic federalists, he tends to see power as a quantity – based on assets and capacities to perform certain tasks and influence other actors.[1] Within the integrated political system, then, federalists wish to see these assets and capacities distributed so as to avoid the monolithic centralization of power. Such centralization may jeopardize not only the democratic responsiveness of the system but also its administrative flexibility and efficiency. Even the supreme Hobbesian values of order and stability, in the federalist view, are better served in the long run by a pluralistic balance of power than by a preponderance of power at the centre.

Federalism, of course, is seen as a solution to the problem of power not only within the state but in the international system. War is taken to be the inevitable product of a system which legitimizes the existence of a multitude of sovereign entities with conflicting goals and the means to pursue them.[2] Federalism as an approach to international integration (as opposed to a theory of the state) takes as its paramount values peace and security, and finds these best served by the abolition or drastic modification of the current international system. In Etzioni's mind, the studies of regional integration and of war and peace are closely related. For him, 'the most compelling appeal of regionalism is that the rise of regional communities may provide a stepping stone on the way from a world of a hundred-odd states to a world of a stable and just peace. Such an achievement seems to require the establishment of a world political community'.[3] The world, in short, must be governed.

Giving such primacy to the values of peace and security is not without its difficulties. In the first place, the problem of peace and security has two faces – one outward-turning and one inward-turning. The former has to do with the recurring argument that protection from some common external threat requires the formation of a large political-military unit. Wheare mentions this as a major factor

[1] For Etzioni's definition of power, see *op. cit.*, p. 8 n. The 'quantity-relationship' debate over power as a concept is discussed on pp. 40–3.

[2] On this point, see I. L. Claude Jr., *Swords into Plowshares*, 3rd edition (New York: 1964) p. 372. In Waltz's terms this is a 'third image' analysis of the origins of wars: *Man, the State and War*, Chs. 6–8.

[3] Etzioni, *op. cit.*, preface, pp. x–xi. See also *The Active Society*, pp. 564–75 for an argument that the prevention of a major war requires supranational control on a global scale, not merely to maintain law and order but to enhance world welfare.

behind the formation of most federations. Etzioni, in a more sceptical frame of mind, discusses the 'common threat' as one of a number of possibly important social and ecological properties affecting integration.[1] Advocates of European federation have consistently stressed external threats to Europe's security, both directly from the Soviet Union and more obliquely from the United States (the long-term implications of economic penetration and strategic dependence).[2] What federalists often neglect to explain, however, is why such threats require more than the classic responses of military alliances or economic cooperation between governments.

The inward-turning face, of course, concerns peace *within* a given state-system. Here this approach accepts the Hobbesian view that the formation of a common supranational government provides an effective restraint on war and violence. In this light international organizations tend to be judged, not as instruments of policy, regulators of diplomacy or even institutions of collective security, but as embryonic federations.[3] To the extent that such organizations advance us toward supranational government, they are deemed successful. Only legal and political controls can check international anarchy. Quite apart from the doubts that might be held on the desire for internal security as a motive for integration, it is of course questionable whether governments have the inherent capacity to provide this kind of security. Recent experiences of violent political conflict within centralized states (France), and of civil war within federations (Nigeria), hardly suggest that the 'domestication' of power-conflicts has much to recommend it.[4]

Even more serious, in the eyes of some critics, is the contradiction between the two faces of peace and security. Far from being 'stepping stones' to world community, Etzioni's regional communities, with their size, self-sufficiency and internal order, may in fact intensify the dangerous fragmentation of the global system. This is the essence of the functionalist critique of federalism: global federation might be acceptable, if set up on flexible lines, but is too remote a possibility

[1] See Wheare, *op. cit.*, pp. 37–8; Etzioni, *op. cit.*, pp. 27–33. Cf. A. Wolfers, 'Amity and Enmity Among Nations', in *Discord and Collaboration* (Baltimore: 1962) pp. 27–9.

[2] For recent arguments of this sort, see J. Pinder and R. Pryce, *Europe after de Gaulle* (Harmondsworth, Middx.: 1969) esp. Chs. 7 and 8.

[3] See H. Brugmans. *L'Idée Européenne* 1918–65 (Bruges: 1965) Ch. 2, esp. pp. 41–2 on the League of Nations.

[4] On this point, see the extensive criticisms on the idea of 'world government' in Claude, *op. cit.*, Ch. 19, Aron, *op. cit.*, Ch. 24, and H. J. Morgenthau, *Politics Among Nations*, 4th edition (New York: 1967) Ch. 29.

to take seriously; regional federations, which are far more practicable and thus offer a tempting form of gradualist strategy, are positively dangerous.[1] Despite such criticisms, federalist literature abounds in optimistic assertions that European federation is the required 'catalyst' or the 'necessary condition' of world federation.[2]

Many of these weaknesses can be traced to the strong flavour of advocacy in much federalist literature, particularly in Europe. Apart from a few scattered claims that federalism is a scientific mode of social analysis, most of the writing in the field is in a strongly prescriptive, often visionary vein. It is not surprising, then, that federalism is often said to serve a wide variety of ends which many political philosophers have held to be incompatible.

The virtue of a federal system, it is claimed, is that unlike other types of supranational state, it is designed as a framework in which such 'centralizing' principles as security, order, authority, administrative rationality, constitutionalism and unity can be reconciled with the 'decentralizing' values of liberty, local autonomy, representation, pluralism, flexibility and diversity. Proudhon, for example, felt that federalism 'solved' the problem of having both freedom and authority in a political system.[3] Others see federalism as 'a technique for organizing political power anxious to conciliate a maximum of community efficacy with a maximum of individual freedom'.[4] On the one hand, then, international federalism embodies the Hobbesian prescription for peace and security, which implies a strongly centralized authoritarian polity. On the other, many writers emphasize the importance of democratic institutions, local communities, small political units and other methods for guaranteeing the responsiveness and representativeness of the domestic political system.[5] In this respect, federalism is often presented as a descendent of the 'American

[1] D. Mitrany, 'The Prospect of European Integration: Federal or Functional', in *A Working Peace System* (Chicago: 1966) esp. pp. 180–7.

[2] See, for example, Pinder and Pryce, *op. cit.*, Ch. 9, esp. pp. 157–60, and R. Aron and A. Marc *Principes du Fédéralisme* (Paris: 1948) pp. 142–6.

[3] Brugmans and Duclos, *op. cit.*, pp. 41, 152. Cf. Friedrich, 'Federal Constitutional Theory and Emergent Proposals', in Macmahon, *op. cit.*, p. 517, and J. J. Chevallier, 'Le Fédéralisme de Proudhon et de ses Disciples', in Berger *et al.*, *op. cit.*, pp. 87–127.

[4] F. Rosenstiel, 'Reflections on the Notion of Supranationality', *Journal of Common Market Studies*, 2: 2, 1963, p. 132.

[5] See, for example, A. Spinelli, *The Eurocrats* (Baltimore: 1966) esp. pp. 11–13; cf. Brugmans' attempt to associate federalism with a vast range of political virtues: Brugmans and Duclos, *op. cit.*, pp. 20–53. For a powerful attack on such claims, see Neumann, 'Federalism and Freedom: A Critique', in Macmahon, *op. cit.*, pp. 44–53.

revolutionary tradition' of pluralism, toleration and liberalism, in direct contrast to the 'French revolutionary tradition' of centralization, authoritarianism and jacobin nationalism.[1] It is certainly open to question whether peace and security – the priorities of the international federalist – will necessarily be maintained in the structurally loose, liberal system favoured by the domestic federalist.

More generally, to claim so many virtues for any political idea is naturally to invite charges of utopianism, and federalism has borne its share of these. Attempts to reconcile or compromise so many apparently opposed values, it is argued, are essentially misguided. Clearly it is possible to argue elaborately, and probably inconclusively, over a great number of these claims. Perhaps it is more important here simply to observe the ambiguities they create in the federalist idea of the goal of integration, and to note the differences of emphasis between the federalists concerned with international problems and those concerned with domestic issues.

Classic federalist theory, then, has two major components: it is a theory of international pacification and a theory of domestic political organization. In the same way, Etzioni's sociological approach, while concerned foremost with the problem of peace, is also an attempt to develop a general mode of analysis of social units on many levels.[2] The international-domestic cleavage thus cuts across the cleavage between classic and sociological federalism. This pattern is evident throughout the development of federalism as a political theory.

There are three major historical sources of federalist ideas. The first of these lies on the innumerable plans devised throughout history for the maintenance of peace and the reorganization of international relations. It is customary to trace the federal institutional pattern back to the various leagues of Greek city-states, even though these seem to have been closer to classic alliances on the pluralist model.[3] Indeed, before Bodin and Grotius, although there had been many proposals for perpetual peace of the 'league' type, the classic federal pattern embodying a 'dual sovereignty' would have been inconceivable. It was only really after the emergence of the United

[1] Brugmans and Duclos, *op. cit.*, pp. 11–12; cf. R. Aron, 'A Suggested Scheme for the Study of Federalism', *International Social Science Bulletin*, 4: 1, 1952, pp. 45–6.

[2] See Etzioni, *op. cit.*, Introduction, p. xviii.

[3] There is considerable disagreement among scholars on this point. Bozeman, for example, describes the Greek leagues as 'federations': *Politics and Culture in International History* (Princeton: 1960) p. 102. Hinsley, however, points out that a terminological ambiguity may be at the core of the problem, since the Latin root 'foedus' means simply 'treaty'. See *Power and the Pursuit of Peace* (Cambridge; 1963) pp. 66–9.

States as a federal system (1787) that peace plans began to urge specifically federal solutions on a European or global scale. And increasingly by the twentieth century, this intellectual impetus was coming out not so much from Europeans as from Americans. This tradition of federalist thought, then, gradually developed into a blend of pacifism, liberalism and constitutionalism, with the overriding assumption that political problems of peace and security could be solved by juridical and institutional means.[1]

The second major source of federalist ideas has been the experience of governing the world's few federal states. The literature derived from this experience has, in the main, the distinctly pragmatic, empirical and legalistic flavour of the old 'political economy'. Not surprisingly, considering the origins of these federal states, most of the sources are in the Anglo-Saxon tradition of constitutional law or in the arguments and reflections of the legally and economically trained practitioners of Anglo-Saxon politics. The primary concern of these writings is with the operation and adjustment of the division of constitutional reponsibilities and with the allocation of economic resources and taxation powers in the federal system. In a rare speculative vein, this type of thought has reached the semi-metaphysical and scholastic extremes of the nineteenth-century German jurists, arguing about the possible constitutional forms of states, but its more usual pragmatic political style is to be found in such sources as the *Federalist Papers* of early American vintage.[2] On the whole, in later writings the existence and the virtues of federalism are taken for granted. The tone is less one of advocacy than of problem-solving.

The third source of federalist ideas is quite different, tracing its origins to medieval European society and denying the federal principle its more familiar associations with the legal constitution of a territorial state. This tradition of thought – primarily European – is far more abstract and philosophical than the ones previously discussed; its analytic bias is toward small groups and sociological variables, and its prescriptive bias is toward fundamental social

[1] For useful reviews of the development of federalist ideas and their historical connection with the peace movement, see Hinsley, *op. cit.*, Chs. 1–7; Brugmans, *L'Idée Européenne*, Chs. 1 and 2; and G. Vedel, 'Les Grand Courants de la Pensée Politique et le Fédéralisme' in Berger *et al.*, *op. cit.*, pp. 31–86.

[2] On this tradition of federalist thought, see Mogi, *op. cit.*, esp. Vol. I, Chs. 2–9; Vol. II, Chs. 5–8; Bennett, *op. cit.*; Lower *et al.*, *op. cit.*, esp. Ch. 1; T. Cole, 'Federalism in the Commonwealth', in Montgomery and Smithies, *op. cit.*, pp. 355–79.

reorganization both below and beyond national boundaries. It is often argued that Proudhon was a pivotal figure in this tradition,[1] to which Althusius and Rousseau were earlier contributors. In the late nineteenth and early twentieth centuries these ideas found their way into such diverse theories as guild socialism, functionalism and pluralism, and were associated with such writers as Gierke, Maitland, Cole, Duguit, and Laski. Of particular influence intellectually (though not politically) was the 'integral federalist' movement which emerged in the 1930s as an eclectic mix of ideas from Proudhon, syndicalism, left-wing Catholicism and a number of other politically eccentric sources. It emphasized the bankruptcy of 'formal' democracy, capitalism and the established ideologies of right and left, and advocated a pluralistic or federal society of communal groups and interests.[2] From such movements derives the sociological concept of federalism which has come to the fore in recent writings. Duclos argues that the introduction of this perspective has led federalist thought to a new and critical phase.[3]

In this light Etzioni's work assumes a new significance. To challenge or to enhance the classic concepts and analytical tools of federalist theory, many dynamic, sociological approaches have been put forward. But most of these – for example Friedrich's concept of 'process', Deutsch's 'security-community', Duclos 'théorie générale de la fédéralisation', the various notions of 'functional federalism', Riker's 'bargaining' approach – apply to broader social processes than the formation of a supranational state out of a system of sovereign states. This is inevitable, as the scope of federalism itself is much broader than the study of international integration. But it does suggest that Etzioni's paradigm, concentrating on sociological variables in integration, is the leading candidate for a systematic sociological model of federalism as it applies to international relations. It remains, of course, to ask if, in moving away from the elegant simplicity of their historically-based classic models and towards the complexities of dynamic analysis, the federalists are not forgetting their own strictures about the inevitability of the 'constitutional question' in the formation of new states.

[1] Brugmans and Duclos, *op. cit.*, pp. 154–60. Cf. Friedrich, 'Federal Constitutional Theory and Emergent Proposals', in Macmahon, *op. cit.*, pp. 511–14, and 'Federalism and Nationalism', *op. cit.*, p. 1015.

[2] For a description of this movement, see Brugmans and Duclos, *op. cit.*, pp. 161–72, and A. Marc, 'Histoire des Idées et des Mouvements Fédéralistes Depuis la Première Guerre Mondiale', in Berger *et al.*, *op. cit.*, esp. pp. 131–6.

[3] Brugmans and Duclos, *op. cit.*, pp. 182–3.

The Integrative Process: Elites, Bargaining and Political Will

Federal theorists see integration as a shift from a classic international system to a single polity with particular constitutional and socio-logical characteristics. In the first section of this chapter we have discussed some of these characteristics and the values and assumptions about political life that tend to accompany them. In this next section we shall examine how the process of change itself is explained.

i) The System: Constitutional issues and social change

On the level of the international system, first, the federalist approach embraces a number of views, ranging from the static, legalistic perspective of classic writers to the dynamic sociological perspective of Etzioni and Friedrich. The older federalists have been more or less content to describe the 'before' and 'after' characteristics of the system, comparing the Hobbesian anarchy of the former with the domestic harmony of the latter. Since their prime interest has been either to make the case for the federal solution to international insecurity or to analyse the workings of existing federal systems and extol their virtues, these writers have not concerned themselves in much depth with the causes and dynamics of the integrative process itself. One finds scattered and brief assertions in their works about the importance of external threats, economic incentives, a common cultural heritage and other factors, but these are generally offered as axioms or assumptions rather than as the central hypotheses to be examined. Even when classic federalists attempt systematically to list the 'background conditions' likely to favour integration, there is little discussion of their relative weight or of the points in the process at which they are most effective.[1]

Recently, however, federalist theory has been concerned less with the stark juxtaposition of international disorder and federal order, and more with how systems move toward the latter condition. This new dynamic perspective owes much to Friedrich's advocacy of a process-oriented federalism. In addition, it draws on other approaches to integration theory, notably that developed by Karl Deutsch. Concluding from numerous case studies that integration must be seen as a dynamic process along a historical assembly-line, Deutsch

---

[1] For the best example of this type of analysis, see Wheare, *op. cit.*, Ch. 3. A good general survey, comparing the explanatory power of the traditional and the newer federalist approaches, is Birch, *op. cit.*, esp. pp. 21–2.

argues that 'the transition from background to process is fluid. The essential background conditions do not come into existence all at once; they are not established in any particular fixed sequence; nor do they all grow together like one organism from a seed. Rather, it appears to us from our cases that they may be assembled in almost any sequence, so long only as all of them come into being and take effect'.[1] Apart from their behavioural and sociological emphasis, and the focus on communications and perceptions, Deutsch's 'background conditions' differ little from those adduced by the classic federalists. Where his approach does differ radically is in its emphasis on the length and indeterminacy of the process of integration, and on such dynamic concepts as 'takeoff'.[2]

Following on from the work of Deutsch and, to some extent, the neofunctionalists, Etzioni has devised a 'paradigm' intended to stress the dynamic aspects of the integrative process. His discussion of the 'preunification state' is really an elaboration, from the viewpoint of political sociology, of the 'unit, environment and system properties' (i.e. background conditions) often mentioned by classic federalists and developed as hypotheses by Deutsch and Haas in particular. Etzioni groups his variables here by examining, first, the state of each unit of the potential union, secondly, the aggregate of these units, thirdly, the environment of the system they comprise, and finally, the degree of integration already present in this system.[3] Throughout his discussion there runs a strong reluctance to identify any particular element as a crucial determinant or even a necessary condition of integration.

Between this discussion and a short exploration of how to analyse the 'termination state', Etzioni focuses on the process of change itself. The kinds, quantities and distribution of 'integrating power' are seen as the crucial determinants of the pattern followed by this process. Here Etzioni puts many federalist notions about power into rigorous, researchable form. Power, and the assets upon which it is based, he asserts, is of three kinds: utilitarian, coercive and identitive. He can then ask, first, which kinds of power in which combinations

[1] K. W. Deutsch *et al.*, *Political Community and the North Atlantic Area*, (Princeton: 1957) reprinted in part in *International Political Communities* (New York: 1966) see p. 48. This analysis applies equally to pluralistic as to amalgamated (i.e. federal) forms of integration.

[2] See, for example, the concept of a broad transitional zone or threshold of integration, which can be repeatedly crossed back and forth: *ibid.*, p. 14; for the concept of 'takeoff' and the comparison with the process of economic development, see *ibid.*, pp. 60–2.

[3] See Etzioni, *op. cit.*, Ch. 2, esp. pp. 16–37.

are most effective at different stages of integration, and secondly, whether this power is distributed equally or is concentrated in a few elite-units, either within or outside the system. Such questions serve to generate a series of hypotheses by which many old federalist notions about the use of power in integration can be tested.[1]

In the pattern of integration itself there are two stages. The first is the 'takeoff', brought about largely by increased shared activities and 'secondary priming'. Here Etzioni's analysis of system-change again owes much to the work of Deutsch and the neofunctionalists. The next stage – once the integrative process has become self-sustaining – is the maturing or stabilization of the system. Here the crucial variables are the scope (the number of societal sectors integrated) and the extent of integration in terms of each power-dimension. Etzioni raises the analytic question of where (in terms of scope and level of integration) a system is likely to find equilibrium, and the tactical question of the sequence in which sectors of the system are best unified.[2]

The work of Deutsch, Etzioni, Friedrich and other 'process-oriented' students of integration has thus introduced a marked change of emphasis into federalist thinking. As a consequence of their relatively static perspective, classic federalist writers have tended to see integration as a sort of constitutional revolution – a dramatic, sudden change from an 'international' to a 'domestic' political system. The archetypal method is a constitutional conference where the members of the system strike a bargain on the form of the supranational state, to which they then yield up at least partial control of the assets of coercive, economic and identitive power. Ideally this is followed by direct, system-wide elections to fill the new institutions. The crucial point in this procedure is the direct broaching of the question of national sovereignty. The federalists' minimal requirement is that a new political system emerge in which not only the legal expression of sovereignty but also its political basis (i.e. the disposition of the assets of power) no longer rests exclusively with the constituent states. Whatever the motivation (fear, external pressure, economic gain), it is assumed to be powerful enough to push even the most recalcitrant state to yield up some of the trappings and the substance of independence.

For the classic federalist, then, the basic index of integration is the

---

[1] *Ibid.*, pp. 37–50. For the hypotheses, see pp. 67–88.

[2] *Ibid.*, pp. 51–60. See also A. Etzioni, 'The Epigenesis of Political Community at the International Level', *American Journal of Sociology*, 68: 4, 1963, pp. 407–21.

seat of sovereignty. Since sovereignty is a legal status derived from and indicating membership in the international system, its abrogation by a state or assumption by a new supranational entity cannot be gradual. An entity is either sovereign or it is not. In legal and constitutional terms, then, the emergence of a federal system from an international system is indeed dramatic and revolutionary.[1]

In practice, of course, the classic international federalists are aware not only of the analytic importance of subtler indices of change (shifts in the locus of the assets of power, rather than the formal trappings) but also of the tactical necessity of gradualism. In part this awareness indicates a shift from the prescriptive to the explanatory mode in federalist thinking. It also reflects the experience of postwar failures in many federations which, while perhaps sound constitutionally, lacked a firm social and political foundation. To understand and then to prepare these foundations before attempting to erect a prefabricated federal structure has thus become the new imperative.

This sense of the sterility of the old methods, as well as the influence of the sociological, process-oriented writers, has stretched the temporal perspective of federalists from their customary focus on the immediate conditions and mechanisms of constitutional change to the longer-term processes which make these changes conceivable and politically practicable. Nevertheless, not all federalists would go as far as Etzioni and Friedrich, in whose analyses the notion of a constitutional threshold plays little or no part. For most, the processes stressed by Deutsch, Etzioni, Friedrich, the functionalists and the neofunctionalists can make the crossing of this threshold less difficult and painful, but they do not provide an escape from the 'constitutional question'. Unlike the neofunctionalists, then, most federalists retain the classic distinction between national and international political systems. Underlying conditions may change incrementally, but integration itself is a qualitative change in the state-system, a revolution consciously directed by the system's elites. The strength of federalism has always been its insistence that this issue must be faced at some point.

The temporal perspectives of the classic federalists and the more sociological theorists differ in another important respect. For the former, political integration tends to be identified wholly with the

[1] On the implications of this analysis of sovereignty, see Rosenstiel, *op. cit.*, p. 138; Spinelli, *op. cit.*, Ch. 1. For sharp criticisms of the 'apocalyptic' federalist view, see Claude, *op. cit.*, pp. 374–80.

emergence of stable federal institutions. For their purposes, once these have been set up, the problem of integration is solved, the process over. For the latter, however, integration is a socio-political process, for which these institutions merely provide a stable, restraining framework. They are not unambiguously dependent variables as in classic federalism, but rather independent variables in a process to be measured by such criteria as communication-patterns, the location of power-assets, social differentiation, or cross-cutting lines of cleavage in the system. Thus, far from being the final seal on the problem of integration, the formation of federal institutions can be seen as a vital stage in a more far-reaching process.[1] In this respect the bifurcation of federalist theory reflects that of development theory, to which it, like the other approaches to integration, has strong ties. Like classic federalism, early political development studies measured success by the emergence and stability of certain kinds of institutions; now they are more likely to look at such social and political indices as attitudes to government authority, class and group cleavages, and the level of violence in the society.

In explaining integration at the level of the system, all federalists are united in emphasizing the primacy of politics. System-change is held to depend less on the vast, impersonal forces of economic or technological evolution, and more on the ability of the system's elites to amass, control and employ the assets of power. In short, this is a non-deterministic philosophy, impressed with the random, willful and dramatic side of political life. Political institutions are seen both as the stage for an ongoing and creative struggle between elites and as the means through which the outcomes of their conflicts are consolidated.

Such an image of political change relies on a clear differentiation between elites and masses and an assumption that elites can often act independently of the political and economic forces in their societies. This is a similar assumption to that which underlies the 'balance-of-power' theory of international relations, where the maintenance of stability depends on the freedom of states' decision-makers to shift coalitions rapidly. This is not to say that elite-mass linkages are not important. But they are important in the sense –

[1] See Friedrich, 'Federalism and Nationalism', *op. cit.*, pp. 1009–10, on federalism as a means of dealing with problems of communal interaction at all levels of a society; also H. Brugmans 'European Unity and the Federalist Idea', *ibid.*, p. 1025, on the 'permanent creative tension and dialectical struggle' which occurs in a federal system. See Macmahon, *op. cit.*, Sec. II, for studies of how 'mature' federal systems deal with continuing problems of integration.

described well by Etzioni – that elites' responsiveness to mass demands provides a vital flow of information to the top and elites' sensitive handling of the reallocation of resources preserves the quiet consensus underlying the federal bargain.[1]

To sum up, then, integration for the federalist is a matter of high politics. Neither the new and salutary awareness of the need to examine background conditions and the dynamics of system-change as a process, nor the liberal-democratic values which permeate classic federalism, have really affected the basic image of system-change. This image still posits a qualitative threshold between international and national politics, relies on the creative capacities of elites in forming the federal compact, and makes allowance for sudden reversals or dramatic accelerations in the process of integration.

ii) *The States: elites and the federal contract*

Of all approaches to integration theory, federalism is the only one which attempts directly to face the Hobbesian paradox posed by states' willing abrogation of their own sovereign power. Pluralists claim that such dramatic renunciations and institutional changes are neither possible nor desirable. Functionalists see sovereignty as being eroded gradually in successive fits of self-interested absent-mindedness. Neofunctionalists evade the paradox, finally, by dissolving the state system into an interdependent network of subnational and supranational political forces pursuing narrow interests across political boundaries.

As we have seen, however, federalists are not inclined to rely on qualities of the system – such as economic and technological interdependence or other such 'background conditions' – to lead inexorably toward greater political integration. In the words of one European federalist: 'In the long run, trade follows politics rather than vice-versa, and all the emerging European economic enterprise could be destroyed just as it has been created.' Moreover: 'Contrary to the theories of those who regard the great anonymous forces of popular sentiment and economic interest as the mainsprings of the political undertakings of peoples, the European unification adventure began with tepid popular support and no popular pressure, over economic questions but without pressure from economic forces.'[2] Such a formulation makes it clear that the socio-economic environ-

[1] Etzioni, *Political Unification*, pp. 74–6.
[2] Spinelli, *op. cit.*, p. 110 and 7. Cf. Brugmans and Duclos, *op. cit.*, p. 16.

ment is to be seen as a passive backdrop for the decisive activities of political elites. The same is true for public opinion and the activities of many interest groups. Not only, then, does the federalist see integration as a revolution begun and consummated by elites; he also defines the elites more narrowly than do the neofunctionalists, who would otherwise share this view.

On this point the federalists are forthright: integration can only be brought about by the states themselves. But when we speak of states as 'acting', we really refer to the elites which act in their name *vis-à-vis* other states – that is, the foreign policy elites. At its very broadest, this group would include top decision-makers beyond the traditional 'foreign office' circles. There are also elites which represent international organizations (such as the European Commission), cross-national groups (such as Monnets' Action Committee) and even states external to the integrating system. For Etzioni, the elites are units which use a large proportion of their power-assets to guide and gain support for 'a process' (such as integration). His definition includes persons, groups or states.[1] All these centres of power compete to lead the process in the direction they desire, or to retard it, and the success of integration depends on the kinds of bargains and coalitions they form. Nonetheless, the point of application remains the elite which makes foreign policy for the state and which has, if only formally, the last word on the acceptable form and degree of integration.

Integration, then, comes about because a shared perception develops among the elites of several states that their problems are so pressing as to require a dramatic restructuring of the system in which they operate. Incremental change is seen as inadequate.[2] Federalists assume dramatic political change is possible partly because, as mentioned earlier, elites are relatively unfettered, free from serious pushes and pulls from transnational interest groups or public opinion and subject only to pressures from their counterparts in other states. This assumption, inherited from 'balance-of-power' theory, is complemented by another of the same vintage – that the 'sovereign' or the top decision-makers virtually embody the national will. From these two assumptions follows the crucial methodological conclusion that the process of integration is best examined in the

[1] Etzioni, *op. cit.*, pp. 45–7.

[2] See E. B. Haas, '"The Uniting of Europe" and the Uniting of Latin America', *Journal of Common Market Studies*, 5: 4, 1967, pp. 327–31. A vivid expression of this 'dramatic' state of mind is Clarence Streit's dictum that 'the most dangerous way to cross a chasm is one step at a time' – quoted in J. P. Sewell, *Functionalism and World Politics* (Princeton: 1966) p. 315.

rarified atmosphere of bargaining among traditional foreign policy elites.

A strong element of this austere view of diplomacy remains in even the most recent sociological federalist thinking. Etzioni, while clearly allowing for a more complex bargaining process than the classical federalists, does tend to associate the notion of 'units' and 'elites' almost exclusively with states.[1] It is these autonomous units, at times almost personified, who act on their own initiative to transcend the limits of their systems of relationships with each other. For the federalist, then, even in going 'beyond the nation-state' there is no escaping the nation-state.[2]

This conception of integration, of course, takes us to the heart of the political dilemma as well known to students of Hobbes as it is to federalist writers. By what political alchemy are these powerful, autonomous states brought to commit the self-willed sacrifice of their freedom of action? It is one thing for federalists boldly to confront this apparent paradox, and quite another to resolve it convincingly. An easy and tempting way out is to personify the states and see federation as involving a conversion or change of heart among them (i.e. among their leaders). But not only does this tell us little about the motives and dynamics of such changes. More seriously, it suggests that federations are easiest formed, not among the democratic, economically advanced states favoured in most federalist literature, but among authoritarian states where the leader's conversion is unlikely to be challenged by group interests or public opinion. Few federalists can be expected to accept such a proposition.

Nevertheless, the idea is worth closer examination. It may be true that integration is more likely to be *sustained* in a federation of highly developed states where liberal-democratic values prevail. On the other hand, the *establishment* of a federation may proceed with more certainty where outside pressure is applied to the system's elites (as with many federations in the British Commonwealth) or where the constituent states lack many attributes of participatory politics. It is conceivable, then, that the most favourable conditions for creating federations are the least favourable for maintaining them.

---

[1] See, for example, his discussion of the necessary 'unit-properties' in the 'preunification state': *Political Unification*, pp. 16–27. The 'units' are assumed to be states, and the elites on which he concentrates are national political decision-makers.

[2] See the comments of Claude, *op. cit.*, p. 103, on supranationality and sovereign states; and S. Hoffman, 'Discord in Community: The North Atlantic Area as a Partial International System,' *International Organization*, 17: 3, 1963, p. 529.

However far one wishes to take this proposition, it is nonetheless clear that a major part of the federalist explanation of integration must lie in how elites interact to create and sustain the federal 'contract'. It is not sufficient simply to expect the outcome of bargaining to reflect the structure and power of the elites' constituencies and the underlying social and economic conditions. The capacities of the elites themselves and the context in which they interact may be more vital to the success of integration. For Etzioni it is not enough to add up the power potential of the elites; much depends on the setting in which these assets must be converted into usable political power and on the skill with which elites perform this task.[1] Riker, looking more closely at the setting itself, argues that two predispositions among the elites are necessary for the conclusion of a federal bargain. One, held by those offering the bargain, is the desire to expand their area of political control without using force. The other, held by those accepting the federal bargain, is a willingness to sacrifice some independence to gain either protection from or participation in some external action.[2] If the central process of integration is pictured in this manner, techniques of analysis such as games theory and small-group dynamics would seem to be of some importance in explaining how the federal contract is formulated.

One might, of course, ask how literally the notion of 'contract' is to be interpreted. The classic federalists certainly had in mind a rather concrete form even if, as Claude notes, their contract theory was rather poor Lockean doctrine since it omitted to assume a pre-existing community.[3] In any case, the written constitution was taken to be the legal expression of this agreement. But among more sociologically oriented theorists, where the notion of contract exists it is taken far more figuratively. In principle, a federal system can operate where there is a tacit agreement among the member-units about the areas of separate and common activity. This view also allows for a much more fluid view of integration as a continual shifting of the locus of power as the various elites engage in a continuous round of bargaining within the 'federal' framework. But here of course it would be less clear than with a strict institutional definition, as to what level of conflict, and what sorts of outcome, are incompatible with the continuation of federalism or a state of integration. The breakdown of institutions is a far less ambiguous measure than shifts

[1] Etzioni, *op. cit.*, pp. 41–3.   [2] Riker, *op. cit.*, pp. 12–16.
[3] Claude, *op. cit.*, p. 378. On Proudhon's concept of the federal contract, see Chevallier, *op. cit.*, pp. 109–10.

of power. The literal notion of contract, then, is of some value even for those who do not accept the legalism of the classic federalists.

A major critique of the federalist approach at this level of analysis relates to the uses of historical analogy, particularly the analogy between international integration and the earlier formation of modern nation-states. One writer has remarked, in connection with the European federalist movement, that we have almost no examples of 'federations of states which had existed for any length of time or in any real sense as independent, sovereign national states'.[1] Another, cutting at the roots of the contract-theory, adds: 'There is as yet no instance of a political federation, in the proper sense of the term, born of the rational conviction that the progress of history necessitates a larger unit than the nation-state.'[2] What these arguments suggest is that the federalist notion of a supranational state set up by contract among smaller states may be an unfortunate intellectual heritage of the Enlightenment and its contract-theories, limited politically to an age when the power of nation-states was not yet overwhelming.

The problem of national power is central to two very different critiques of the federalist approach. On the one hand, the 'realist' critique holds that a federal contract of any kind among sovereign nation-states is in practice impossible, even if in principle the ideal solution. On the other hand, the functionalist critique rejects it both in practice and in principle for being based on the old, dangerous 'individual index of power'. In short, according to the 'realists', the world is not yet ready for federalism; according to the functionalists, the era of federalism has already passed. Both of these criticisms are clearly based on conceptions of the nation-state quite at variance with that held by federalists. It is only the federalists who manage to feel, and attempt to reconcile, both the continuing value and the increasing dangers of the nation-state system as a way of organizing world politics.[3]

In a sense these criticisms sum up the difficulties of this approach to integration. In the general context of integration theory, to insist on a direct assault on national sovereignty has come gradually to appear an almost tragically 'realistic' view: only concerted political power can overcome separate political power; only a direct confronta-

[1] K. C. Wheare, 'Federalism and the Making of Nations', in Macmahon, *op. cit.*, p. 40.

[2] Aron, 'A Suggested Scheme for the Study of Federalism', *op. cit.*, p. 54.

[3] On the historical dilemma of federalism and nationalism, see Friedrich, 'Federalism and Nationalism', *op. cit.*, passim, and Aron, *Peace and War*, pp. 749–52.

tion can overcome national autonomy. And yet, like the pluralists, these theorists may underestimate the cumulative force of functionalist gradualism. And in their search for dramatic integration through conflict and contract, they may have lost the modest resignation of the pluralists and merely gained an overpoliticized notion of integration which gets them no further either practically or conceptually.

iii) The Individual: Political will and divided loyalties

We must now turn briefly to the third level of analysis and examine what federalists say about the role of individual attitudes and behaviour in integration. Both classic and sociologically-oriented federalists seem to share a remarkable reluctance to make explicit many of their assumptions about what this role might be. By and large, their few statements on the subject tend to complement the general emphasis on the central role of national elites.

At the first glance, this stress on elites contradicts many of the assumptions and values held by the older federalists who, as Claude has observed, tended to accept the Wilsonian view that 'the peoples of the world are ready and eager to make the federalist plunge'.[1] As we have seen, there is a conscious stress in federalist writings on democratic values, popular support, and the elites' responsiveness to individual opinion in the formation and maintenance of the supranational state. A strongly populist philosophy clearly lay behind the revolt of the radical wing of the European federalist movement in 1956; this was a reaction against the incipient 'gradualism' of the majority of the movement, who sought to collaborate with national governments and economic elites in the hope of arriving eventually at federalism through economic cooperation. For the radicals, the failure of EDC showed the futility of hoping that national governments would adopt such a goal. Hence, they concluded, the federalist movement ought to 'go to the people'.

In this strategy a serious contradiction becomes evident. As Claude notes, this populist faith among federalists coexists uneasily with a belief in propaganda campaigns to persuade people to support the federalist solution.[2] As a European federalist describes the radical federalist view in 1956: 'seul un combat révolutionnaire pouvait encore sauver l'Europe. . . . A cet effet une nouvelle réalité populaire devait *être suscitée*: celle d'un "peuple européen" au singulier, d'une collectivité politique continentale, s'affirmant par-dessus les frontières

---

[1] Claude, *op. cit.*, pp. 375–6. [2] *Ibid.*, p. 376.

malgré les différences de nationalité, de langue et de culture'.[1] The people ought to be on the side of the federalists against reactionary and divisive national governments. If perchance they are not, their support must be generated by those elites who wish to change the system.

In Etzioni's approach this manipulative notion of the relation between popular attitudes and political change is even more apparent. One of the important aspects of his 'political community' is that it forms a focal point of political identification for its citizens. The community becomes a focal point because its leaders and institutions possess assets capable of being used to build up 'identitive power'. This power, 'is based on the identification of the subject with norms, values, symbols over which the holder of power has control. . . , or on an identification with his personality that makes his approvals and disapprovals powerful'.[2] By such means as education, religion, national rituals, propaganda and the manipulation of symbols, the integrating elites can harness or create a supporting popular will. This will, in turn, provide a justifying ideology or a degree of legitimacy for integration.[3]

But the view that popular opinion, when it does not already support federation, is mobilized in the struggle of elite-groups to bring about political change, presupposes that the desirability of such changes is accepted by significant groups among the political elites themselves. In the last analysis, as we have seen, it is the attitudes and behaviour of these people that are held to be decisive. Clearly the elites may arrive at a belief in the value of integration through a variety of processes. It could be the rational economic judgement that economic welfare or viability requires larger units; it could be a perceived threat from an outside power; it could be a mystical belief in some inexorable historical process, or in some mythological unity; it could be a calculation about personal, group or national political advantages in the larger political unit. Whatever the deeper motivation, there must be an underlying stability of outlook and a lack of deep ideological and social cleavages among these elites, so that this political will can lead to productive bargaining.

There tends to be a great reliance on this notion of 'political will' among federalists. Etzioni is inclined to take the existence of integrat-

---

[1] Brugmans, *L'Idée Européenne*, p. 177. Emphasis added. '. . . only a revolutionary struggle could still save Europe. . . . To this end a new popular fact had to be instigated: that of a "European public" in the singular, a continental body asserting itself across frontiers despite differences of nationality, language and culture.'

[2] Etzioni, *op. cit.*, p. 37 n.   [3] *Ibid.*, pp. 37–41, 71–2.

ing elites as his starting point, and thus not to worry about the sources of their motivations. But federalists often seem to think in more mystical terms, as if 'political will' were a kind of *deus ex machina* or magic elixir which, once injected into selected members of the political elite, will produce a 'conversion' carrying all before it. This idea has particular appeal, of course, to the more apocalyptic federalists; in times of crisis, however, even the gradualists come to rely on it. Needless to say, they have little idea how this 'will' is to be created.

One difficulty with this reliance on such elusive factors is that it leads to a great emphasis on the personal, the unpredictable and the unique in the integrative process. In particular, it leads to a 'great man' theory of integration, where the requisite political will is seen as residing in the person of a great leader or group of leaders.[1] In times of crisis, this can lead to futile messianic longings and to a nostalgia for bygone constellations such as that of Adenauer, de Gasperi and Schuman. The 'great man' approach suggests that integration is a rather haphazard, indeterminate process subject always to instant accelerations and reversals at the whim of the powerful. As a reaction to the smooth technological determinism of the older functionalists, this assertion of free will is helpful, but may go rather too far the other way. It may play down too much the slow growth of a popular consensus which not only supports gradual advances in integration, but also prevents drastic and arbitrary steps backward.

The less dramatic federalists, and those who, like Etzioni, take a sociological perspective, have much more confidence in this consensus. To a great extent this confidence is based on a belief in the effects of institutions and power on political attitudes. Many studies have demonstrated the effects of federal institutions (established or emergent) on patterns of political behaviour and attitudes.[2] These studies recall Monnet's belief in the formative capacities of institutions, common decisions and activities.[3] Etzioni, taking a broader

---

[1] Rosenstiel, *op. cit.*, p. 138, talks of the necessity for any federalist revolution to be along 'egotistical' lines.

[2] See D. B. Truman's classic article, 'Federalism and the Party System', in Macmahon, *op. cit.*, pp. 115–33; cf. D. Sidjanski, 'Federal Aspects of the European Community', in Montgomery and Smithies, *op. cit.*, pp. 416–17: 'Constructed pragmatically according to the necessities or vagaries of history, the European Community contributes by its functioning to the insensible transformation of political reality. It establishes new habits of collaboration, new decision-making mechanisms, and may even give birth to new attitudes or mentalities.'

[3] J. Monnet, 'A Ferment of Change', *Journal of Common Market Studies*, 1:3, 1963, pp. 204, 211.

view, sees the emergence of consensus as a product of the distribution and composition of power in the system.[1] The general assumption among all these writers is that the configuration of power and institutions in an integrating system, if sufficiently authoritative, is effective in shifting the preoccupation of the units and their members from the violent hostilities of international life to the more legitimate and less dangerous rivalries of domestic politics.

The political attitudes of individuals, then, are held to have a structure congruent with that of their political community. In a federal system, this clearly implies that the shift of loyalties towards the centre which integration entails is not total. Even Etzioni's demanding definition of 'identification' leaves some loyalties focused on the local units.[2] Federalism thus accepts the possibility of multiple levels of political orientation: men can participate in and feel loyalty to several sets of political institutions at the same time and in the same space without experiencing inner conflict. Their attitudes to the local community, the province and the nation-state, while not of similar intensities, are essentially of the same kind. They do not, however, compete for primacy, nor are they incompatible with loyalty to new levels of organization which may develop.[3] In the last analysis it is on the possibility of this kind of distribution and co-existence of individual political attitudes that the value and stability of a federal system must depend.

Federalism and European Integration

In postwar European politics, federalist ideas have manifested themselves in a variety of ways. Most obviously, of course, they were championed by the many groups and organizations which formed during World War II – often as part of national resistance movements – and later coalesced as the driving force of the European Movement. Although they differed widely in origins, social bases, ideology and strategy, these federalist groups generally shared an abhorrence of the old European nationalism and determination to construct, as quickly as possible, a United States of Europe.

---

[1] Etzioni, *Political Unification*, pp. 37–50, 68–70.   [2] *Ibid.*, p. 4.

[3] On this concept, see H. Guetzkow, *Multiple Loyalties: Theoretical Approach to a Problem in International Organization* (Princeton: 1955). One European federalist, however, suggests that the idea of divided loyalties remains foreign to the French, implying that it is a cultural characteristic not easily acquired in a centralized state. See Brugmans, 'European Unity and the Federalist Idea', *op. cit.*, p. 1023.

But federalism has been more than the doctrinal preserve of explicitly federalist groups. In a broader sense it has provided a semi-articulate set of assumptions which have helped legitimize or justify a number of disparate groups and policies concerned with integration. The belief is widespread in Europe that whatever the eventual form, the means used, and the time taken, some kind of European supranational state will eventually emerge. For some, like the Gaullists, the prospect is very distant, and depends on a number of unlikely national changes; for others, like the functionalists, a federal state is probable but undesirable; for the neofunctionalists in Brussels it is desirable and almost inevitable. Thus, whatever the fortunes of federalist groups, many ideas fundamental to federalism have remained at the focus of debate over Europe's future.

As an explicit doctrine and as an underlying belief, federalism in Europe has had both pragmatic and academic aspects. In its pragmatic state, federalism has represented the medium by which a concrete body of political and administrative experience from other parts of the world has been applied – with varying degrees of success – to European problems. This is certainly its most familiar aspect. In addition, however, many federalist groups have sought to develop and implement a pure, indigenous form of federalism which draws on European traditions of political thought and social organization and is uniquely suited to contemporary European conditions. These federalists have had relatively little impact on postwar European politics and have remained in somewhat frustrated exile from the main centres of the integration movement. As in many such cases, the consequences has been an increased stress on the doctrine and on pure analytical theory.

Especially where it has taken this latter turn, federalism has found itself in a curious relationship with the ongoing process of European integration. Because federalist theory has such a strong normative streak and has shown little tendency to formulate testable hypotheses, and because it usually prescribes dramatic structural change rather than piecemeal growth, it can gain little feedback from the world of political experience. On the one hand, federalists ideas pervade the working assumptions of most of those striving toward European integration; on the other, federalist theory cannot grow or change, as neofunctionalist theory has done, according to political developments, because its propositions are rarely cast in testable or refutable form. Where European federalist theory has developed, then, it has done so in splendid academic isolation, as rarified conceptual analysis or as normative political philosophy.[1]

On the other hand, some of the difficulties of European federalists originate in the very predominance of the pragmatic wing of federalist thought. The European pragmatists have tended to take for granted the applicability of models and practices drawn from American experience or from comparative studies of federal systems. It is typical of political scientists (especially Americans) to see the problem of Western European supranationalism as 'in the stream of national federalism'.[2] But many European writers have questioned this assumption. Pryce has pointed out the great problems in applying often rigid and perhaps alien notions of federalism to modern Europe.[3] Others have suggested that the federal ideal requires too much of Europe without recognizing its uniqueness, or that the federal solution may prove unnecessary for many of Europe's economic problems.[4] Of course, many of these reservations are premised on the classic, dualistic notion of the federal state, and avoid the more interesting and perplexing question of whether the 'cooperative federalism' model, with its less rigid conception of the divisions of powers, might not prove highly appropriate for Europe.

Perhaps the best way to trace the links between federalist theory and the politics of European integration is to follow the fortunes of those who attempted at various times to turn the development of postwar Europe in an explicitly federal direction. It is striking that interest in federal solutions has tended to recur in moments of crisis in the European integration movement. Sometimes federalist tactics have caused the crises or at least contributed to them; more often, however, Europeans have returned to federalism when other approaches seem to have failed, and federalist groups have been quick to seize the moment. Neofunctionalism, 'federation via confederation' and other eclectic, indirect strategies of integration, they insist, are really just sophisticated forms of escapism or procrastination. What these periodic crises demonstrate, according to the

[1] For one of the more stimulating examples of such theory, see Brugmans and Duclos, *op. cit.*, esp. Part II. That many federalist propositions can be cast in testable form is made clear in Riker, *op. cit.*, passim.

[2] A. W. Macmahon, 'Introduction' to Part IV, Macmahon, *op. cit.*, p. 409. Cf. C. J. Friedrich and R. R. Bowie, eds., *Studies in Federalism* (Boston: 1954) as a practical guide to aspiring European federalists.

[3] R. Pryce, *The Political Future of the European Community* (London; 1962) pp. 56–61.

[4] S. J. Bodenheimer, *Political Union: A Microcosm of European Politics 1960–66* (Leyden: 1967) p. 19; M. Camps, *What Kind of Europe?* (London: 1965) p. 129.

federalists, is the overriding need to face the 'constitutional issue' and to transfer some powers from the nation-states to a common government. From the federalist perspective, then, the history of European integration shows continuous and wasteful vacillation between subtle, gradual (and ultimately ineffectual) attempts to erode national sovereignty, and bold resolution to broach it directly.

For the federalists, the first critical period came in the early post-war years when numerous political forces competed to determine the direction of economic and political reconstruction in Europe. In this period of pushing and pulling among diverse groups and parties, the federalists went from the leadership to the periphery of the European unity movement in the space of a few years.

Nearly all the countries of Western Europe had spawned federalist organizations during or immediately after the war. Predominant among these were the Anglo-American Federal Union, the French Committee for European Federation, and the Italian Movimento Federalista Europeo. Most of these groups coalesced into the Union of European Federalists (UEF) in a series of conferences culminating at Montreux in August 1947. The UEF brought together and attempted to coordinate the policies of many different species of federalist groups, ranging from 'world' federalists (who saw European unity as the first stage), to 'international' federalists (who stressed the importance of retaining considerable decentralization and diversity) to 'integral' federalists (who wanted to build the new Europe on the basis of traditional national sub-groups).[1]

Avowedly federalist organizations were not, however, the only groups pressing for European unity, or even for unity of a federal nature. Among the more important organizations participating in the debate on Europe's future were the British-led United Europe Movement, the European League for Economic Cooperation (founded by Joseph Retinger and Paul van Zeeland), the French Council for a United Europe, Coudenhove-Kalergi's Inter-Parliamentary Union, and André Philip's Socialist Movement for a United States of Europe. The federalists' aims were compatible with those of some, although not all, of these groups. In addition, while the federalists relied on a militant membership and popular support, most of the leading political figures were to be found in the other groups. Thus, whereas federalist ideas had gained a wide currency,

[1] See Brugmans, *L'Idée Européenne*, pp. 99–104, and Macmahon, 'Introduction' to Part IV, in Macmahon, *op. cit.*, pp. 411–12, for descriptions of these groups, the proliferation of which was astonishing.

177

federalist groups themselves had little direct influence on, or participation in the major decisions of the early postwar integration movement.

Their weakness was reflected in the events which led up to the formation of the Council of Europe. The Council was the product of a political process catalyzed by the Hague Congress of May 1948, which was organized by the International Committee of the Movements for European Unity. This Committee, later renamed the European Movement, united the UEF and several of the groups mentioned above. At the Congress, the divergence of views, particularly between the more radical federalists and the cautious, predominantly British, pluralists, was striking. The former, hoping the Congress would act as, or bring about, a Constituent Assembly for Europe, called for the immediate creation and implementation of federal political institutions (in particular a directly elected Assembly) and federalized economic and administrative structures. The latter argued for more traditional forms of cooperation among European states, perhaps leading in time to closer ties, and for an Assembly drawn from national parliaments. In the end, it was this view which prevailed.

Nevertheless, the Hague Congress was an important and impressive show of strength and solidarity for the European unity movement, and federalist ideas were strongly in evidence throughout. 'The time has come', read the main resolution, 'for the nations of Europe to transfer some portion of their sovereign rights and henceforth to exercise them jointly so as to coordinate and develop their resources'.[1] It was the aftermath of the Hague Congress which demonstrated the federalists' real influence. Both the enthusiasm generated by this 'grande manifestation publique'[2] and any force its resolutions might have had, were gradually dissipated in the complex negotiations which followed, and which finally produced, in May 1949, a Council of Europe which satisfied hardly any of the federalists' demands.

Federalists in the Council's Assembly continued nevertheless to press for more than the general consultative powers which it had been given, demanding a European political authority with 'limited functions but real powers'.[3] Increasingly, however, the federalists had become a minority isolated from the mainstream of resurgent

[1] Quoted in *ibid.*, p. 411. For a detailed description of the Congress, see Brugmans, *L'Idée Européenne*, Ch. 5.

[2] *Ibid.*, p. 107.

[3] *Ibid.*, p. 116. U. W. Kitzinger, *The Politics and Economics of European Integration* (New York: 1963) p. 8.

national politics, and these demands, too, met little response. Gradually the Council came to the point where, as the federalists argued, it could either go on producing 'platonic wishes' or it could absorb itself in 'functional' and 'neutral' projects. In effect it never made the choice, and most ardent 'Europeans' (such as Spaak) soon abandoned it for the greater promise of 'functional' or 'partial' federation.[1]

Thus, despite an abundance of the conventionally favourable conditions for federation – a strong external threat, recent experience of internal war, a decline in nationalism and national capabilities, evident need for common efforts at economic and social reconstruction, strong encouragement from an 'external elite' (the United States) which also provided an institutional model, and numerous organizations with high-level contacts and propaganda skills capable of spreading the federalist gospel – despite all these conditions, the 'federal revolution' somehow slipped away. Clearly, British opposition had a great effect, but in other European governments, too, there was considerable hesitation about supranationality. Whatever the root cause, it is little wonder that the federalist movement receded in some confusion and disharmony as other methods came into vogue in the early fifties.

After 1950, however, the Schuman plan gradually became the prototype on which many European federalists remodelled their ideas about integration. (Some, of course, refused this 'little European' alternative.) The project for a European Defense Community (EDC) seemed to offer a fortuitous combination of the 'sector approach' with that common control of the armed forces of member-states which federalism traditionally stressed. The Pleven Plan, on which the EDC scheme was based, was a French attempt to bring German rearmament – demanded by the Americans because of their Korean commitments – under joint European control. 'Des l'été de 1950' writes Brugmans, 'il était clair que la question allemande coincidait avec celle de l'Europe unie, même sur le plan militaire'.[2] Thus the EDC was seen, not merely as part of the 'German problem', or as a military question, but as a 'rapid and dramatic means of making a further breakthrough in European integration . . . in a jealously guarded domain that was highly and patently political'.[3] By May 1952, the

[1] Brugmans, *L'Idée Européenne*, pp. 117–23.
[2] *Ibid.*, p. 141. 'As early as the summer of 1950 it was clear that the German question coincided with that of European unity, even in the military sphere.'
[3] W. Hallstein, *op. cit.*, p. 14.

Treaty, modelled on the ECSC Treaty, had been signed by the Six – Britain, as usual, expressing support but refusing to take part.

While the Treaty was undergoing its arduous examination by the various political groupings in the Six, the Foreign Ministers of these countries had encouraged the creation of an *Ad Hoc* Assembly based on the ECSC Assembly; this body, after much deliberation and study, produced in March 1953 a draft treaty for a European Political Community (EPC). This is perhaps the closest any European countries have ever come to forming a federal community. The EPC, which was to incorporate the ECSC and the EDC, was to have as its main organs a bicameral legislature (a Senate chosen by national parliaments, and a Peoples' Chamber elected directly by universal suffrage, each country being represented proportionally), an Executive Council (which could be removed by the Senate, or censured by the Chamber), an advisory Council of Ministers (to represent the ECSC and the EDC), a Federal Court, and an Economic and Social Council. Its functions, besides control of the two other Communities, were to be the progressive establishment of a common market, the encouragement of coordinated economic policies in a number of fields, and the promotion of cooperation in foreign policy.[1]

The EPC, with its characteristic institutional pattern, its direct links to the European electorate and its partial control over military power, clearly represented an effort to plant the roots of a federal system for the Six. One of the theorists behind it claimed that its decision-structure would provide an 'inner compulsion to growth' so that more and more functions would come under its control.[2] But even in its original condition, the EPC came considerably nearer what the federalists had hoped for, but failed to achieve, in the Council of Europe. In the Draft Treaty the influence of American ideas and practices is clear. It is worth noting the importance, in the Assembly's studies, of the work of Friedrich and Bowie, both American experts on federalism. In Brugman's words: 'Sans doute l'exemple des Etats-Unis y était-il comme référence constante, ce qui

[1] See *Ad Hoc* Assembly, *Draft Treaty Embodying the Statute of the European Community* (Strasbourg: 1953).

[2] Bowie, 'The Process of Federating Europe', in Macmahon, *op. cit.*, p. 508. But see A. Zurcher, *The Struggle to Unite Europe*, 1940–58 (New York: 1958) p. 104, where it is argued that the EPC represented no increase in supranationality from that found in the ECSC structure. It is worth noting here that stronger measures were contemplated. An early draft of the EDC, later rejected, gave the 'federal' authorities the right to intervene, i.e. to use force if necessary in member states, even without parliamentary advice: A. N. Holcombe, 'Coercion of States in a Federal System', *op. cit.*, pp. 137–8.

n'était peut-être pas sans inconvenient politique, puisque les différences énormes éxistaient entre la situation américaine vers la fin du dix-huitième siècle et celle de l'Europe au milieu du vingtième.' However misleading it may have been in other respects, however, at least the American influence forced the Europeans to face the concrete issues to do with the division of powers.[1]

The failure of the French National Assembly, on 30 August 1954, to ratify the EDC Treaty, collapsed the whole edifice.[2] The trauma induced by the death of the Treaty, after such a long and agonizing debate, affected not only those who saw the EDC–EPC scheme as the federalists' direct constitutional challenge to national sovereignty, but also those who saw it as the next in a series of incremental, functional schemes, and those who merely hoped for improved collaboration among the European states. As important as the immediate political setback was to the integration movement, then, the longer-term effects on its intellectual under-pinnings were potentially more serious. The federalist movement itself, thrown into new disarray, accurately reflected the bafflement and frustrations rife in broader European circles. Faced with the dramatic '*relance*' marked by the Messina Conference of 1955, the federalists were once more forced to choose between their doctrinal purity and pragmatic collaboration in yet another gradualist project of uncertain prospects.

For many, the defeat of the EDC marked what Brugmans called 'le démasque final'. No longer in their view, could federalists harbour 'l'illusion que les gouvernements et le personnel politique national . . . adopteraient des solutions fédérales'.[3] This group, in which Spinelli was particularly prominent, split from the UEF at Luxembourg in March 1956 to form the Mouvement Fédéraliste Européen. The MFE, which consisted mainly of French, Belgian and Italian social-democratic federalists and which drew as well on the traditions of 'integral', socially-oriented and Catholic federalist thought, aimed

---

[1] Brugmans, *L'Idée Européenne*, p. 161. 'Undoubtedly the example of the United States was taken as a constant reference, which was perhaps not entirely convenient politically, since there were enormous differences between the American situation toward the end of the eighteenth century and that of Europe in the middle of the twentieth.' Bowie, like many other framers of the Draft, was clearly impressed with the analogy so mistrusted by Brugmans. See 'The Process of Federating Europe', in Macmahon, *op. cit.*, pp. 498–9.

[2] The best analysis of the prolonged and soul-searching debate is D. Lerner and R. Aron (eds.), *France Defeats EDC* (London: 1957); see also F. R. Willis, *France, Germany and the New Europe*, 1945–67 (New York: 1968) Chs. 6 and 7; Brugmans, *L'Idée Européenne*, Ch. 7.

[3] *Ibid.*, p. 177. '. . . The illusion that governments and national political officials . . . would adopt federal solutions.'

at a radical transformation of European society through an immediate propaganda-campaign culminating in a Constituent Assembly. Its influence steadily diminished in relation to that of the other faction, which was based on the Dutch and German (and some French) federalist organizations, and which chose to seek the federalist goal by gradualist means. This group, known as Action Européen Fédéraliste (AEF) took a pragmatic position: it was preferable to work with, rather than against, national forces since these remained an undeniable political reality; this in turn, entailed working through such organizations as the emergent EEC.[1]

Thus, for a great many federalists, the EEC became the new vehicle upon which Europe would be carried to the political goal they envisaged. However, many of those supporting or active in the EEC (such as Spaak, Monnet and Hallstein) could only be said to hold to a pragmatic and flexible set of ideas about integration which derived eclectically from federalism, functionalism and numerous other sources. Some of the ideas of these 'federal functionalists' or 'gradual federalists' came later to be distilled (largely by Americans) into the distinctive blend now known as neofunctionalism. Once again, then, federalists found themselves marginally influential in a move toward integration which drew selectively on their ideas and in which they tried to find followers who would keep federalist proposals to the fore. At the same time numerous federalist groups kept up contacts with the political parties, and during the French debate over EEC, were influential in getting the Treaty accepted.[2]

The great successes of the EEC from 1958 to 1963 naturally provided a period of ascendancy for these pragmatic federalists, whose philosophy of 'federalism through collaboration' appeared on the point of vindication. But with the increasing difficulties of the early sixties a number of new issues became clear. Many more doctrinaire federalists, temporarily won over, began once more to question the premises behind the gradualist movement. And they began to find fault with the structures and practices of the EEC itself.

The three main areas in which familiar federalist ideas began to reappear were, and remain, the central issues of European integration: the problem of democratic control and political responsiveness; the problem of geographical scope; and the problem of finding a

[1] On this split in the federalist movement, see also Brugmans and Duclos, *op. cit.*, pp. 143–9; Spinelli, *op. cit.*, pp. 190–3; and M. Forsyth, 'The Political Objectives of European Integration', *International Affairs*, 43: 3, 1967, pp. 489–91.

[2] Willis, *op. cit.*, pp. 236–7, 257–8.

new impulse toward further integration. It would be useful to look briefly at each of these.

The issue of democratic control has inspired a considerable literature, in which two main themes can be discerned. The first has to do with the latent suspicions of federalists concerning the bureaucratic and technocratic tendencies of the 'sectoral' or 'community' approach to integration. In the writings of Spinelli and Brugmans, for example, a recurrent motif refers to the centralist, authoritarian inclinations of the 'Eurocrats' who operate 'L'Europe des offices'. As Brugmans observes: 'Nous aboutissons donc à la situation paradoxale, où une Europe qui veut s'intégrer "pour rester libre", sacrifie le principe parlementaire dans le domaine le plus important: celui de l'intégration.'[1] The federalist prescription, of course, is a European Parliament directly elected by universal suffrage, to which the Commission would be responsible and which would have ultimate control of the Community budget. Such a Parliament would provide a more credible check on a bureaucratic system seen by many as remote and irresponsible, would attract politicians of standing and ability, would reflect more accurately the balance of political forces in the Community, and would provide a focus for popular participation in its affairs.[2] In the long run, this Parliament could help to build and harness the consensus for a new '*relance*' toward greater integration.

The second element of the federalist approach to the problem of democratic control has to do with decentralization as a means of increasing the responsiveness of the political system. In a sense this marks a return to the more radical branch of federalism, which owes much to Rousseau's ideas about the virtues of small political units. Thus, in place of a federation of European nations, some have advocated a federation of regions, with direct links between Brussels and the local administrations.[3] The concept of a 'Europe of regions' is a happy combination of the two faces of federalist theory: the one

[1] Brugmans, *L'Idée Européenne*, p. 192. 'We are ending up in the paradoxical situation where a Europe desiring to unite "in order to stay free", sacrifices the parliamentary principle in the most important domain: that of integration.' Cf. Spinelli, *op. cit.*, esp. pp. 23–5, on the dangers of the European 'functionalist establishment'; Chs. 4 and 5; and pp. 151–72 on the European Parliament and the reluctance of the Commission to allow it a decisive role.

[2] For proposals of this kind, see Pinder and Pryce, *op. cit.*, Ch. 10. In contrast, see *The Economist*, 16 May 1970, pp. 63–4, for the view that a democratically elected President, who appoints the Commission, is a superior solution.

[3] On this idea, see Brugmans, 'European Unity and the Federalist Idea', *op. cit.*, pp. 1026–8; A. Sampson, *The New Europeans* (London: 1968) Ch. 22, esp. pp. 430–4; Pinder and Pryce, *op. cit.*, pp. 52–5.

seeking to integrate national states; the other seeking to decentralize them. There is, of course, considerable debate on how power ought to be distributed among these two, or perhaps three, tiers of government – supranational, national and regional. Are the regions to have genuine autonomy in some fields, or are they merely to perform administratively devolved tasks? How such questions are answered depends perhaps less on administrative and constitutional rationality than on national governments' perceptions of political threats from dissident regions.

Whatever their prospects, these federalist proposals do indicate an awareness that the political and social bases for European integration may be shifting drastically. The demand for European elections and for sensitivity to regional interests and peculiarities, the increase of European functional ties, and the support for ideas of economic or corporative federalism – all these would seem to indicate increasing challenges to the assumption that the political structure of the nation-state system accurately represents European social and political relationships. The distinctiveness of federalism is that is does not look simply to supranationality and larger units to solve Europe's problems, but places equal, if not more, value on small, diverse and responsive regional governments. In this concern for internal differentiation according to need, federalism comes at times to resemble the older functionalism.

The recurrent question of the geographical scope of European integration has also engaged federalists in a new round of argument. As we have seen, most federalists accepted the 'little Europe' approach in the early fifties, largely because the alternatives seemed so hopeless. In recent years, however, a number of internal and external changes relating to the Six have turned many federalists back to the original vision of a broad European union. Many internal weaknesses and dangers of the Community, it is argued, would be offset by an increase in membership. The addition of British and Scandinavian institutions, practices and cultures, it is claimed, would provide an increasingly necessary stability to the Community, while that other federalist ideal, the internal 'balance of power', would be improved by the addition of a large state to offset France, and more especially, Germany.

The most prevalent arguments for geographical expansion, however, have to do with Europe's external relations. British technology, military power, financial influence and diplomatic experience are seen as valuable assets for a Europe struggling to come to terms not only with the long-standing Soviet presence to the east, but also with the threat of American technological, economic, strategic and cultural domination. Beyond these defensive arguments, federalists often return to the theme that a large, united Europe can reclaim its former primacy in world politics, acting as a pillar of the Atlantic community, or as a benefactor of the Third World, or finally, as a rival of, or mediator between, the two superpowers. On occasion, too, federalists will still make the case that a large, growing federal Europe is the best possible point of departure for a federal world.[1]

On the third issue, concerning further increases of integration, much of the debate between federalists and other observers of the Community arises from differing definitions. As we have seen, the common claim of Community officials is that the existing patterns of decision-making and bargaining in the Community represent a considerable degree of integration, perhaps even a *de facto* federalism. Against this, federalists assert that, by any of their indices, the gradualist method has failed to produce anything approaching federalism. Some federalists invoke the powers of the European Parliament as the true index of integration;[2] other theorists insist on examining the locus of fiscal and police power, of 'essentially political' decisions, of powers of revision, or of external sovereignty.[3] To the federalists the failure of the Community to make inroads on such powers, is a harsh but realistic index of the failure of integration.

From the conclusion that the incremental 'community method' has failed, it is but a short step to the reassertion of the venerable federalist principle that we must, once more, try to face directly the problem of national sovereignty. One way to do this would be to negotiate a new Treaty of Rome, subsuming the Community and committing the Six and those states wishing to join them, to new and definite steps toward positive economic and political union. Such a Treaty would necessarily embody some federal institutions. Moreover, the inclusion of new members, it is argued, would provide an impetus for growth. As an alternative, the European states might set up, alongside the EEC, a 'political community' performing the sorts of functions envisaged by the Gaullists but with the vital difference

[1] See Forsyth *op,. cit.*, p. 489 and Pinder and Pryce, *op. cit.*, esp. Chs. 7–9.

[2] Brugmans, *L'Idée Européenne*, p. 201.

[3] Sidjanski, 'Federal Aspects of the European Community', in Montgomery and Smithies, *op. cit.* pp. 417–20; Spinelli, *op. cit.*, pp. 95–9, and Ch. 6.

that it operate by majority voting and with democratic controls.[1]

The federalists, then, argue that the sorry condition of European integration calls for drastic remedies. They would like to believe that the risks involved in a dramatic new round of treaty-making, which will inevitably raise emotional issues of sovereignty, would be preferable to a continuation of the stagnation and frustration of the Community and the whole European movement in the last ten years. But the dilemma is nonetheless very real: how to guarantee that in the drama of change integration does not recede rather than advance. As Brugmans wrote, referring to an earlier impasse: 'the federalist movement . . . finds itself in the deplorable condition of a doctor who would have liked to operate on his patient, but knows that such an an operation would probably mean death'.[2]

Federalist ideas, then, remain central to any discussion on the future of European integration. However minor the influence of particular federalist organizations may have become, federalist priorities and standards have permeated the Community and help to define both its problems and its responses. They compete in this respect with the neofunctionalist ideology of Brussels and the strong pluralist inclinations of Britain, Germany and France. At present, federalist prospects must remain mixed. Democratic control, apart from tentative moves to increase the competence of the European Parliament, has made little headway. On the other hand, the Community is moving to expand its membership, although the cost may be a further stalling of the drive to supranationalism. Finally, some new initiatives – in the monetary field, for example – have been taken towards further integration, although again their implications for federalism are by no means clear. The Community, in short, is still in a state of uncertainty. As we have seen, it is at such points that federalism appears to offer the clearest, strongest alternative to national retrenchment. It remains to be seen if this persistent 'conscience' of European integration, the federalist ideal, can move the present national leaderships to undertake the dramatic political changes it has called for consistently over the last twenty-five years.

[1] For examples of such proposals, see, J. Pinder in *European Community*, May, 1969, pp. 10–11; the 'Brown Plan', *ibid.*, April, 1969, p. 7; Lord Gladwyn in *The Times*, 15 November, 1968.

[2] H. Brugmans, 'The Dynamics of European Integration', in Haines, *op. cit.*, p. 164. Cf. Lord Gladwyn, *The Times*, 15 November 1968, on the reluctance of some 'Europeans' to apply the supranational principle to new institutions, lest it 'weaken, by comparison, the present rather tottering Community'.

PART II
Problems in Integration Theory:
Three Levels of Analysis

PART II Introduction

The attempt at interpretation and criticism in the preceding four chapters leads us to some rather unsettling impressions of the present state of integration theory. On the one hand, there is an unmistakable, if inchoate, order in the field; the four approaches – pluralism, functionalism, neofunctionalism, federalism – are distinctive and internally cohesive in most important respects. On the other hand, they differ so dramatically from each other that we might well ask if integration theory has any central core of problems, axioms, themes or hypotheses. The four approaches diverge seriously over: (a) the purposes and scope of integration; (b) the nature of the end-product; (c) fundamental assumptions about international politics and social change; (d) the other disciplines and traditions of theory on which they draw; (e) the major variables by which they explain the integrative process, and the levels of analysis on which they operate; (f) their proportions of prescriptive fervour and empirical analysis; (g) the degree and form of success they have achieved in postwar Europe, whether in predicting or in influencing events. Reviewing these differences, one is reminded of Stanley Hoffmann's dictum that 'a flea-market is not a discipline'.[1]

And yet, we need not be routed by the apparent diversity and chaos of the field. With some sorting out, presumably flea-markets can *become* disciplines. In the first part of this book we have examined the current condition of integration theory. This exercise has raised numerous questions about its future development, some of which will be confronted in the next three chapters. In addition, however, it has shown that, within the embrace of a broad definition of integration, these are areas of compatibility as well as contradiction, both of which can be subjected to empirical scrutiny.

The general definition is worth recalling: international political

[1] S. Hoffman, *Contemporary Theory in International Relations* (Englewood Cliffs, N.J.: 1960) p. 7.

integration was described as a process whereby a group of people, organized at the outset in two or more independent states, comes to constitute a political whole which can in some sense be described as a community. From this general definition, two major questions were derived – concerning the nature of the 'political whole' envisaged as the outcome of an integrative process, and the dynamics of the process itself. The four approaches are defined fundamentally by their answers to these two questions.

The following tabular summary gives an indication of the distinctiveness of each approach:

		PLURALISM	FUNCTIONALISM	NEOFUNCTIONALISM	FEDERALISM
I.	*The End-Product:* Structure	Community of states	Administrative network responsive to community needs	Supranational decision-making system	Supranational state
	Evidence	Probability of peaceful conflict resolution; communications (flows intensity).	Degree of 'fit' between structures & functions; need – satisfaction.	Locus of decisions (scope & level).	Distribution of power (formal & informal).
II.	*The Process:* System	Self-sustaining growth of interdependence & informal structures	Technical self-determination; imperatives of functional needs & technological change	Political development: growth of central institutions through 'forward linkage'	Constitutional revolution: dramatic redistribution of power and authority
	State	Increase of capacity for decision-making, information & responsiveness	Reluctant cooperation to solve technical & economic problems	Bargaining process where governments pursue interests among other groups	Bargaining resulting in Hobbesian contract among elites of states
	Individual	Social learning through communications & interaction (elite & mass)	Habits of cooperation derived from satisfaction of utilitarian needs by new institutions	Effects of successful decision-making & conflict resolution on elite attitudes	Differentiation of loyalties according to level of government.

From this crude juxtaposition of the approaches it is tempting to conclude that we are faced with yet another instance of the blind men and the elephant. International political integration appears to be a rather large and unfamiliar phenomenon of which various theorists are aware of only a small and often misleading part. Yet in the context of integration theory this fable may need modifying. In the first place, we are not sure that every theorist is quite as blind ('blinkered' might be a better word) as the next; some may turn out to have an accurate picture of the whole creature, at least in outline. In addition, two or more theorists may in fact have hold of the same part of the animal, even though they call that particular part by different names. And finally, there are a few theorists who, distrustful of descriptions of the whole animal – derived as they are from such partial analyses and aided by familiar and thus often misleading experience – suggest that the creature may be unlike anything we have seen before.

This last point in particular suggests the direction which an attempt at further exploration of integration theory might take. In the first place, on the basis of the approaches discussed in the previous chapters and of recent European experience, it might be possible to derive a model of the sort of 'political whole' in which integration could culminate, without relying on the more familiar models of state, organization or community employed by most theorists. Such an operation starts from the assumption – common to all the approaches we have examined – that this condition of political integration is a property of a political and geographic whole which, originally at least, could be described as an 'international system'. It is not, in other words, a property of the states or individuals in that system, even though these both may undergo changes which complement (or even determine) those on the level of the system. The first step in further interpreting and reformulating some of the ideas discussed in earlier chapters, then, is to develop a way of looking at system-change as the dependent variable in a theory of integration. To this task the first part of the next chapter will be devoted.

The second task of this further exploration will be to develop, through an extension of the critical framework used in the previous section, a way of ordering some of the more important independent variables upon which a theory of integration might be based. This is not an attempt to put forward a new theory or general overarching explanatory system. It is simply an attempt to construct a loose framework for the analysis of integration, in which it might become clearer where the four approaches we have discussed complement each other, where their hypotheses are contradictory, and where there are theoretical gaps that need filling.

The basis of this framework is the belief that a satisfactory explanation of the process of international political integration will only be derived from the analysis of independent variables on three distinct levels – the system, the state and the individual. Although it is on the level of the system that we must take the condition of integration to be manifested, the factors bringing about that condition may arise on all three levels, and as we have seen, each approach in fact relies on some hypotheses or assumptions on each level.

Each of the next three chapters, then, will deal with one level of analysis. In each we shall draw together and organize some of the hypotheses and variables relied upon by the approaches we have criticized. The postwar European experience remains the touchstone for this discussion, while some of the analysis will draw on the general literature of political science, on foreign policy theory and on social psychology. These last chapters are thus an attempt to go beyond textual and philosophic criticism, and – on the basis of the four main approaches, the postwar European experience, and theoretical work in related fields of social science – to set up an arena for the intellectual contention and conflict out of which a theory of integration might emerge.

6 Political Integration as System-Change

Integration, like its cousin, peace, is foremost a property of the international system viewed as a whole. In our general definition, the integrative process is seen as culminating in a community-like political form which embraces a group of people who, originally at least, were organized politically as a system of sovereign nation-states. It might be possible, of course, to see integration as a quality of the states or the individuals in the system. As Waltz points out, some writers on international relations have seen peace as more or less synonymous with the emergence of a certain type of state, while others have seen it as a condition of the 'minds of men'.[1] Theorists of integration, as we have seen, often rely on similar assumptions about the social structures and decision-capacities of states, or about the growth of a psychological and cultural community. But this does risk confusing the dependent and the independent variables in the integrative process. It is still implicit in these theories that while such qualities of states or individuals may invariably be associated with peace or integration, they are associated as contributors to a particular condition of the system as a whole.

In its most general sense, this theme of integration as system-change runs through all the approaches discussed in the previous chapters. But the character of change envisaged varies greatly. For the pluralists, it is an increase in the 'mutual responsiveness' of the states in the system, measured by the intensity of their interactions and communications and not necessarily accompanied by any institutional changes compromising their sovereign capacities. For the functionalists, however, a radical structural change is prescribed, whereby the states and their relationships are gradually overlaid and made irrelevant by a network of flexible organizations responsive to the needs of technology, economics and human welfare. In the neo-functionalist view, system-change involves, at the very least, the

[1] K. N. Waltz, *Man, the State and War* (New York: 1959) esp. Chs. 2 and 4.

evolution of new patterns of decision-making and conflict-resolution for the system as a whole, but it is clearly intended that this shift in the quality of inter-state relationships should lead ultimately to a structural change from a 'diplomatic' to a 'domestic' system. The federalists, finally, envisage system-change as a redistribution of legal and political authority, from exclusive residence within each state to partial control by common political institutions.

.) In one way or another, all these approaches have their implied notions of the ideal condition toward which the system aspires. Since, for most theorists, the analysis of political integration involves comparisons of the existing, unsatisfactory state of the international system with some improved, if not ideal, future state, it is clear that justifiable charges of teleological or utopian thinking will occasionally be made. Indeed, many of the writers discussed in the previous chapters have come under such criticisms at one time or another. The tendency to minimize the autonomy of states and over-emphasize the needs and goals of the system is most marked in functionalist and, to a lesser extent, neofunctionalist literature. While functionalists do not argue that men and states are the helpless pawns of economic and technological forces, they do rely on these forces and the requisites of a cross-national social whole increasingly to condition the behaviour of statesmen. From a slightly different viewpoint, however, federalists or neofunctionalists could be accused of a similar teleological bias: they tend to attribute, to systems in conditions of conflict or disequilibrium, a 'natural' tendency to adjust themselves through a redistribution of powers which often involves increased allocations to central authorities.

It must be added that this teleological or utopian tendency seems to have more to do with the individual scholar's purposes and values than with the systems perspective as such, although the latter certainly enhances any such tendencies. It is largely in one type of systems approach – what Haas refers to as the system-dominant, abstract type – that the teleological and utopian writers tend to congregate. And even here, 'system-need' can be a rationale equally well for a conservative state of social equilibrium as for a sweeping transformation of the international system.[1] In any case an attempt will

[1] See E. B. Haas, *Beyond the Nation-State* (Stanford: 1964) esp. pp. 52–68. The debate over the teleological and utopian implications of systems theory really centres on the question of what is to be considered as 'change'. It can be argued that those using models derived from the work of Parsons are really discussing change *within* rather than *of* social or international systems, and that their analysis thus tends to be narrow and conservative. See R. Dahrendorf, 'Out

POLITICAL INTEGRATION AS SYSTEM-CHANGE

be made, in the model of system-change developed in this chapter, to mitigate what Haas has called the 'tyranny of *telos*'.[1]

As we have seen, integration theorists have found a variety of models for the condition to which the current system is to change. Most of these models, not surprisingly, are derived from familiar political experience, Both the federalists and, with a few reservations, the neofunctionalists, adopt the nation-state as their model and tend to view international integration as nation-building on a new level. Other theorists, finding this model inappropriate or undesirable, strike out in different directions. The pluralists combine a preference for the familiar – the nation-state system – with a nostalgia for that elusive 'golden age' of European diplomacy when the system actually worked to prevent wars; they merely attempt to refine and rationalize the processes of international adjustment. The functionalists go to the other extreme, and envisage replacing system and states with a set of institutions corresponding to the ideal of a flexible administration concerned less with geopolitical and legal boundaries than with solving specific problems.

Only occasionally do integration theorists venture beyond the familiar. In speculations about the future of Europe, scholars, statesmen and journalists have occasionally suggested that what will emerge is a new and barely describable political animal, for which our traditional models are of little use.[2] It is another premise of this chapter that models of European integration, if they are to lead to useful explanations, must derive less from familiar, concrete political experiences than from the mixture of evidence, concepts and explanations thrown up by the many diverse studies of recent European developments – in short they must draw eclectically on the approaches we have been examining in this study.

Whatever their model of the end-point of the integrative process, most of these writers conceive of system-change as requiring the crossing of a qualitative threshold. In the federalist approach, of course, this is most sharply defined, since a fundamental legal-political distinction is drawn between the nature of the system before

of Utopia: Toward a Reorientation of Sociological Analysis', *American Journal of Sociology*, 64: 2, 1958, pp. 115–27. For a concise review of problems in systems theory and a useful reformulation, see J. P. Nettl, 'The Concept of System in Political Science', *Political Studies*, 14: 3, 1966, pp. 305–8.

[1] Haas, *op. cit.*, p. 65.

[2] See, for example, R. Pryce, *The Political Future of the European Community* (London: 1962) esp. pp. 22–5, 56–9. Cf. A. Buchan (ed.), *Europe's Futures, Europe's Choices* (London: 1969) pp. 156–62.

and after the federal 'revolution'. Etzioni talks of a 'takeoff point', after which integration becomes self-sustaining.[1] Deutsch, too, describes a fluid but discernible threshold between a classic diplomatic system and a 'security-community'.[2] In the functionalist and neo-functionalist approaches, where integration is seen as a gradual process of blending institutions, out of which a new community emerges, such a definite threshold is less easy to detect; nevertheless, the need for such a criterion, even if arbitrarily imposed, is implied in the efforts of Haas and Lindberg to distinguish more and less integrated types of decision-making.[3] Even for the most impression-istic or qualitative judgements, a threshold or standard seems to be required; what it is, of course, depends primarily on how integration is defined.

The first step in this reformulation of the idea of integration as system-change must therefore be to suggest a model of the sort of political whole towards which the system evolves and from which we can derive a standard or set of indices to employ as a measure of the extent of integration in any system. If we call this model 'political community' it is not because it resembles any particular state, organization or community now in existence, but because the term is sufficiently broad to embrace a variety of social and political systems including those toward which Europe may be developing. It is also close to being the standard term for the end-product of an integrative process. How, then, might we describe this end-product?

A way of thinking about integrating political communities which would seem to hold much promise is the multidimensional perspec-tive.[4] To adopt such a model is to acknowledge the breadth and

[1] A. Etzioni, *Political Unification* (New York: 1965) pp. 51–5.

[2] K. W. Deutsch *et al.*, 'Political Community and the North Atlantic Area', in *International Political Communities: An Anthology* (New York: 1966) pp. 13–17.

[3] Haas, *op. cit.*, pp. 103–13; L. N. Lindberg, 'The European Community as a Political System', *Journal of Common Market Studies*, 5: 4, 1967, pp. 356–63; and 'Political Integration as a Multidimensional Phenomenon Requiring Multi-variate Measurement', *International Organization*, 24: 4, 1970, pp. 672–9 and 703–8.

[4] There have been a number of attempts to develop multidimensional models of integration. See, for example, K. W. Deutsch, 'Integration and the Social System: Implications of Functional Analysis', in P. E. Jacob and J. V. Toscano (eds.), *The Integration of Political Communities* (Philadelphia: 1964) esp. p. 191; J. S. Nye, Jr., 'Comparative Regional Integration: Concept and Measurement', *International Organization*, 22: 4, 1968, pp. 855–80; J. Galtung, 'A Structural Theory of Integration', *Journal of Peace Research*, 5: 4, 1968, pp. 375–95, and esp., Lindberg, 'Political Integration as a Multidimensional Phenomenon' *op. cit.*, pp. 649–731. An earlier version of the model developed here is in C. C. Pentland, 'The Dimensions of Political Integration', unpublished M.A. Thesis, University of British Columbia, 1966.

complexity of the integrative process and the possibility that different approaches cover different aspects of it, i.e., are complementary in many respects. Drawing on the approaches examined earlier, we can define political community as the condition of a system which is integrated above a certain level in each of four dimensions. These four dimensions have to do with decision-making, the performance of functional tasks, patterns of social behaviour, and political attitudes. A degree of integration in each of these can be stipulated as the minimum requisite for political community. Beyond the minimal points however, a wide variety of systems – as defined by the four dimensions – would be compatible with the notion of political community.

The decision-making dimension refers to the structures and processes through which conflicts are resolved and choices made among scarce values in a society. Narrowly defined, decision-making structures are those institutions of government, such as the legislative, executive, bureaucratic and judicial, whose study has been seen traditionally as the core of political science. More broadly, these structures include political parties, interest groups and less formalized patterns of organizations and interaction. Decision-making is thus a process occurring within or among such structures.

Much recent political science is centred on more or less abstract formulations of this process. The competitive models of politics, deriving many ideas from economic analysis, which have been developed by such writers as the group theorists, the 'distributive' theorists, the democratic pluralists and those who employ strictly economic analogies, are attempts to formalize this continuous process of institutional conflict and decision.[1] Theories of systems as abstract models of decision-processes, such as those of Easton, Deutsch or Almond and Coleman, and the theories of more concrete organizational processes, also seem to be based on a notion of decision as central to politics.[2]

Among the writers on integration, the neofunctionalists come closest to concentrating exclusively on this particular dimension. Their interest in the cross-national interactions of interest-groups,

---

[1] See D. B. Truman, *The Governmental Process* (New York: 1951); H. D. Lasswell and A. Kaplan, *Power and Society* (New Haven: 1950); R. A. Dahl and C. E. Lindblom, *Politics, Economics and Welfare* (New York: 1953); A. Downs, *An Economic Theory of Democracy* (New York: 1957).

[2] See D. Easton, *A Framework for Political Analysis* (Englewood Cliffs, N.J.: 1965); K. W. Deutsch, *The Nerves of Government* (New York: 1966); G. A. Almond and J. S. Coleman (eds.), *The Politics of the Developing Areas* (Princeton: 1957); H. A. Simon, *Administrative Behaviour*, 2nd edition (New York: 1965).

197

political elites and bureaucrats, in the modes of conflict resolution, and in applying systems-theory, makes them impatient with approaches that rely on social indices or on the 'non-political' unifying effects of pure functional cooperation. Neofunctionalists see no intrinsic interest in the number of contacts between bureaucrats in Brussels or the structure of the European coal industry: these are of relevance only in so far as they feed into 'the political system' and influence how decisions are made and conflicts resolved among the six countries.

The functional dimension, on the other hand, is concerned, not with these purely 'political' phenomena, but with the material content and consequences of decisions. It is concerned with the structures and practices through which the basic needs of individuals and groups in the fields of welfare and security are met in society. These include such social structures as administrative agencies, the industrial complex, the agricultural system, the military and police organizations, the communications media and so forth. If a technocratic utopia could be imagined, without the purely political superstructure, it would no doubt be described in terms of these functional organizations.[1]

That these phenomena generally come under the purview of economists, sociologists and students of public administration has not prevented political scientists from giving them a primacy in the process of political change. Not only the functionalists, but many other theorists of integration, tend to see political change as led by or described in terms of changes in the performance of 'basic' economic, social or military functions in a system. We need not accept the complete Marxist picture of social change to see that a system where the decision-process is isolated from demands and support arising in the functional organizations, or superficially imposed upon it, is likely to be unstable. Thus, even if we take the 'essence' of the political to be 'decisions', a 'political community' may require a somewhat broader definitional base. For example, to know how decisions are made in agricultural matters in the EEC will not tell us much about the prospects for 'political community' there unless we also know about the pressures building up from the present inadequacies of the European agricultural structure.

The third dimension of political community has to do with patterns of social behaviour which, while being regular and often predictable, are less stable than what we call 'institutions' or

[1] Cf. J. Meynaud, *Technocracy*, trans, P. Barnes (London: 1968).

'structures'. These are the more or less habitual actions of individuals which, in the aggregate, give us pictures of overall patterns of social mobility, communications flows, interaction and political behaviour in a system. Indicators of this sort of social behaviour are familiar enough: communications data (mail, telephone calls, telegrams, literacy-levels, circulation, etc.); trade figures and flows of finance; labour mobility, tourism and other forms of travel; horizontal and vertical social mobility; elite interactions (numbers of meetings); voting and mass participation in politics.

Deutsch's work, both on the national and on the international level, is well known for its emphasis on such data. It is possible to quarrel with interpretations of these indicators – particularly as regards their psychological or political significance. But it is also possible to take them more at face value, as representing unregulated but nonetheless regular social patterns which give both cohesion and distinctive character to a political community. According to some, it is more useful for an understanding of European integration to know whether intra-European social contacts are increasing at the same rate, or gradually tapering off, than it is to know about the European industrial structure or the powers of the Commission. Whether or not one accepts this view, the argument at least makes clear not only the distinctiveness of this dimension but also the reasoning through which it can be said to have political relevance.

The fourth dimension of political community is the social-psychological one, to do with the aggregate patterns of political attitudes in the system. It is concerned with how the elites and the public perceive the political system and their society, and what emotions they feel towards them. The sources of evidence about these attitudes are many and varied: they can be inferred from policies and behaviour, analyzed from their expression in literature, speeches and communication media, or probed in opinion polls and depth-interviews.

Political scientists have rarely agreed on the significance of these patterns of attitudes in political life. Some, particularly elite-oriented theorists, regard only a small group as important in this respect, the attitudes of the public being considered at the least irrelevant, at the most a sort of acquiescent background against which the struggle for power is enacted. Others, however, have taken the problem of 'political culture' more seriously and attempted to describe and explain political systems in terms of the level of public political awareness, loyalty and participation.[1] In integration theory there has been some work of this kind, most notably by Deutsch, who has surveyed public opinion and elite attitudes toward European integration, and by Inglehart, who has attempted to construct a model to assess the influence of public preferences on decision-makers in integrating systems.[2] Other writers, such as Haas and Lindberg, have also discussed the 'shift of loyalties' implied by integration, but neofunctionalist literature is on the whole unclear on how and when this shift might occur, and on what weight to give it *vis-à-vis* shifts in the locus of decision-making.[3] In any case, to talk of political community without considering the problems of legitimacy, compliance, popular will, political culture or loyalties, would seem to be extremely risky. The fact that integration theorists have made only tentative efforts to deal with this dimension need not prevent us from including it in the concept of political community developed here.

A political community, then, is a system (clearly, whether formally 'international' or 'domestic' is not important here) in which there is a certain degree of integration in the structures and processes of decision-making, in the performance of functional tasks, in patterns of collective social behaviour, and in collective political attitudes. These four dimensions embrace the major themes of the literature we have examined. As a comprehensive way of describing a political system they perhaps recall Parsons' functional subsystems referred to by Deutsch. They are, however, not as abstract as these, nor are their interrelationships as systematically spelled out.[4] They do imply a broader notion of political community than is found in the multi-dimensional models of Lindberg and Nye, both of which are really centred on decision-making. Nye distinguishes between economic, social and political integration, while Lindberg concentrates on differentiating numerous dimensions within a decision-making model of community. Nye and Galtung both draw further distinctions

[1] See, for example, G. A. Almond and S. Verba, *The Civic Culture* (Boston: 1965), and L. Pye and S. Verba (eds.), *Political Culture and Political Development* (Princeton: 1965).

[2] See esp., K. W. Deutsch, L. J. Edinger, R. C. Macridis and R. L. Merritt, *France, Germany and the Western Alliance* (New York: 1967); R. Inglehart, 'Public Opinion and Regional Integration' *International Organization* 24: 4, 1970, pp. 764–95.

[3] See, for example, L. N. Lindberg, *The Political Dynamics of European Economic Integration* (Stanford: 1963), p. 6; L. N. Lindberg and S. A. Scheingold, *Europe's Would-Be Polity* (Englewood Cliffs: 1970) esp. pp. 36–60, and Ch. 8.

[4] See Deutsch, 'Integration and the Social System: Implications of Functional Analysis', *op. cit.*, p. 191.

between types of political integration.[1] But our four dimensions, it should be clear, do not refer to different types, but to four necessary aspects of a single process which may lead to a new and unfamiliar form of political community.

Clearly there are significant differences between this four-dimensional model and those espoused by the theorists discussed in earlier chapters. Federalist and neofunctionalist writers, as we have seen, tend to focus on the decision-making dimension, paying little or no attention to the other three. Within the decision-making dimension, however, their criteria for integration may be quite high – requiring, for example, real legal and political competence for central institutions, or a predominant pattern of decision which 'upgrades the common interest'. It may be that a more inclusive conception of political community need not be so demanding in any one dimension. Again, the functionalists' overriding concern with the second dimension would seem less compelling if mechanisms, inherent in the other dimensions, could be discovered whereby integration could be advanced on a broader front. From time to time integration theorists have criticized each other for narrowness or inappropriateness of focus: Lindberg has charged Deutsch with being more interested in 'social' than 'political' community.[2] Haas and Claude have suggested that functionalists assume, unrealistically, a divorce between the worlds of welfare and politics.[3] A broader model of political community might relieve these charges of some dead weight, while still allowing the debate over the relative importance of variables to carry on in an ordered framework.

But clearly such a framework will only be of use to the extent that it provides its own criteria by which theorists might assess the degree of integration in a system. In order to do this, we must attempt to describe the logical range of integration in each dimension, and postulate for that dimension a minimal threshold, which is at least intuitively satisfying and below which we would not consider the system to be integrated.

In the decision-making dimension, the system can be described as integrated to the extent that peaceful processes of conflict-resolution and stable structures for decision predominate over the threat or use

[1] For these models, see Nye, *op. cit.*, pp. 860–74; Lindberg, 'Political Integration as a Multidimensional Phenomenon', *op. cit.*, pp. 660–1; Galtung, *op. cit.*, esp. pp. 375–80, 383, 388.

[2] Lindberg, 'The European Community as a Political System', *op. cit.*, p. 345.

[3] Haas, *op. cit.*, pp. 21–2; I. L. Claude, Jr., *Swords into Plowshares*, 3rd edition (New York: 1964) p. 250.

of violence and the classic diplomatic patterns of self-help. The extreme case of an unintegrated system in these terms would thus be something like a continuing 'state of war', where violence is the norm and no settlement more than an expedient truce with no recognized legitimacy. This is conceivable in actual international wars (particularly where restraints on 'total war' are non-existent) and in ongoing feuds and vendettas between social groups such as gangs. At the other extreme, a totally integrated system would be one of absolute order, where all decisions are taken in a single, authoritarian centre and where, out of fear of coercion or through total identification, these decisions are unfailingly accepted throughout the system. While this is clearly an 'ideal type' of totalitarian, monolithic system, it is worth recalling that some critics of integration theory have seen it implied, at least logically, in the functionalist and neofunctionalist models: these are criticized for the possibility that they would lead an unresponsive, centralized and technocratic system of government.[1]

But where, between these two conceivable extremes, should we place the minimal point at which we can refer to a system as 'integrated'? Reasonably this point would be when it is possible to detect, in the system, institutions and political actors who are generally accepted as representing the interests of the system as a whole, whose demands are considered and regularly reflected in the outcome of decision-processes in the system, and who possess the influence to see these outcomes enforced. This description clearly contains several statements in need of more precise formulation. What, for example, constitutes 'general' acceptance? Evidence of this might be that the political elites of each country indicate in policy-statements that they perceive and accept these institutions and actors as playing a system-wide role. Such seems to be the case in the EEC, where the Commission and the Brussels institutions are held, even by French elites, to represent the interests of the system as a whole. The same could not be said unequivocally of the United Nations system, since the institutions (notably the Secretary-General) are frequently seen by different groups of states as being predominantly concerned with the interests of other groups of states, there being little general consciousness of a persisting common political interest. Again, how does one measure the 'regular' reflection of these common interests in the system's decisions and the amount of influence the institutions possess? Following the lead of Haas, it is possible to distinguish types of

[1] Such is one of the main themes of A. Spinelli, *The Eurocrats* (Baltimore: 1966) passim.

settlement, roughly by the extent to which they reflect the common interests, even if this judgement will always be somewhat impressionistic as to the sample of decisions examined and the detection of these interests in them. Amounts of influence are perhaps more easily assessed: one can examine the common institutions' capacities for enforcement and their access to legal and financial resources. Again, by such standards the EEC would appear to be integrated, if only minimally, in the decision-making dimension. The UN system, on the other hand, appears to wobble back and forth across the threshold, while the broader 'Europes' of the Council of Europe or of the UN Economic Commission possess few attributes of integration.

In the functional dimension, the extent to which a system can be described as integrated depends on the number of sectors of activity in the fields of welfare and security which are organized on a system-wide rather than on a local or national basis, and on the proportion of the total activity in those sectors which is carried out in the common structures. At the nether extreme of this dimension it is possible to imagine a system of states where the principle of autarchy is reduced to its absurd logical implication: all economic activities, administration, policing and defense, are undertaken by individual states, in 'splendid isolation' and in total rejection of international cooperation. Of course even the best-known examples of isolated states in recent history, such as the United States up until World War I, were not able to attain such a pristine degree of functional detachment. At the other pole of this continuum, every conceivable functional task would be carried out for the 'common good' by the institutions of the system as a whole, without respect for political demarcations. It is important to note that total integration need not imply total centralization. In this dimension the criterion of integration is rationality of functional performance as measured against common needs. In some sectors, rationality might require centralization, in others, devolution to the state-level or below. To the extent that rationality implies structural differentiation and flexibility, of course, it makes coordination difficult and costly. Like the 'centralization' continuum of the decision-making dimension, then, this 'rationality' continuum is characterized by potentially pathological conditions at each extreme, and puts in graphic form some classic political dilemmas.

As a minimal criterion for integration it can be suggested that at least one important functional sector must have the preponderance of its activities organized on a system-wide basis for the common

203

good. Here again there are problems in the precision of wording. What is the measure of 'importance', and how much is a 'preponderance'? If one is to avoid an infinite semantic regress, at some stage an arbitrary, intuitive judgement must be made about such matters. In this case, then, a sector is 'important' according to the number of people who depend on it for their welfare or security, and according to the proportion of the system's resources it draws upon or produces. Thus the military sector is important because of its overall protective function, and because of the size of national defence budgets. The ECSC dealt with an important economic sector because of the strategic position of coal and steel in the European economy and the scale of the industry. 'Preponderance', too, can be defined arbitrarily. In this case it is taken to mean simply and literally that the system-wide organizations command more resources and are the focus of more activity and attention – in short, have more 'weight' – than the national ones.

Although it is difficult to judge, it seems fair to say that in these terms the EEC has at least passed the threshold of functional integration. The coal and steel industries and the Common Agricultural Policy are indicative of this. But it is hard to be sanguine about this dimension of integration: further development requires those steps toward 'positive integration' that the Six have been reluctant to take. Nevertheless, functional integration is more advanced there than in any other system. The military integration of NATO or the Warsaw Pact, the various agencies of the UN for functional cooperation, and the structures of international business and finance do not seem generally to exhibit the qualities demanded by our criteria. Some instances of economic and social cooperation, such as the Nordic Council, moving toward economic integration, can be considered on the very threshold.

In the third dimension, that of social and political behaviour, theorists are perhaps best equipped with indices for measuring integration, even if the implications of what they measure are often not well understood or agreed upon. The more these patterns of behaviour indicate that individuals habitually act with reference to the system rather than to their states or to other systems, the more that the system can be described as integrated. Thus integration involves not only the lessening of internal barriers to communication and interaction, but often an increase in the differentiation of the system from other systems. A completely unintegrated system in this dimension would be one in which the members of each state – both elites and public – were totally indifferent to, and uninvolved with, the members of the other states. There would be, in short, no trade, communication or social mobility of any kind – a complete absence of international intercourse most closely approximated historically by the relations (or paucity thereof) between the Roman and Chinese empires, or, until very recently between the United States and China. At the upper extreme of integration, the behaviour of individuals, as mapped by the volume and intensity of communications, inter-actions and mobility, would be unchannelled by state boundaries and would be organized instead in a centralized, system-wide pattern. From the standpoint of the system, then, the integration-continuum of social and political behaviour runs from total indifference (or preoccupation with traditional roles and boundaries) to total mobilization.

At what point along this continuum can it be said that the system first becomes integrated? To insist on the emergence of common structures facilitating the growth of these patterns might be too demanding. A system of states, after all, can support a high degree of cross-national communication and interaction without developing formal institutions. On the other hand, to say that any amount of cross-national contact constitutes evidence of integration renders the index so minimal as to be useless. Clearly, then, we must establish a level of intensity of contacts or mutual responsiveness between states, beyond which it can be reasonably agreed to talk of them as integrated. One way to do this would be to discern certain fields of social and political activity, such as consultations and exchanges between leaders, participation by individuals and groups in political life (voting, lobbying, propaganda, etc.), migration of labour, and exchange of goods and services, and to argue that a system is integrated to some degree when one of these patterns of activity persistently overlaps national boundaries and develops system-wide characteristics. Increases in integration can thus be measured by the multiplication of such patterns, as well as by their intensity and their political importance.

In the EEC there are several indications that such patterns exist. From 1958 to 1963, intra-EEC trade increased two and a half times, a figure that is not solely accounted for by national economic expansion or by the general increase in international trade.[1] In other

[1] For useful tables of these trade-flows, see H. Alker and D. Puchala, 'Trends in Economic Partnership: The North Atlantic Area 1928–63', in J. D. Singer (ed.), *Quantitative International Politics* (New York: 1968) pp. 312–13.

cases, where the policies of national governments are not so indulgent toward transnational behaviour, the indices, while ambiguous, do show tendencies for social patterns to flow over national boundaries. Within the Six, work permits and passports are still required, but this has not prevented almost 150,000 Italian workers per year entering West Germany since 1960, or over 5,000,000 German tourists per year going to Italy.[1] It is easy to be dazzled by such figures, of course, and to overstress their socio-political weight, their historical uniqueness and their pre-eminence in the Six alone. In fact, in Europe on a broader scale such patterns are almost as striking, which may mean that the social patterns described by such behaviour, if it persists or increases, will not be congruent with emerging political and economic patterns.

In the fourth dimension of political community, to do with attitudes, integration can be described as a shift of the awareness and the loyalties of individuals from a particularistic focus on their local or national communities, to a wider focus on the system as a whole. At the lower, unintegrated end of this continuum, we can discern two logical possibilities. One is the total preoccupation and identification of each individual with his local community or national state, such as occurs for brief periods when populations are mobilized to face a national emergency. The other is a situation where individuals are completely uninvolved in and unaware of political life, such as seems to be the case in less developed and unmobilized societies. In the first case, the process of integration would be a contest between states and system for already mobilized loyalties and perceptions; in the second case, the development of political awareness could have effects on both levels at once.[2] The other extreme of the continuum is more easily characterized. It would be a replication on the systems level of the first alternative described above – the total mobilization and expression of political loyalties and awareness, and their fixation on one particular political system, such as might occur on occasions of mass indoctrination or collective hysteria. From the point of view of the system, then, the continuum ranges between the two poles of parochialism (or apathy) and total identification.

[1] H. S. Feldstein, 'A Study of Transaction and Political Integration: Transnational Labour Flow within the European Economic Community', *Journal of Common Market Studies*, 6: 1, 1967, p. 49. A. Sampson, *The New Europeans* (London: 1968) Ch. 12.

[2] The second case is particularly relevant for integration in less developed areas, where the emergence of 'modern' national political cultures might be necessary not only for national political development, but for forms of regional integration.

Locating the threshold of integration in this dimension raises a number of problems. Studies of political attitudes and political culture have by no means made it clear that a particular level of political awareness or popular support is a requisite of integrated societies; Almond and Verba found wide variation on such indices between the United States and Mexico, which points up the difficulty of settling on a minimal requirement.[1] On the other hand, merely to look for a flickering awareness of transnational society on the part of a certain number of individuals will almost certainly not suffice. It might be suggested then that a useful threshold to postulate is the point when the system as a whole becomes competitive with the individual states in general popular awareness and affection. This would occur when statements indicating that the system is perceived as a political community with at least some impact on daily life, are made by a majority of the population, or appear in communications media with the same frequency as statements about national life. As for expressions of positive loyalty, it would seem likely that a much lower incidence of these would be compatible with the existence of political community. A system-wide figure of around twenty per cent would indicate a substantial and politically weighty body of favourable attitudes toward the system as a whole.[2]

From this perspective the EEC system would appear, on the basis of the scanty information we have, to be on the threshold of integration in this dimension. For example, in the Gallup survey of early 1962, while there was very wide popular support for the 'European idea' (from sixty to eighty per cent of the respondents in all six countries favoured it, at least moderately), this support and the level of information about the EEC were both somewhat superficial, and loyalties and affective responses were at best mixed. Most strikingly, national rather than European problems remained salient in the news.[3] Other studies have supported this impression.[4] On a broader European scale the figures would undoubtedly be lower all across the board. Even though our criteria fall below the level of awareness

[1] Almond and Verba, *op. cit.*, Chs. 2 and 3.

[2] In most democratic systems, such a body of attitudes would represent a potentially powerful political force, whether this were expressed in the form of votes for a political party or in the concerted actions of interest groups.

[3] Gallup International, 'Public Opinion in the European Community', *Journal of Common Market Studies*, 2: 2, 1963, pp. 101–3, 106, 108–9.

[4] Deutsch *et al.*, *France, Germany and the Western Alliance*, esp. Ch. 21. R. L. Merritt and D. Puchala, *Western European Perspectives on International Affairs* (New York: 1968). Lindberg and Scheingold, *op. cit.*, pp. 38–60.

and loyalty found in many developed countries, they are thus approached by very few of the many regional integrating systems today.

To sum up, then, the process by which a political community is formed can be analyzed in terms of distinct processes of integration in four dimensions. In each of these, polar extremes can be conceived which are logically possible, if empirically unlikely. More important, a threshold can be postulated for each, and the stipulation made that a political community cannot be said to exist unless all four thresholds have been passed by the system in question. Naturally, different theorists will have different ideas about where this threshold should be placed. But the articulation of such a dimensional model should at least make it easier for different scholars' criteria to be broken down and compared.

There are, of course, disadvantages to this method of looking at integration. The model is less elegant and less clearly related to historical or empirical examples of political community, than the state-analogies, the pluralist model or the functionalist idea. In addition, it encompasses a potentially broad range of variables and, in so doing, raises the recurrent question of their relative weight. To some, then, it might seem that, far from clarifying matters, this model introduces new and unnecessary complications into the study of integration.

To this, one reply would be that the development of models always requires a choice between the values of simplicity and manageability on the one hand and comprehensiveness and sensitivity on the other. At the present stage of theorizing about integration, the need seems to be for a framework which can suggest how propositions from various approaches can be related, and which corresponds more closely to the salient features of the best studied integrating systems. The four-dimensional model seems to be 'closer' to the European experience in this sense, while its inclusiveness makes it potentially more sensitive to data than models derived from more traditional ideas of political community.

There is no denying the problem of weighting the variables. This problem arises in many theoretical formulations in political science; it is resolved generally by a reliance on a powerful single factor, by ruthless but explicit trimming and simplifying of the model, or by an agnostic falling-back on the presentation of the model as a 'conceptual framework'. The last alternative, for all its inconclusiveness, has a certain utility for a study in the chaotic state in which integration-theory finds itself today.[1] One problem of weighting, of course, is dismissed by definition, if we take some degree of integration in each of the four dimensions to be a necessary minimum for political community. Clearly, however, this still leaves the major issues of, first, weighting variables within each dimension and, secondly, determining linkages between dimensions. Resolving the former will require further choices based on variables referred to most frequently in the literature, tempered by judgements as to researchability. The latter problem sensitizes us to the complex but promising concept of inter-dimensional tension, which will be examined later in this chapter.

One advantage of this model is that it minimizes the problems of teleology and unilinearity. The upper extreme of integration in each dimension, while the logical extension of the process, is clearly neither inherently compelling or desirable. In all cases it is possible that a more stable and desirable level of integration will be found somewhere in the middle ranges, but no assumptions need be made about the stability of integration at any level. In addition, by setting the threshold of integration at a fairly modest level in each dimension, we remove the limelight from it and can raise the more interesting question of what types of political community – in terms of combinations of levels of integration in each dimension – can be conceived. This question may prove as important as the more usual one of the conditions pushing systems across the threshold.

It should be evident that there will be a wide variety of possible types of community, according to the extent that the system has become integrated in each dimension. As the basis of a crude typology let us take four ranges of points on each dimension: non-integration (below the threshold); low integration (just above the threshold); medium integration; and high integration (approaching, but still well below, the theoretical maximum). It should then be possible to describe groups of states according to where they fall along each dimension. Some systems have clearly attained – at least for a brief period – a moderate level of integration in at least one dimension.

The states of the Warsaw Pact-Comecon system, for example, could be considered moderately integrated on the decision-making and functional scales, and perhaps lowly integrated on the other two.

---

[1] A good example, in another field, of the strengths and weaknesses of a conceptual framework of this kind, is R. C. Snyder, H. W. Bruck and B. Sapin (eds.), *Foreign Policy Decision-Making* (New York: 1962).

The Arab League states, in certain periods, have shown an appreciable degree of decisional, functional and attitudinal integration often reaching into the middle range. Several groups of less developed states have become integrated – at least for a brief period – in one or two dimensions. This would apply to Kenya, Uganda and Tanzania, which achieved a low degree of functional integration, and perhaps to the Central American states in the functional and behavioural dimensions. In few other state systems outside Western Europe does it seem possible to make such assertions.

In Europe different groups of states exhibit varying levels of integration. The highest overall levels would be found in the Benelux system, the Nordic Council states and the Six, although in none of these could we judge any dimensions to be integrated beyond the medium level (the functional dimension in each, and perhaps the attitudinal and behavioural dimensions in the Nordic system would reach this level). Except in the functional and behavioural dimensions in the EFTA states and possibly in Britain-and-the-Six and the Council of Europe states, there is little evidence of integration in other possible groupings – least of all, of course, among the states represented by the UN Economic Commission.

It bears repeating that these are impressionistic judgements which are meant to serve as illustrations of the method, and which would require empirical substantiation on a greater scale than is possible or necessary here. It would, however, be feasible to elaborate the criteria of each dimension so as to arrive at a rough scale on which to rank more precisely the various state-systems according to their level of integration.[1] Another point worth stressing in that this model gives only a static picture or a 'snapshot' of the condition of integration at a given time. As there is little apparent reason to assume that a system's level of integration in any dimension will remain stable for long periods, regular reassessments must be made.

[1] One might, for example, set up a scale for each dimension, with the extreme of integration at 1, that of disintegration at 10, and the threshold set at, say, 7. The problem then is to judge where each system might be placed – that is, the old problem of correspondence between data and scale. Lindberg's solution seems to be to rely on rather intuitive judgements about how to rate the items on his list of functions, according to the extent that they are decided upon in the Community system rather than by the states' governments. See Lindberg, 'The European Community as a Political System', *op. cit.*, pp. 356–9, Lindberg and Scheingold, *op. cit.*, Ch. 3, and Lindberg, 'Political Integration as a Multidimensional Phenomenon', *op. cit.*, pp. 662–79. The other, more inductive, solution is Deutsch's, where the emphasis is on 'hard' empirical data, and the measurement of integration relies on far less precise criteria, i.e., a less explicit scale. In neither case is the problem of inference really avoided or overcome.

In this way, as with the economy or demographic patterns, trends and rates of change over time can be determined.

This, then, is the framework in which the process of integration, seen as change on the level of the international system, might be formulated as the dependent variable in a theory of integration. We must now turn to the question of independent variables on the level of the system. Drawing on the approaches examined in previous chapters we shall try, first, to delineate both the general background conditions and the major process variables for integration in each dimension, and secondly, to assess how changes in one dimension affect changes in the others. These sets of questions encompass most of the causal problems raised in the various approaches to integration on the system level.

The notion of a 'background' condition has both a temporal and ecological connotation – that is, it can refer both to long-term, relatively stable factors as compared to more immediate situational factors, and to political, socio-economic and other conditions existing outside the integrating system. The term will be used here in both these senses, on the argument that the fundamental distinction to be made is between the background cond tions taken as a general group, and the 'process' conditions. The essential problem of the former has to do with their predictability and stability. As Nye has pointed out, integration theorists have often held a remarkable number of such conditions as 'constant', to the detriment of the general applicability of their conclusions. At the same time they have ignored the possible effects of dramatic change or intervention by an external variable.[1] The process variables, as indicated, are the more immediate and emphemeral conditions operating in a process of change. It would be useful to try and group the background conditions and process variables according to the dimensions in which they are likely to have the most effect.

Among the major background conditions relevant to the decision-making dimension, the one most frequently mentioned is a standing threat or compulsion from the external political environment. From

[1] J. S. Nye, Jr., 'Patterns and Catalysts in Regional Integration', *International Organization*, 19: 4, 1965, p. 882. Cf. J. S. Nye, Jr., 'Comparing Common Markets', *International Organization*, 24: 4, 1970, esp. pp. 811–12. Elsewhere in this article, Nye draws a useful distinction between 'structural conditions which are conceived as relatively stable variables more determined by factors other than the integration process and perceptual conditions which are quite volatile during an integration process and are determined more by the integration process itself.' (p. 812).

the Turks to the Russians such threats have been constant fare in arguments for European union. Beside the perception of military or economic threats, integrating states have been motivated by the general structure of the international system (i.e. the position of Europe as a 'pawn' between two super-powers) or by the support of powerful outside states (the US, in the case of Europe). Other background conditions relevant to integration in this dimension would include the origins and composition of political elites in the system (the problem of compatibility), the existence of traditional political ties, common institutions or habits of cooperation and consultation, and the relative capacities of states to make and enforce decisions. Geographical factors are also weighty insofar as they encourage or inhibit the growth of common practices of decision and conflict-resolution.

The crucial process variables here centre around the style and context of decision-making in the system. They include many of those brought out in the neofunctionalist literature on the European 'community method': a convergent pattern of group and national interests in the particular issue; the growth and manoeuverability of institutions and actors representing the 'common interest'; situational pressures of an institutional, legal and psychological kind which push negotiators to resolve their conflicts; and the pattern of conflict-resolution itself (whether it 'upgrades the common interest', is enforceable, and has the effect of leading to new problems and decisions).

For functional integration perhaps the most important background conditions have to do with the state of technology and the general level of socio-economic development in the system. Complex industrial societies, it is generally held, are more amenable to the formation of the sorts of cross-national administrative cooperation stressed by both functionalist and neofunctionalist writers. This has been one explanation of the failure of less developed regions to follow the example of the EEC.[1] Geography, in terms of both topography and natural resources, is another important background condition here. Related to this is the existence of common functional needs and problems in the system as a whole, such as the perceived necessity for postwar reconstruction or technological development

[1] See, for example, E. B. Haas, '"The Uniting of Europe" and the Uniting of Latin America', *Journal of Common Market Studies*, 5: 4, 1967, pp. 315–43. Cf. A. Segal, 'The Integration of Developing Countries: Some Thoughts on East Africa and Central America', *ibid.*, 5: 3, 1967, pp. 252–82.

in Europe, or for economic development and political independence in Latin America.

The main process variables in this dimension have to do with the condition of the existing patterns of functional performance, and the problems to which they give rise. A shift in the uses of energy-sources in Europe, for example, has given rise to fundamental structural changes in the coal industry. Integration can be enhanced or impeded according to how many sectors of the economy are affected by a particular functional problem, and by the extent to which each functional sector depends on and influences others. It seems, finally, that some sectors are more potent than others in inducing broader functional integration, but there is little consensus among theorists whether these honours are due to the industrial, the social welfare or the military sector.

In the dimension of social and political behaviour, the important background conditions have to do with the origins and composition of populations and the degree of communications and interaction between them. Relevant to the first are not only problems of linguistic and ethnic background, but also the degree of social pluralism and the patterns of social cleavages (whether cross-cutting or congruent) in the system. The second set of conditions includes the general level of social exchanges and contacts in all strata of the population, as well as the degree of social and spatial mobility in the system. In general, integration theorists, taking their cues from the modernized system of Western Europe, have assumed that high measures in all these cases are advantageous for integration.

For this dimension the more immediate process variables would reflect increases in the capacities of both individuals and institutions to handle social communication and interaction. Aspects of this 'social learning' process – which many theorists see as self-reinforcing – would include diffusion of languages throughout the system (French, German and English in West Europe; Russian in East Europe), easing of restrictions on exchange (lowering of tariff barriers, removal of restrictions on labour and tourist movement), and the emergence of new structures for elite-consultations. In this dimension, as one writer has observed, the distinction between background and process is not always easily maintained.[1]

The important background conditions in the attitudinal dimension, finally, have to do with the sharing of cultural traits and the com-

[1] On this point, see B. M. Russett, *Community and Contention* (Cambridge, Mass.: 1963) p. 33.

patibility of the major values of groups in the system. Cultural traits in this case have to do with the religious, literary and mythical traditions prevalent in the system, as perpetuated or evolved in practices of upbringing, education and socialization. The more ephemeral value-systems represented in ideologies and in patterns of social and economic motivation (such as the 'Protestant ethic' or the 'need for achievement') must also be considered here. Neofunctionalist assertions about the irrelevance of 'operative myths' of a tradition of European unity stretching back to and beyond the Carolingian era, may be somewhat premature; in addition, ideology and myth seem to have played some part in integration schemes elsewhere.[1]

Process variables in this last dimension would include the configuration of values and interests among groups and individuals over particular issues, and the way in which discrepancies are resolved or explained. Other process variables would centre on the linkage between political attitudes and the sources of gratification for basic functional needs. Social contacts and patterns of communication (the effects of symbols) are also important. In order to understand more fully how these aggregate patterns of attitudes change, it is thus necessary to examine prevailing theories of individual attitude-change. These ideas, traces of which are found throughout the literature on integration, will be developed more fully in the chapter on the individual level of analysis.[2]

In its skeletal form, then, this model associates sets of background conditions and process variables with specific dimensions of integration, rather than with the process viewed as an undifferentiated whole. Clearly the reality is not as well packaged as this; but to set down these associations systematically does not preclude examining 'cross-dimensional' effects. For example, a background condition like the degree of social pluralism or mobility, associated most closely with the third dimension, will not be without effects in some cases in the functional dimension as well. The same holds for a process variable such as the prevalent pattern of conflict-resolution, which would normally be associated with the decision-making dimension. But it is a truism that social scientists can sooner or later discover everything to be related in some way to everything else. What is important is to specify the strongest, most regular and most persuasive relationships.

[1] See, for example, J. S. Nye, Jr., *Pan-Africanism and East African Integration* (Cambridge, Mass.; 1965).   [2] See *infra*, Ch. 8.

This does, however, raise the problem of how the processes of change within each dimension influence those in the others. It would be useful to approach this problem by speculating about the stability of different patterns of political community. It might be suggested, for example, that a political community where the level of integration in all four dimensions was roughly the same would be more stable than one where, say, the decision-making dimension was highly integrated and the rest hardly at all. Such a hypothesis has a number of implications. Not only would it mean that, in a system highly integrated in all dimensions, political change or decay would be a very long-term proposition; more important, for a system like the European Communities, integrated to a small degree in each dimension, further movement up the scales would be a very slow, balanced and complex process. What it does not suggest is whether the best strategy for advancing integration in such cases is a comprehensive attack on all four fronts, or a more selective effort to increase the level of integration in one dimension, creating tension which may be resolved by some overall increase. This hypothesis also gives a new perspective on systems which exhibit wide discrepancies in the levels of integration of their dimensions. Assessing the prospects for overall integration or disintegration becomes a matter, not simply of measuring the presence of so many conditions or variables, but of inquiring which direction the level of integration in each dimension would have to move to restore an overall balance.

Clearly, to impute a 'natural' tendency to equilibrium to an integrating system would risk falling back into the teleological trap. For this reason it must remain a hypothesis. Such problems are also mitigated if we conceive of any such 'tension' between dimensions in terms of their relative weight and the overall costs of integration for the system. The notion of inter-dimensional tensions is implicit in much of the literature on integration: different writers take different views about which dimensions have the most 'pulling-power' and accordingly, which strategy is most likely to suceed. Functionalism, for example, can be seen as the argument that integration in the functional dimension – particularly its economic sectors – works gradually but decisively on the other dimensions and induces change, first in behaviour and attitudes, then ultimately in decision-making as well. With this sequence neofunctionalists would most likely agree, with the important proviso that the functional and decision-making integration are more closely interwoven in the leading role. The federalists, however, would stress the importance of integrating the decision-making dimension first, the other dimensions following obediently, while Deutsch and other pluralist writers seem to give an important place to behavioural and attitudinal change as the prerequisites of integration in the other dimensions. Most of these writers, of course, are interested in the positive – that is, integrative – effects of one dimension or another; presumably the process would also work in reverse.

In any case, there seems to be little consensus as to the relative influence of each dimension. Moreover, it is deceptively easy to assume that, at all levels, an increase of integration in one dimension will induce some increase – not necessarily comparable – in at least one of the others. But if, as mentioned, the background conditions and process variables often have effects in more than one dimension, it could well be that at some stages integration is, as it were, a *competitive* process between dimensions, for 'scarce resources'. In short, change in one may have counter-inductive effects on another. For example, concentration of decision-making or centralization of functional tasks beyond a certain point in the present European Community system might induce an emotional retrenchment of local attitudes and an increased alienation from the 'European' social structures. Or integrating systems might undergo an experience common to many new states, where the social mobilization of the population has preceded the development of stable political institutions and hindered integration in the functional and decision-making dimensions. What such examples suggest is that, past a certain optimal level, further increases in the integration of a particular dimension may not necessarily induce similar increases in the others.[1]

This model, then, has some important implications for the kind of evidence we seek and, ultimately, for the sort of theory we develop in explaining integration. Most of the approaches we have examined are unilinear, assuming the process of change to occur along one dimension. In many, there is a flavour of determinism, both in the sense that certain mixes of factors are seen as causally compelling and in the sense that integration is seen as an irreversible, steady progress to a predetermined goal. By contrast, the four-dimensional model attempts to express the open-ended and undetermined nature

[1] Similar problems are beginning to be raised in the literature on political development. See, for example, E. A. Nordlinger, 'Political Development: Time Sequences and Rates of Change', *World Politics*, 20: 3, 1968, pp. 494–520; and C. S. Whitaker, Jr., 'A Dysrhythmic Process of Political Change', *ibid.*, 19: 2, 1967, pp. 190–217, esp. p. 216.

of integration as at least a workable alternative hypothesis. The great unknowns in the equation then become the relations between processes of change in respective dimensions – how each affects the direction, intensity and type of change in the others.[1]

The four-dimensional model will also influence the kinds of analogies we use to describe the process of system-change. Federalists, as we have seen, tend to talk in terms of an integrative 'revolution.' Such a notion of rapid political and constitutional change, implying an unambiguous threshold, may be applicable only to the decision-making and, perhaps, some aspects of the functional dimension. On the other hand, more evolutionary analogies – using the ideas of 'stages', 'epigenesis' or 'assembly' – may apply to the functional dimension, where there are discernible sectors which can, in some sense, be assembled gradually. And finally, analogies of diffusion – such as those of social learning and innovation (or, indeed, the spread of epidemics) – may be most appropriate to the behavioural and attitudinal dimensions.

In summary, then, each dimension, besides being associated with certain background conditions and process variables, may require a distinctive analogy to explain the process of integration within it. This complements the main argument of this chapter, which has been that what we call the process of political integration might more usefully be seen as four distinct but interrelated processes of integration. Such a perspective not only serves to illustrate the links between variables and hypotheses developed in different approaches to integration, but also suggests a number of new and potentially fertile questions about the process of change on the level of the international system.

[1] For a discussion of the principle of indeterminacy in the physical sciences, and its implications for the social sciences, see F. W. Matson, *The Broken Image* (Garden City, N.Y., 1966) esp. pp. 124–31, and Ch. 7.

7 Political Integration and the Behaviour of States

To many students of international relations, who would accept that political integration is a process which manifests itself on the level of the system as a whole, it will not necessarily follow that the important explanatory variables are also to be found on that level. As indicated in the preceding chapters, a strong current of opinion among integration theorists is nevertheless behind some such claim. Certain writers might stress the functional requisites of the system, others its qualities as a rudimentary society or polity, and others the need, deriving from a Hobbesian 'state of war', for order or equilibrium. In many cases the background conditions and process variables discussed in the previous chapter will appear decisive in the integrative process. This perspective does, however, risk begging an essential question, which is whether or not the qualities and actions of individual states are in the last analysis more important for the success of integration than the condition of the international system.

A powerful tradition both in the study of international relations and among its practitioners, would hold that indeed explorations of such processes must start from the assumption that the self-determined actions of states, rather than any characteristics of their patterns of interaction, are the fundamental movers of international political change. This 'realist' viewpoint is expressed well by Claude '. . . it is evident that the long-term evolution as well as the current functioning of the Community institutions is fundamentally a matter to be determined by the national governments concerned. Supranationality has contrived no genuine escape from sovereign states. It may be a step toward federal unity, but it is a step taken by *governments*, which retain the capacity to decide whether to take further steps forward, to stand still, or to retreat'.[1] Among integration theorists, those closest to this position are the pluralists and the

[1] I. L. Claude, Jr., *Swords into Plowshares*, 3rd edition (New York: 1964) p. 103.

federalists, who, as we have seen, come to widely divergent conclusions from similar assumptions about the primacy of the nation-state in international relations. While, in general, the functionalists and neofunctionalists show more interest in the systemic variables, they are certainly aware of the *negative* impact of state policies on integration, as the writings of Mitrany and Haas, in their very different ways, make clear.

Theorists who consider the modern nation-states still to be the ultimate arbiters of their own destiny can logically come to a number of different conclusions about the process of international political integration. They can, in the manner of eminent 'realist' writers like Morgenthau, Claude and Aron, conclude that the prospect of such changes is, at best, extremely distant and that what presently passes for a process of political integration in Europe is really little more than the continued exercise of diplomacy by other – mainly economic – means.[1] A second conclusion, close to this, is that of the pluralists, who simply define integration in such a way as to make it compatible with the uncompromised expression of state sovereignty.

The third conclusion – in this context the most interesting one – is in the form of a paradox, evident in many writings on integration: how is it that these apparently dominant, autonomous political units can become engaged in a process whose logical outcome is the reduction and perhaps ultimate abolition of their power and self-determination? Federalists, recognizing the paradox as the classic one of social contract theory, rely on a version of that theory for their answer. Functionalists and neofunctionalists place more faith on the subtleties of a gradual, indirect attack which relies on the pursuit of self-interest by the political elites and the public, both oblivious to the long-term implications of their actions. Such solutions of the paradox, however, are generally little more than summary dismissals of the problem to make way for others seen as more important or interesting.

Nevertheless, for each of these three points of view – particularly the last – the question arises as to whether, or in what ways, a state behaves differently toward other states with which we describe it as 'integrating', than it does toward states outside this system. To put it another way, to what extent do our usual conceptions of 'foreign policy' apply to states involved in a process of political integration?

[1] *Ibid.*, pp. 101–5; H. J. Morgenthau, *Politics Among Nations*, 4th edition, (New York: 1967), esp., pp. 511–14; R. Aron, *Peace and War* (New York: 1966) pp. 457–63.

It seems clear that, if we accept the traditional distinction between domestic and foreign policy, the behaviour of an integrating state toward its partners is still, technically, to be explained largely as representative of the latter. But most theorists of integration would also agree that such a simple characterization is inadequate, and that in many ways the patterns of policy-making in integrating states resemble those of domestic political processes. In short, the 'community policy' of a state (its policy toward other members of the integrating system) can be described as a subtype of foreign policy behaviour marked by many features of domestic political processes. A useful way to make this distinction clearer would be, first, to develop James Rosenau's discussion of foreign and domestic policy as 'issue areas'.[1] We can then go on to delineate some of the variables influencing the behaviour of integrating states.

'Issue areas', according to Rosenau, are 'categories of issues that affect a political process in sufficiently similar ways to justify being clustered together'.[2] A particular issue area consists of: '1. a cluster of values, the allocation or potential allocation of which 2. leads the affected or potentially affected actors to differ so greatly over (a) the way in which the values should be allocated or (b) the horizontal levels at which the values should be allocated that 3. they engage in distinctive behaviour designed to mobilize support for the attainment of their particular values'.[3] Rosenau argues that, seen in this light, the foreign and domestic issue areas exhibit some important differences. His discussion provides clues about the possibility of a 'community policy' issue area as well.

The first distinction Rosenau draws between the foreign and domestic issue areas refers to the types of motivation found in each. For the general public, foreign policy, being largely beyond their interest and control, is the subject of more intense, clear-cut and unambiguous motivation than are the more immediate, understandable and often complex issues of domestic policy. For the political elites, however, this is not the case. The intensity of their motivation is as low and the objects of it as extensive as in the domestic arena; moreover they are more aware than the general public of the interdependence of foreign and domestic politics. Thus the foreign

[1] See J. N. Rosenau, 'Foreign Policy as an Issue Area', in J. N. Rosenau (ed.), *Domestic Sources of Foreign Policy* (New York: 1967) pp. 11–50.

[2] *Ibid.*, p. 15.

[3] J. N. Rosenau, 'Pre-Theories and Theories of Foreign Policy', in R. B. Farrell (ed.), *Approaches to Comparative and International Politics* (Evanston, Ill.: 1966) p. 81.

policy issue area, unlike domestic policy, is characterized by a 'motivational gap' between citizens and policy-makers.[1]

The pattern of motivation in community policy would seem to be quite different again. What 'motivational gap' can be said to exist, seems to be based not only on immediacy and levels of information, but on perceptions of the relations of specific issues to the integrative process. Among the general public, in the first place, most issues are perceived and acted upon as domestic issues, whatever meaning observers and elites might place on them for the progress of integration. But within the policy elite itself a further pattern of motivation is apparent. Some members of the elite tend to treat the issues as domestic, and the involvement of other states' interests as merely additional resources or obstacles in the battle. Others reverse this position, and attempt to make diplomatic gains from the interdependence of states' economic and political systems. A third group tends to see such issues as opportunities to increase the level of integration in the system as a whole. Even among these last policy-makers, as Lindberg observed, the perceptions of what integration involves are likely to vary greatly.[2] Community policy, in short, is unique in that it is made in an environment where the nature of the political game itself is more than usually ambiguous and where different groups see it in different terms. This comes out particularly in neofunctionalist writings. Even the pluralists, however, would insist that in an integrating state the motivations of the public are somewhat less stark, simple and intense than tends to be the case in pure foreign policy issues.

A second distinction between the foreign and domestic issue areas Rosenau finds in the numbers and types of political roles pertaining to each. Issue areas, he argues, can be seen as structures of roles, not all of which are occupied or enacted at all times.[3] In general, there are far more roles in the domestic than in the foreign policy issue area, although most of these have reference only to a single issue. Such a role typically would be the leadership of an interest group concerned with one very narrow field of policy. Domestic policy as an issue area is thus marked by a high degree of structural differentiation. On the other hand, foreign policy roles tend to be few, multi-faceted and organizationally concentrated. Representative of

[1] Rosenau, 'Foreign Policy as an Issue Area', *op. cit.*, pp. 24–34. See also the table on p. 46.

[2] L. N. Lindberg, *The Political Dynamics of European Economic Integration* (Stanford: 1963) pp. 108–9.

[3] Rosenau, 'Foreign Policy as an Issue Area', *op. cit.*, pp. 36–7.

these are the roles of government leader, foreign minister and senior officials.

In community policy, it is clear that the latter type of role predominates. And yet the process of integration – certainly as witnessed in the EEC – has increasingly engaged actors playing traditionally domestic roles, both of the multiple – issue type (i.e. leaders of large interest groups and 'power-brokers') and of the single-issue type. The main reason for this is that a state involved in a fairly advanced process of integration such as that in the EEC, represents the archetype of what Rosenau elsewhere has called the 'penetrated political system'. This he defines as a political system in which 'nonmembers of a national society participate directly and authoritatively, through actions taken jointly with the society's members, in either the allocation of its values or the mobilization of support on behalf of its goals.'[1] National systems, he notes, permeate and depend on each other, and their functioning increasingly embraces actors not formally part of their society. Moreover, groups now strive to attain their goals in a social and political structure that is becoming a 'composite of subnational, national and supranational elements.'[2] Thus the penetration of national societies, not only by each other but by international organizations, has a multiplying effect on the number of foreign policy roles; it adds to the number of roles played by senior officials (i.e. the foreign minister becomes a member of the EEC Council of Ministers, and senior bureaucrats work on Community policies); and it projects the domestic political roles of each society into the international arena.

The third distinction which Rosenau draws between the foreign and domestic issue areas has to do with patterns of interaction. The

[1] Rosenau, 'Pre-Theories and Theories of Foreign Policy', *op. cit.*, p. 65. Cf. A. M. Scott, *The Functioning of the International Political System* (New York: 1967) Chs. 13 and 14. For an application of this idea to a study of foreign policy, see W. F. Hanrieder, *West German Foreign Policy* 1949–63 (Stanford: 1967).

[2] Rosenau, 'Pre-Theories and Theories of Foreign Policy', *op. cit.*, pp. 63–4. For a more recent attempt to systematize these ideas, see J. N. Rosenau (ed.), *Linkage Politics* (New York: 1969) esp. Chs. 1–3. An illustration of this phenomenon with respect to the European Communities is Feld's finding that twenty-two per cent of the members of national economic interest groups he interviewed thought that placing demands on the Community organs was more advantageous than placing them at the national level. While this does, of course, support Feld's main point, namely that the major efforts of these groups continue to be directed toward national governments, it also illustrates the intermingling of subnational, national and supranational structures described by Rosenau. See W. Feld, 'National Economic Interest Groups and Policy Formation in the EEC', *Political Science Quarterly*, 81: 3, 1966, p. 394.

pattern in foreign policy, he notes, is largely hierarchical, or 'executive', while that of domestic policy is horizontal, or 'legislative'. That is, the foreign policy process is typically carried out in a restricted, centralized decision-structure, while in the domestic policy process there are many dispersed centres of power and responsibility, each with claims on the society's resources, which must be considered and accommodated. Furthermore, the relatively small number of roles in the hierarchical foreign policy structure, as well as the concern of policy with resources outside the state, tends to restrict the frequency of interactions and conflict between groups in the society. As Rosenau observes: 'Foreign policy controversies . . . do not require the participants to treat each other as rivals for scarce resources'.[1] By contrast, domestic policy is marked by a highly complex, intense and competitive pattern of interactions throughout the society.

In this instance community policy, at least as it is evidenced in the EEC states, again deviates significantly from the pure model of foreign policy. One reason, already touched upon, is the interpenetration of states' political systems and the effect of this interpenetration on the structure of foreign policy roles. Connected with this, but more important in this context, is the increasing fragmentation and internal conflict which characterize the foreign policy process – moving it toward Rosenau's 'legislative' pattern – as a state becomes more deeply engaged in integration. It could be argued that integration only intensifies what in fact is a more general experience in contemporary international relations. Our language, inherited from an era when foreign policy was purely 'diplomatic-strategic action' and, as such, the preserve of the sovereign or one or two ministers, encourages and sustains the hierarchical view of foreign policy, where those divergent interests that exist are coordinated under the 'national interest' and all the instrumentalities orchestrated smoothly to that end. Some of the ambiguity and paradox surrounding the behaviour of integrating states might be removed if, instead of this ideal picture, we held fragmentation and contradiction increasingly to be the norm in the foreign policy process. As the techniques and instances of 'informal penetration' have increased, and the range of issues on which states must have dealings across their borders has expanded, the traditional foreign policy hierarchy has been unable to coordinate all the policies advocated and pursued by different departments and agencies – all

[1] Rosenau, 'Foreign Policy as an Issue Area', *op. cit.*, p. 45.

with their different foreign and domestic clientele, different priorities and perceptions, different methods, personnel and contacts. It is in a rather developed example of this kind of environment that the pattern of interactions peculiar to the community policy process takes place.

These observations on the patterns of motivation, roles and interaction in community policy-making suggest that while it can be described as a blend of the characteristics of the domestic and foreign policy processes, it also possesses enough unique qualities to be described, for some purposes, as an issue area in its own right. Not only those three patterns just mentioned, but the types and sources of values sought, the types of actors conflicting and cooperating over their pursuit, and the types of political behaviour in which they engage, differ markedly from those in most accepted models of either diplomatic or domestic political behaviour.

It follows from this that care must be exercised in any attempt to specify the variables likely to influence the behaviour of states engaged in integration. Conceptual frameworks applicable to the study of foreign policy, while a useful point of departure, may need some modification for the analysis of a policy process with so many properties of domestic politics.

Approaches to the study of foreign policy have generally emphasized, in varying proportions, two main sets of theoretical problems. The first of these has to do with the sources of policy and the relative weight of influences on a state's behaviour arising in its non-human or non-political environment, in its external political environment, and in its domestic political and social systems. Some writers, particularly those interested in small states or convinced by the 'third image' of world politics,[1] naturally stress the external factors. Thus neutralism can be explained as the response of small states to a particular distribution of power in the global political system, rather than as a product of indigenous forces. Others, often inadvertently, concentrate almost exclusively on internal factors. The list of 'significant factors in the study of foreign policy' given in one recent text refers to external influences only marginally, under the general category of 'trends and issues'.[2] Increasingly, however, scholars are raising the question of the relative weight of internal

[1] See K. N. Waltz, *Man, the State and War* (New York: 1959) Ch. 6.
[2] R. C. Macridis and K. W. Thompson, 'The Comparative Study of Foreign Policy', in R. C. Macridis (ed.), *Foreign Policy in World Politics*, 2nd edition (Englewood Cliffs, N.J.: 1962) p. 5.

and external factors in a more systematic – if not always more satisfactory – manner.[1]

The other set of problems has to do with the structures and processes through which foreign policy decisions are formulated and executed. The studies by Frankel, Modelski and Snyder are good examples of this general approach, which sees the various influences on foreign policy essentially as inputs into a decision-process, and the process itself as of primary importance.[2] The pre-occupation with the decision-making process has much in common with theories of organizational decision-making developed by Simon and Lasswell, and with the input-output models of political systems associated with Easton, Almond and other contemporary political scientists.[3]

Drawing on these two approaches to the study of foreign policy, as well as recent European experience and the four approaches to integration theory we have identified, it should be possible to put forward some of the more important variables affecting a state's behaviour toward its colleagues in an integrating system. Looking first at the sources of policy, we can discern three main categories of influences: (a) needs and constraints arising in the general non-political environment of the state's decision-makers – that is, from geographical, economic, technological and cultural sources; (b) influences arising in political systems formally external to the state, including the global and regional international systems, the integrating system, and the domestic systems of other states; and (c) influences arising in the state's domestic political and social system. Having identified these variables we can then go on to examine how they feed into the structure and processes of community policy-making in a state.

To some extent, the general non-political environment can be said to provide certain objective limitations on a state's policy toward integration. The influence of the Channel, for example, on

[1] See, for example, Rosenau, *Domestic Sources of Foreign Policy*, and the articles by R. Rummel and M. Haas in J. D. Singer (ed.), *Quantitative International Politics* (New York: 1968) pp. 187–214, 215–44.

[2] See J. Frankel, *The Making of Foreign Policy* (London: 1962) R. C. Snyder, H. W. Bruck and B. Sapin, (eds.), *Foreign Policy Decision-Making* (New York: 1962); G. A. Modelski, *A Theory of Foreign Policy* (New York: 1962).

[3] See H. A. Simon, *Administrative Behaviour*, 2nd edition (New York: 1965) esp. Ch. 1, 4, 5 and 11; H. D. Lasswell and A. Kaplan, *Power and Society* (New Haven: 1950); D. Easton, *A Framework for Political Analysis* (Englewood Cliffs, N.J.: 1965); G. A. Almond and J. S. Coleman (eds.), *The Politics of the Developing Areas* (Princeton: 1960).

British policy toward Europe is not fully explained by the 'state of mind' theory. The conjunction of geographic fact and the level of technological development impeded, and indeed continues to impede, a wide range of contacts and transactions. Similar phenomena have been pointed out in other cases of unsuccessful integration.[1] For the most part, however, it is more useful to describe this environment as influential on state policy to the extent that it is perceived in certain ways by decision-makers. It is in this perspective that the sharing of cultural traits, transport and communications, the relative size of populations, types of economic systems and relations between them (trade and competition), geographical factors (size, shape, borders, distribution of resources), and the level of scientific and technological development, assume their most important role in community policy.

Thus the apparent cultural and social similarities of European states, which to outsiders have often appeared clear and objective forces leading toward unity, have in earlier eras of nationalism been less than evident in expressions of state policies.[2] Similarly, the geographic proximity and compactness of the Six, so favourable a factor in the view of those who foresaw the emergence of a new state, did not determine the behaviour of those states in earlier times when, contrary to its 'logic', they turned to overseas expansion. Finally, the economic interdependence of France and Germany was a fact, objectively observable by any economist, long before the perception by policy-makers of its possible importance for the political relations of the two states. The ECSC and the EEC were not so much 'necessary' outcomes of this interdependence, but products of a political need which suddenly made it politically relevant.

This distinction between the environment as an objective determinant of, or limitation on, state policy, and as an influence which must be perceived in order to have effects, has been drawn most exhaustively by the Sprouts.[3] While the student of integration who

[1] Cf. A. Etzioni, *Political Unification* (New York: 1965) pp. 123, 170–2, for the effects of geographical discontinuity on the union of Egypt and Syria, and on the West Indies Federation; see also R. L. Merritt, 'Noncontiguity and Political Integration', in Rosenau, *Linkage Politics*, pp. 237–72.

[2] European historiography has naturally reinforced these perceptions of traditional distinctiveness. Some historians have attempted to counteract this by pointing out the long tradition of European cultural unity. See, for example, G. Barraclough, *European Unity in Thought and Action* (Oxford: 1963).

[3] H. and M. Sprout, *The Ecological Perspective on Human Affairs* (Princeton: 1965) esp. Ch. 1.

stresses the independent variables on the systemic level may rely, at least implicitly, on propositions about the objective effects of changes in the patterns of these variables, the scholar who takes the state as the ultimate arbiter of its own destiny is obviously obliged to filter these influences through the perceptions of statesmen. In short, he reasserts the primacy of politics. All he can suggest about the 'compellingness' of the non-political environment on the policy of a state towards integration, is that certain combinations of variables increase the *probability* that steps favouring integration will be taken.

When we turn to discuss the more directly political influences on a state's policy, many of these conceptual difficulties disappear, since by definition such influences must be communicated and perceived, in order to have any effect. In the discussion which follows, three sources of external political influences will be identified: the global or regional international system; the integrating system; and the domestic systems of other states.

Integration theory contains many references to the importance of influences arising in the general international political environment of states. Etzioni formalizes the notion, popular among federalist writers, of the 'external elite', whose presence or policy compels states to seek closer ties.[1] An apparent political and military threat from the Soviet Union, and more latterly an economic and technological threat from the United States, have repeatedly been claimed as decisive forces turning European states towards integration. Alternatively, the active encouragement of the United States, in the different forms it took under Marshall, Dulles and the Kennedy 'Grand Design', has been felt by European states throughout the postwar period, although not all of them have accepted American exhortations with the same degree of trust or enthusiasm. Aside from the policies and pressures of the major powers, of course, there are the many demands voiced from less influential quarters of the global system: from former colonies concerned about their preferential trade-relationships (i.e. the British Commonwealth, and the former French African states), from developing states concerned about the distorting or discriminating effects of a large economic unit (i.e. Latin American states) and from those who see integration as forming a new power likely to pose a threat or disturb the nuclear balance (i.e. neutrals and Eastern European states). Finally, the integrating states themselves may perceive the growth of new powers

[1] Etzioni, *op. cit.*, pp. 45–7.

227

(i.e. Japan, China) as threats to their traditional, separate international influence, and seek to regain it, as France and West Germany have tried, through concerted European action.

Aside from the policies and perceived actions of single states, an important influence on community policy from this source is the way in which statesmen read the alignments in the global system. In the early postwar period, for example, as the gulf between the two protagonists of the Cold War became apparent, Western European leaders talked less and less of broad European organizations. Britain's Commonwealth alignment restricted the scope of potential economic arrangements even further. More recently, the atmosphere of *détente* and the expectations of multipolarity in the two camps tended to revive thoughts of European union going beyond the Six and perhaps even extending to Eastern European countries. The same has occurred as the Commonwealth has not only evolved, but been *seen* by both British and West European statesmen as having evolved, into a less weighty and cohesive economic and political organization.

A third influence emanates from the presence, in the global system, of international organizations which encourage or compete with regional organizations. Many states have been quick to take advantage of the provisions of the UN Charter on regionalism, and in fact the various regional Economic Commissions have been major instigators of economic cooperation in Europe, Latin America and Africa, albeit with somewhat mixed success.[1] Not all states have been able to accept an easy compatibility between their commitments to various international organizations. British vacillation between Europe and the Commonwealth is the best-known example. West Germany has been the major European arena in which the debate between the ideas of a narrower European economic union and the broader free trade areas based on an Atlantic system or GATT has taken place. Similar arguments over defence have been rife particularly in French and German policy deliberations. The prospect of a new attempt to form a European defence community, equipped with nuclear weapons, is likely to revive these controversies. In short, the existence of international organizations introduces a delicacy and ambivalence into the making of a state's policy toward integration on a narrower basis.

[1] On this, see J. Siotis, 'The Secretariat of the UN Economic Commission and European Economic Integration', *International Organization*, 19: 2, 1965, pp. 177–202; and R. W. Gregg, 'The UN Regional Economic Commissions and Integration in the Underdeveloped Regions', *ibid.*, 20: 2, 1966, pp. 208–32.

These three sets of influences have their equivalents in the more limited confines of the integrating system. It borders on tautology to say that the policies of a state's partners in an integration-scheme tend to be more salient than those of other states; what is less evident is that in most such systems there are one or two leading states from whom the others persistently take their cues. In military alliances like NATO and the Warsaw Pact the influence of the nuclear super-power is overwhelming; even the more intransigent allies, such as France and Rumania, are incapable of forming alternative poles of influence within the system, but must, on the whole, act purely negatively. As the EEC states are well aware, this pattern of dominance also exists, perhaps less evidently to outsiders, in systems whose basic rationale is economic. Formal voting power aside, it has been observed often that when France and Germany agree, the others must ultimately give way; when they do not, little can be achieved. The rarity of such absolute cases of accord or discord is what gives smaller powers their scope for action.

This relates closely to the second source of influences on policy, which lies in the pattern of alignment between states in the integrating systems. Certainly, the myth or reality of a 'Paris-Bonn' axis must be a constant consideration in the policy-processes of the other four states. Whether the impending threat of a coalition of the 'Five' ever had a comparable influence on French policy toward British entry or on the advancement of integration, is somewhat more doubtful – partly because the 'alliance' was strenuously denied and, in any case, it was unenthusiastically supported by West Germany. The probable entry of Britain and three small states into the Community will render the patterns of alignment considerably more complex. The existence of a tripartite (or, if Italy is included, quadripartite) balance of big powers should provide more flexibility for these states and more options for the smaller ones. Whether it will result in stability and growth is, however, another question.

Integration theorists have always placed a great deal of importance on the role of system-wide organizations as influences on the policies of states. Particularly the functionalists and neofunctionalists tend to attribute to these organizations important resources for affecting the behaviour of their member-states, whether this be through persuasion and example, the creation of multiple cross-national ties and habits of cooperation, or the use of their limited financial and legal powers. This type of argument, as we have seen, is developed in most studies of regional organizations and in some writings on the development of global organizations.[1] It runs counter to the more traditional and widely-accepted assumption that the behaviour of international organizations can really only reflect the outcome of the power-contest between its member-states. Which of these views is more accurate in a given case depends partly on the immediacy of the international organization's function for the state, and partly on the extent to which its activities penetrate the national society. Thus French indifference to the UN has been a consequence, not only of the anticolonial accusations of the fifties but also of the French preoccupation, in the early postwar years, with pressing European rather than more distant world problems.[2] The symbolic impact of the EEC institutions, on the other hand, is matched by the increasing influence of their activities in the everyday economic and social life of its member states.

This is not to say that the presence of such organizations invariably has a positive effect on a state's policy toward integration. Tactically its officials may make damaging errors, as the Commission did during the events leading up to the crisis of 1965-6, seriously alienating the French (or, according to some, creating the opportunity for France to express a much deeper opposition). Not only failures of the skills and capacities of the organization's officials, but the very assumptions, tacit agreements and entrenched habits on which its position is based, can be allies for states determined to slow the pace of change. The Commission's caution about upsetting the delicate balance of interests by which the present level of integration is sustained, grows naturally from its role as guardian and overseer of the Community's development. But this caution by itself tends to ally the Commission with those national policy-makers who fear the consequences of increased supranationality.

Most of the influences on community policy from the global international system and the integrating system are transmitted through the formal channels of foreign policy relationships. A third

[1] Two studies of global organization from this perspective are E. B. Haas, *Beyond the Nation-State* (Stanford: 1964); and J. P. Sewell, *Functionalism and World Politics* (Princeton: 1966). Haas deals with the International Labour Organization, Sewell with the various UN agencies for financing economic development.

[2] Cf. J. B. Duroselle, 'France and the United Nations', in N. J. Padelford and L. M. Goodrich (eds.), *The United Nations in the Balance* (New York: 1965) pp. 331–49, esp. p. 338.

set of influences, however, occurs in less regular and controlled ways. These are the influences that pass from the government and society of one state into the society of another without the mediation, and often without the knowledge, of its government. Andrew Scott refers to this type of relationship as 'informal access', and distinguishes five main types.[1] The first is informal governmental access, where the agents of governments seek to influence the policies of other states through such devices as cultural exchange, various kinds of aid, communications and other political activities. This can, of course, have sinister overtones, depending on the state of relations between the two countries concerned. But clearly the theory behind the French and German governments' support of the postwar programme of Franco-German cultural exchanges was that the resulting change of popular attitudes would filter up into the political process and be a source of favourable policies. In the present European system opportunities for this kind of informal access are legion.

A second form of access Scott calls 'quasi-governmental'. Here organizations and activities with some special governmental connections seek to influence other governments' policies. Fears of this kind of influence are presumably an important ingredient in the hesitation of European governments to encourage the takeover of national corporations by those of other countries. A third type is nongovernmental access, where businessmen, tourists and similar groups of private citizens make contacts and exchanges across state boundaries. Clearly such contacts form the bulk of informal access in Western Europe, although the political effects of the information and influence thus transmitted can easily be exaggerated.

The fourth type mentioned by Scott, informal access by an international organization, has already been discussed as an influence from the international system. The EEC has penetrated national societies to a substantial degree, in that political parties, interest groups and individuals have representatives in, and dealings with, its institutions quite apart from their own governments; and conversely these contacts serve to transmit the organization's influence back to the national societies. By the same process – and this is Scott's fifth type – states can gain access to these groups, parties and individuals through the medium of the international organization and thus indirectly gain access to their society.

Thus there are a number of ways in which a state's policy can be

[1] Scott, *op. cit.*, pp. 193–4.

influenced informally by other states. An integrating system such as that of the Six has great scope for such techniques and processes, all of which underline the blurring of the classic distinction between domestic and foreign affairs, or between the internal and external sources of policy.

This point is worth bearing in mind when we turn to those influences on a state's community policy which, formally at least, can be said to arise in its own political and social system. The following analysis focuses, not on the environment in which a state acts, but on whether certain types of states are more likely than others to engage in a process of integration. Each of the theorists whose work we have criticized has advanced a number of propositions as to which internal characteristics of states have a bearing on integration. Some of these propositions are more or less unanimously accepted, while others are contradictory. The anarchic conditions of integration theory are nowhere better illustrated than in this area.

Many of the variables judged important by these writers pertain to a state's economic system. Neofunctionalists, comparing the level of integration in Western Europe with the inconclusive attempts elsewhere in the world, are more or less agreed that advanced industrial states are more likely than the predominantly agricultural, primary-product states of the less developed world, to undertake the types of cross-national economic contacts seen as preliminary to political integration. A more orthodox functionalist or federalist, however, might argue that increased perception of a common need such as industrialization and security against the vicissitudes of the world market, will act as substitutes for the more familiar capitalist drive for broader markets. The argument is certainly attractive, and consistent with a respectable line of integration theory. However, as yet the experience of Latin American and African states has not borne it out. Latin American states, for example, have discovered the difficulty of integrating on a continental basis economies that can hardly be described as integrated nationally.[1] At the same time, high levels of economic development are usually so strongly correlated with favourable political and social factors (such as social pluralism) that it is risky to place too much weight on this element alone.

[1] See C. W. Anderson, *Politics and Economic Change in Latin America* (Princeton: 1967) pp. 18–44, and 47–66; E. B. Haas and P. C. Schmitter, 'Economics and Differential Patterns of Political Integration', in *International Political Communities* (New York: 1966) pp. 259–99.

Another problem arises over the degree of planning and governmental involvement in the economy most likely to enhance integration with other states. The EEC, with its broad range of official economic philosophies, gives no clear lead in this matter. On the surface, at least, the more centrally controlled the economy, the more it would seem to be an effective asset of governmental policy: if that policy favours political integration, much economic leverage is possible; if the government is against integration, there will be few autonomous market-forces able to act across borders and gradually change the policy.[1] A free-enterprise system, on the other hand, may set up more persistent pressures towards integration, while being less amenable to mobilization in support of specific governmental policies in that direction.

Beyond these broad economic issues are a host of more immediate ones. Short-term economic changes can be an important force to shift government policy. Fears of decrease of French industrial competitiveness after May 1968 were said to be one reason for that government's hesitancy about British entry to the EEC. The debate in Britain over the Community has likewise focused on the immediate issue of prices and on whether the cold wind of competition will invigorate or freeze particular industries. The costliness of the agricultural sector of the West German economy, and the need for development capital and a market for surplus labour in Italy are well-known examples of specific economic problems acting as an impetus toward integration, rather than a source of doubts about it. Theorists have also delineated a great many sociological variables said to influence governments to support integration. Many of the issues raised here parallel those raised over economic factors. It is held, for example, that modernized societies, characterized by stability, social mobility, pluralistic group-structure and a universalistic scientific ethos, are more likely to throw up demands for integration than are less developed societies. Neofunctionalist thought has stressed the value of pluralism, where governments have to steer a precarious course between the converging and conflicting demands emerging from different social sectors and often coalescing with interests in other states. It is this kind of socio-political environment which neofunctionalists claim enables those desiring integration to fashion favourable, if unstable, constellations of support. By the same token, pluralism usually requires gradualism

---

[1] Comparisons of the EEC and Comecon would be useful for exploring this hypothesis.

as well. Rapid federation, on the other hand, is more likely to come about between like-minded rulers of more monolithic and less developed societies.[1]

Other theorists, like Deutsch, stress different patterns of social behaviour and attitudes as likely to increase a state's propensity to seek international contacts. With many of these forces, however, it is difficult to discern their effects on integration, because they are often directed to national political change as well. Social and spatial mobility – however it be measured – is a condition for national political modernization as well as for international integration; in this sense, the two processes are drawing on, or competing for, the same social resources. This makes it difficult to assess the weight of the variable in either instance. It is easy to suggest lists of the sociological factors which might affect governmental support for integration. Such factors as the size and composition of population (by such attributes as age, ethnic origin, education, literacy, occupation, income, urbanization) and the predominant patterns of social behaviour and attitudes (communications flows, media consumption, travel, opinions) spring to mind immediately, and are easily measured.[2] The productive, and more difficult, stage of such analysis, is the judgement of the relative weight and effective combinations of such variables, and the explanation of their correlation with policies favouring integration.

Related to the economic and social attributes of the state is a rather more nebulous group, often referred to as 'cultural attributes'. This would include such long-term influences on policy as the prevalent pattern of education and socialization, the literary, artistic, mythical, and historical tradition, and the dominant religious and ethical values and philosophical systems in a society. Also related to this group of factors is the state of scientific and technological development of the society; this is often reflected in economic life, for example through the communications and transport systems. Despite the difficulty of measuring precisely the political effects of these cultural traits, theorists of integration, like writers on foreign

[1] The formation of a federation of sheikhdoms in the Persian Gulf, for example, appears to be largely a matter of persuading a handful of men that it is in their best interests to collaborate on defence. While this may not prove easy, it is likely to require less complex tactics than those necessary to increase integration in the European Community.

[2] See K. W. Deutsch, 'Toward an Inventory of Basic Trends and Patterns in Comparative and International Politics', in J. N. Rosenau (ed.), *International Politics and Foreign Policy* (New York: 1961) pp. 461–6.

policy, are reluctant to leave them off the ledgers. One can certainly see that some cultural qualities, such as the extent to which education and patterns of family life are authoritarian or encourage the perpetuation of ethnocentric values, could have a significant effect on a state's approach to integration.

Many influences on a state's inclination to engage in integration can be traced to its political institutions and to the quality of its political life. Some of these political characteristics, such as the degree of governmental legitimacy, participation, pluralism or coherence, are closely related to the economic, social and cultural characteristics mentioned earlier. In addition, the political qualities of the state are manifested in the way decisions are made in domestic, foreign and community policy. A useful way of tying together this examination of internal factors would thus be to look at the policy-process and show the points at which different influences feed into it. We can distinguish three stages of the policy-process: (1) the 'input' stage, where demands and support for actions by the government are expressed, and information obtained; (2) the decision-making stage, where a series of choices are made and conflicts resolved, within the governmental structure, as to future policy on specific issues; (3) the 'output' stage, which involves the execution, enforcement and appraisal of governmental decisions.[1]

Demands and support for policies are usually expressed through three types of medium – interest groups, political parties and public opinion. The first of these, the interest group, is a widespread and extremely varied creature. There are broad interest groups, such as the large national trade-union or industrial organizations, whose concern is usually only marginally with matters of foreign policy, but which, like the Trades Union Congress and the Confederation of British Industries, inevitably find themselves deeply and continuously involved in governmental deliberations over economic integration. There are narrower groups whose interests may from time to time be raised in questions of foreign policy but whose preoccupation is with domestic affairs. There are *ad hoc* groups and 'ginger groups' like the Action Committee for a United States of Europe, specifically concerned with the goals of integration. And there are the various advisory groups and coalitions of interests close to or within the governmental structure itself.

---

[1] On these processes, see esp. Easton, *op. cit.*, and Almond and Coleman, *op. cit.*, pp. 3–64.

Clearly the role and relative influence of these types of group will vary from state to state and from issue to issue. In foreign policy, traditionally, the role of interest groups has on the whole been minimal, while in matters of integration, where the pattern of decision-making more closely involves domestic considerations, their role is likely to be greater. In some cases, interest groups perform the functions of 'interest articulation' – they form nodes of opinion and demands, seeking access to the governmental system to realize their desires. Methods can include petitions, shows of voting or financial strength, threats, and presentation of reasoned arguments in the press, in pamphlets, or in governmental meetings and memoranda. In other cases, of course, the process may be reversed, and governments and parties may use the interest groups as allies in intramural struggles.[1]

A recent study of the behaviour of national economic interest groups in the EEC demonstrates that the cross-national, 'umbrella' organizations of interest groups are of less significance, and that attempts to gain access to the EEC organs remain far less frequent, than activities on the national level.[2] But to say that national governments continue to dominate the channels of political influence does not preclude the possibility that their policies will evolve to support increased supranationality if the force of their national interest groups is sufficiently behind such a development. All this, however, assumes a fairly special type of political culture, in which the interplay of interests has replaced the clash of ideologies, and in which power is sufficiently diffused so that governments can and must respond to the expression of group interests. This type of political culture – close to Almond and Verba's 'civic culture'[3] – seems to be a vital requisite of the neofunctionalists and others who would reach political integration through the economic sectors of society. It is less clear that if political integration were approached more directly, this sort of pattern of interest groups would be necessary, or even an advantage.

Political parties share this function of expressing demands and support in the political system, but they also serve as aggregators of interests, that is, coalitions of groups whose demands, while more or less compatible, may not be identical, but who see advantages in

[1] Cf. L. Milbrath, 'Interest Groups and Foreign Policy', in Rosenau, *Domestic Sources of Foreign Policy*, esp. p. 250.

[2] Feld, *op. cit.*, pp. 401–11.

[3] G. A. Almond and S. Verba, *The Civic Culture* (Boston: 1965) Ch. 1, esp. pp. 5–10.

combining their political weight. European party systems tend to be mixtures of very large parties, such as the two main German and British parties, the Gaullist party in France, and the Italian Christian Democrats, which are aggregations or loose coalitions of this kind, and very small parties such as those in France and Italy, formed either out of specific interests (such as the 'poujadist' movement) or out of ideological schisms (such as the variety of left-wing factions in France).

As the French experience over the ratification of the EDC demonstrated rather well, the stability of a national party system can affect decisively that state's ability to develop a consistent community policy. In West Germany and Italy, where large Christian Democratic parties have dominated postwar politics, or in the Fifth French Republic, some continuity of policy could be·expected. One would also expect that where smaller parties are the rule, or where government consists of unstable coalitions, a state's relations with the integration-movement are likely to be less predictable, this in turn conditioning the behaviour of interest groups toward the integrating institutions. The latters' preoccupation is likely to be more with getting and maintaining influence on the domestic scene. Such, however, has not always been the case. The EDC experience aside, French policy toward Europe under the Fourth Republic was on the whole remarkably consistent, largely because throughout the regular rise and fall of cabinets, the same men tended to reappear in the posts most relevant to foreign affairs. Moreover if, under the Fifth Republic, the general basis of policy has been more evident and consistent, it cannot be said that in execution and tactics it has been particularly predictable.[1]

Public opinion feeds into the national policy-process indirectly through groups, parties and representatives, and more directly through its expression in communications media. Its weight, however, is notoriously difficult to assess. It is possible to discern certain cases, such as the change in French European policy after the narrow verdict of the election following the 1965–6 crisis, where a government can be said to have responded to a dramatic expression of popular opinion. On the other hand, public opinion also tends to be passive, and is moulded by the very way in which issues are formulated. For example, the expressions of elite and mass opinions

[1] This, however, may have more to do with personalities and with the constitution than with the party system, the latter having been reshaped to a great extent by these two forces.

tabulated in Deutsch's study[1] are grouped in terms of the alternative concepts of European unity as developed and presented by governments and the press. Patterns of opinion might look significantly different if a number of hypothetical models were included, or if some of the alternatives were arbitrarily removed by the questioners.

Again, the influence of public opinion on a state's policy toward integration will depend, like the influence of groups and parties, on the responsiveness of the governmental system – which can be a function of the extent to which participation is possible, and valued, in the society, and to which the ruling group feels its position vulnerable. The British parliamentary system, with the four- or five-year stewardships it usually affords strong majority governments, permits determined leaders to ignore or mould public opinion over long periods. In the face of the current opposition to EEC entry in British opinion, the Conservative Government will clearly find this a helpful asset. Much of the strength and boldness of French policy toward Europe in the early 1960s derived in much the same way from de Gaulle's domestic invulnerability, backed as he was by a solid majority in the National Assembly. On the other hand, where divergent views on integration are represented at the highest level, as in recent Italian coalition governments, policy is bound to be hesitant, contradictory and reactive.

At the actual decision-making stage, many other variables come into play. Governmental decisions tend to be complex and continuous processes of interaction between political leaders, the representatives of interest groups, advisers and civil servants – the composition of the 'decisional unit' varying over time and from issue to issue.[2] As the breadth of Snyder's framework indicates, a vast number of variables are potentially relevant, among them being the role-structure, the personalities and motivations of individuals (or what Rosenau calls 'idiosyncratic' variables[3]), their 'definition of the situation', organizational pressures, and the amount of information available. It is, for example, at this point in the policy process that the abilities and experience of senior bureaucrats become particularly relevant. It is here, presumably, that the effects on bureaucrats of international contacts or a period of

[1] K. W. Deutsch, L. J. Edinger, R. C. Macridis and R. L. Merritt, *France, Germany and the Western Alliance* (New York: 1967) pp. 74, 76, 163, 165.

[2] Snyder *et al.*, *op. cit.*, pp. 92–7.

[3] Rosenau, 'Pre-Theories and Theories of Foreign Policy', *op. cit.*, p. 43.

secondment to Brussels, are expected to make their impress on national policies.

Another important influence will of course be the institutional system in which policy is made. The more executive-dominated it is, like the Fifth Republic, the less the influence of interest groups is likely to be – on routine community policy at least – and the more its making will resemble the foreign policy process. The more influential the legislature in the governmental system, as, by comparison, in Italy or West Germany, the more the making of community policy is likely to resemble a domestic legislative process. It is tempting to add that the more a state is able to treat community policy as foreign policy, the more it will do so, and the more its policy is likely to show either powerful support for, or powerful opposition to, integration. On the other hand, perhaps the more the community policy-process resembles domestic policy, the less the government's freedom of action; this means that both its ability to halt integration and its capacity to give it a dramatic push forward, are seriously restricted.

In the third stage of the policy-process, which concerns the execution, enforcement and appraisal of the decisions, the relevant variables again have to do with the capacities of the bureaucracy, and of the military and other agencies through which policy is carried out. It is often claimed, for example, that the quality of French bureaucrats and diplomatic officials (in particular their detailed knowledge of the Treaty of Rome and their facility in the legal and political labyrinth of Brussels) accounts for the effectiveness of France's European policy. And the effectiveness of that policy, as judged in Paris, then becomes, by the process of feedback, an 'input' into future decisions.

The analysis of a state's capabilities – economic, administrative, military – can also indicate the extent of its dependence on other states for the success of its policies. The functionalist argument holds that an increasing awareness by states of the limits of their capabilities drives them to seek cooperation with other states and increasingly to tailor their policies to fit the common interest thus created. Federalist theory, too, relies on a sort of capability-analysis: as states perceive themselves less and less able to guarantee the security of their citizens or to perform the rudimentary functions of government, they are driven to amalgamate with others in the same predicament so as to create a new unit with the necessary capacities.

It should be clear that there are many more variables which might affect a state's policies toward integration. In this chapter we have been able to touch on a few of those mentioned frequently in the literature on integration, and to suggest how the policy-process through which they find expression in the integrating system differs from both the classic model of foreign policy, and the normal processes of domestic policy.

In the previous chapter it was argued that political integration is best seen as a condition of the international system as a whole, and that important variables for explaining change can be found in the system as it evolves according to its own dynamics. In the present chapter we have noted that the system can also affect integration by influencing the behaviour of its units, the states, and, moreover, that much of the integrative process can not be explained except at the level of the nation-state as actor.

In one sense, this represents a vindication of the approaches, like pluralism, which focus primarily on the ingredients and processes of decision-making in the autonomous nation-states which constitute the integrating system. In fact, neofunctionalist theory now places considerable emphasis on the nation-state as a unit of analysis.[1] It is clear to most theorists that examining some of the factors surveyed in this chapter is helpful in offsetting the somewhat misleading picture of automaticity and determinism to which a purely systemic analysis often leads.

In another sense, however, this treatment of the state as a major actor in integration diverges considerably from the classic realist picture of foreign policy which lies behind many pluralist and federalist assumptions. The notion of the 'penetrated state' and the suggestion of a distinctive 'community policy' issue area which blends characteristics of the foreign and domestic issue areas, both serve to dissolve two of the certainties of the classical view. The concept of the impermeable, autonomous state, and the concrete distinction between foreign and domestic policy, are simply not tenable in the context of integration. If integration theory is to develop, then, it must draw on studies of the behaviour of particular states in integrating systems. But these studies are likely to be in an idiom unfamiliar to other theorists who traditionally have stressed this level of analysis.

[1] See, for example, L. N. Lindberg and S. A. Scheingold, *Europe's Would-Be Polity* (Englewood Cliffs: 1970) esp. Ch. 3.

8 Political Integration and Political Man

The previous two chapters have concentrated on the levels of analysis most familiar to students of international relations. One chapter examined political integration as a process of change in an international system; the other explored it on the level of the state, as a problem in foreign policy analysis. It may be, however, that despite their seeming comprehensiveness these two levels of analysis do not subsume all the important variables which might account for international political integration.

The literature on international relations, including that on the subject of integration, contains numerous references to a third level of analysis – having to do with the attitudes and behaviour of individuals as political actors. As Kenneth Waltz has shown, an important body of thought in international relations holds that the nature of man, rather than the state or the international system, is the ultimate source of war. Pessimistic thinkers of this school, seeing change in human nature as unlikely and any other solution as superficial, view the condition of peace as fragile and ultimately dependent upon the varying skills of statesmen. Optimists, on the other hand, seek the key to peace in man's increasing understanding of his own behaviour and attitudes. If the former group have at times been guilty of conservative obscurantism, the 'solutions' of the latter have often been simplistic and naive.[1] In recent years, however, as the study of elite images and public attitudes has become a widespread and accepted feature of international relations literature both the modesty of its claims and the sophistication of its results have increased.[2]

Explanations of political change in terms of the qualities of individual leaders or the preferences of the common man are not, of

[1] K. N. Waltz, *Man, the State and War* (New York: 1959) esp. Chs. 1 and 2.
[2] The best introduction to recent social-psychological work on international relations is H. C. Kelman (ed.), *International Behaviour* (New York: 1965).

241

course, new to students of politics. Indeed, whether in polemical popular writings, in histories or even in the works of social scientists determined to examine processes and systems, there are recurring references to the crucial role of individual leaders in postwar European integration. It is often a deceptively simple picture of strength and dedication, hesitancy or intransigent opposition: Churchill rallying the European Movement and then disillusioning the federalists; Monnet operating through informal contacts to create political and institutional innovations and initiatives; Adenauer manoevering West Germany back into the front rank in the context of European organizations and *rapprochement* with France; and de Gaulle, the epitome of individual political will, vision and cunning, stemming and perhaps even turning the European tide.

On a broader scale, too, it is natural to believe that a major political change such as European integration will require a transformation of the way the average European thinks and acts. For some, the more extreme 'melting pot' theories might be compelling; for others, European Man is likely to remain rooted in his national culture but with an overlay of new political allegiances and cultural perspectives. In any theory of political change – particularly one with strong doctrinal components – propositions about the emergence of a 'new man' of some kind are rarely difficult to find.

The task of the political scientist is clearly to put such notions to the test. To what extent do the personalities, attitudes, images and behaviour of individual leaders or 'men in the street' really affect the process of integration? To what extent, in turn, does the process affect them?

It is not necessary to define integration in terms of individual patterns of behaviour or mental dispositions, in order to accept that explanations of change in individual attitudes and behaviour can contribute to the development of a theory of political integration. And while social-psychological variables may prove to be of fundamental importance in integration, to seek an all-embracing explanation on that level could probably prove as misleading as theories of peace in terms of 'mental health'. But in the four approaches to integration which were examined in earlier chapters, there are many important assumptions or propositions – not always made explicit – about the role of individual attitudes and behaviour in the integrative process. Having drawn some of these out, we can now go on to suggest ways of developing them more systematically, and to show where social-psychological propositions might fit in a broader approach to integration. Change on the individual level might well prove to be a precondition of, or at least complementary to, change both in the behaviour of states and in the international system.[1]

It should be clear, then, that to advocate that more attention be paid to this level of analysis is not to claim that the whole of integration theory ought to fall under the purview of Pavlov or Freud. It is merely to suggest that the work of theorists who have sought explanations of social and political change on this level might help us explain many puzzling or obscure problems of integration. Economists, sociologists and political scientists concerned with problems of socio-economic and political development have often used psychological insights in this way. Max Weber, for example, advanced, in a heavily qualified and elaborate form, the argument that the psychological effects on individuals of their membership in Protestant sects were a crucial source of modern capitalism. Following this lead, David McClelland has undertaken a detailed profile of the kinds of attitudes associated with historical cases of economic expansion. Other theorists have examined the social-psychological conditions prevalent in 'backward' and modernizing societies.[2] None of these writers offers anything approaching a single-factor explanation of social change; all stress the interdependence of sociological, psychological, cultural, economic and political variables.

Central to any analysis of integration on this level are propositions about the nature, formation, change and effects of individuals' political attitudes. 'An attitude', according to a recent text on social psychology, 'is an organized and consistent manner of thinking, feeling and reacting with regard to people, groups, social issues, or, more generally, any events in one's environment. Its essential components are thoughts and beliefs, feelings (or emotions), and

[1] In exercises of this kind, charges of reductionism are always liable to be raised. Here there is no claim that explanations of integration must ultimately derive from psychological analysis. The best comparison is perhaps economic theory, where explanation on the level of the system (macro-economics) and of the firm (micro-economics) is complemented by a generally accepted set of social-psychological assumptions which, despite their lack of interest for most economists, are not in principle unresearchable. Discoveries that 'economic man' is not quite what economic theory assumed him to be will not necessarily bring the edifice crashing, but will show the limits of explanation on the other levels and perhaps clear up many anomalies.

[2] See M. Weber, 'The Protestant Sects and the Spirit of Capitalism', in H. H. Gerth and C. W. Mills, *From Max Weber: Essays in Sociology* (New York: 1958) pp. 302–22; D. C. McClelland, *The Achieving Society* (Princeton: 1961); E. C. Banfield, *The Moral Basis of a Backward Society* (Glencoe, Illinois: 1958); D. Lerner, *The Passing of Traditional Society* (New York: 1958).

tendencies to react.'[1] As employed by social psychologists, the notion of attitude is only marginally related to the fascinating but difficult psychological subjects of personality and motivation. As Brown explains, an attitude is 'a concept used by the social psychologist in order to explain without complicated references to individual psychology, with which he is not primarily concerned, what happens between stimulus and response to produce the observed effect.'[2] An attitude, then, is an attributed quality designed as an explanation of behaviour.

Social psychologists have stressed different aspects of this general concept. Some have placed most emphasis on the elements of perception, cognition or orientation – what an individual 'sees' of the world, and how he structures this knowledge. Asch, for example, defines an attitude as 'an organization of experiences and data with reference to an object. It is a structure of a hierarchical order, the parts of which function in accordance with their position in the whole . . . (as well as) a quasi-open structure functioning as part of a wider context.'[3] Newcomb's definition, although broader, also stresses cognition and structure: 'An attitude is the individual's organization of psychological processes, as inferred from his behaviour, with respect to some aspect of the world which he distinguishes from other aspects. It represents the residue of his previous experience with which he approaches any subsequent situation including that aspect and, together with the contemporary influences in such a situation, determines his behaviour in it.'[4] In this sense, attitudes are closely related to what Boulding calls the 'image'.[5] They are the personal theories or models by means of which we interpret the world around us. In their pathological form they are often referred to as stereotypes or paranoid delusions.

Other theorists place more stress on the affective emotional aspect of attitudes. The preferences, loyalties and values of individuals are, in practice, inseparable from their perceptions and images, The former shape, and are in turn shaped by, the latter. Nevertheless, an analytic distinction is often made. As Klineberg observes, the

[1] W. W. Lambert and W. E. Lambert, *Social Psychology* (Englewood Cliffs, N.J.: 1964) p. 50.

[2] J. A. C. Brown, *Techniques of Persuasion* (Harmondsworth, Middx.: 1963) p. 37.

[3] S. E. Asch, 'Attitudes as Cognitive Structures', in M. Jahoda and N. Warren (eds.), *Attitudes* (Harmondsworth, Middx.: 1966) p. 32.

[4] T. M. Newcomb, 'On the Definition of Attitude', in Jahoda and Warren, *op. cit.*, p. 22.

[5] K. E. Boulding, *The Image* (Ann Arbor, Michigan: 1956).

term 'attitude', as opposed to 'opinions', is used 'to refer to affective or emotional components, our feelings for or against others, as well as our readiness for certain forms of behaviour. The distinction is difficult to maintain, however, since opinions and attitudes are usually closely allied.'[1] According to another writer, an attitude is 'a disposition to react favourably or unfavourably to a class of objects.'[2] On the surface, at least, attitudes in this sense are of particular relevance to political science, which is centrally concerned with conflicts over values and with the loyalties of individuals to their social groupings. This sense, too, is perhaps closest to the layman's understanding of the term.

A third body of theorists ties attitudes more closely with behaviour, seeing their significance primarily in the individual's assessments of his own capacities for influencing his environment, and his propensity to undertake such activities. According to Allport: 'An attitude is a mental and neural state of readiness, organized through experience, exerting a directive or dynamic influence upon the individual's response to all objects and situations with which it is related.'[3] In his approach to foreign policy analysis, Snyder also uses this concept of attitude, linking it both with internal qualities such as motivation and with the cognitive and affective aspects summed up in the phrase 'definition of the situation'. Attitudes, he writes, are 'the readiness of individual decision-makers to be motivated.'[4] What Almond and Verba refer to as the 'evaluational orientation' of individuals towards the political system is also close to this usage. Evaluation involves the combination of cognition and emotion to produce judgements about political objects, judgements implying decision and action.[5]

We can thus discern three aspects of an individual's political attitudes: his perceptions and theories about political life; his feelings and emotions toward political objects, symbols and groups; and his sense of personal competence, efficacy and involvement in political matters. Clearly the nature of, and the relationships between, these aspects of an individual's political attitudes and their effect on

[1] O. Klineberg, *The Human Dimension in International Relations* (New York: 1964) p. 48.

[2] I. Sarnoff, 'Social Attitudes and the Resolution of Motivational Conflict', in Jahoda and Warren, *op. cit.*, p. 279.

[3] G. W. Allport, 'Attitudes in the History of Social Psychology', in Jahoda and Warren, *op. cit.*, p. 20.

[4] R. C. Snyder, H. W. Bruck and B. Sapin (eds.), *Foreign Policy Decision-Making* (New York: 1962) pp. 137–67, esp. p. 149.

[5] G. A. Almond and S. Verba, *The Civic Culture* (Boston: 1965) pp. 14–15.

integration will vary with his position in society. To this problem we must turn next.

As we have seen, nearly all the literature on integration relies on a clear distinction between elites and the general public, whether the basis of this distinction be access to communication and information, technocratic and administrative expertise, functional specialization, interest group leadership or simply the distribution of the assets of political power (wealth, symbols, force).[1] Since, by definition, these elites either exercise political power directly or consistently, or are in a position to influence strongly those who do, it would seem a productive and economical research strategy simply to concentrate on their complex of attitudes towards integration. If we know what the elites perceive, reason, believe and intend, can we not predict their actions and hence the direction of integration? If so, matters are simplified enormously; there is no longer any need to examine the whole range of background conditions which in some way contribute to change if we can have direct access to the focus of that change.

Matters, unfortunately, are more complicated than this. The extent to which elite attitudes are reliable indicators of the probable direction of integration depends on such factors as the internal homogeneity of the elite groups, the structure of the decision-making institutions, the general distribution of political skills in the societies concerned, and the degree to which particular issues affect deep-seated values or merely superficial feelings among the general public.[2] Clearly elite attitudes would be almost all we needed to study if the elites were homogeneous and consistent, the decision structures monolithic, political skills monopolized by the elites, and if the issues were of superficial, passing interest to an unmobilized public. Needless to say, this is rarely the case, especially in Western Europe.

To some extent crisis situations or recognized points of rapid change provide a semblance of these conditions, if only by narrowing the focus of decision-making to a small group or even an individual. Because of their strategic location, their access to points of leverage and their personal commitment, we have rightly focused

---

[1] A good discussion of the concept of elites is in T. B. Bottomore, *Elites and Society* (Harmondsworth, Middx.: 1966). For basic definitions, see esp. pp. 9 and 14. Cf. H. D. Lasswell, *Politics: Who Gets What, When, How* (Cleveland: 1958) Ch. 1; G. A. Almond, 'The Elites and Foreign Policy' in J. N. Rosenau (ed.), *International Politics and Foreign Policy* (New York: 1961) pp. 269–70.

[2] On these points, see R. Inglehart, 'Public Opinion and Regional Integration' *International Organization* 24: 4, 1970, p. 764–73.p

at different times on de Gaulle's vision of Europe in contrast to Monnet's.[1] More recently we have seen the importance of a personal 'meeting of minds' between Prime Minister Heath and President Pompidou at a critical juncture in Europe's development. At certain times, then, to know how leaders think may indeed be to know how events will go.

For other purposes, however, it might prove more fruitful to examine the nature and distribution of political attitudes in the general public. For most of the public, even in the mobilized societies of developed, Western democracies, interest and participation in politics is at best sporadic.[2] A much smaller section, the 'attentive public', will exhibit a continuing awareness of political life, a well-developed set of loyalties and a sense of civic competence. With the proviso that the boundary between these two groups is flexible, it is largely on the latter that studies of public attitudes focus.

The attitudes of the general public are important for integration in two main respects: first, how they are related at any given time to the attitudes and actions of the elites; and secondly, how they develop over time. To examine the first means not only to see what channels are available for the expression of public attitudes at the level of decisions. It means also studying the degree of congruence between aggregate public attitudes, elite attitudes and government policies.[3] Beyond looking at the congruence of aggregate patterns, it would be very valuable to conduct individual interviews in search of an incipient syndrome of European Man.

In many ways, the study of changes in public attitudes towards integration over fairly long periods of time seems even more promising. In a very significant set of findings, Inglehart has shown that attitudes of individuals toward their own nations and towards European integration can be predicted more accurately from the historical circumstances in which those attitudes were formed and the 'age cohort' to which the individual belongs, than from the alleged effects of the life-cycle.[4] In short, an individual does not

[1] See, for example, J. B. Duroselle, 'General de Gaulle's Europe and Jean Monnet's Europe' in *World Today*, 22: 1, 1966, pp. 1–13.

[2] For evidence on the size of the politically aware public in different countries, see Almond and Verba, *op. cit.*, Chs. 2 and 5 to 7. Cf. Inglehart, *op. cit.*, pp. 768–9.

[3] See Inglehart, *op. cit.*, p. 779, for evidence that in Germany and Britain, but not in France, congruence between elite preferences and government policy (1961–65) was high.

[4] *Ibid.*, pp. 786–95.

necessarily become more conservative or more nationalistic as he grows older. If his attitudes and those of his generation were formed in a period of general enthusiasm for the 'European idea' and general disillusionment with nationalism (such as the aftermath of World War II), these attitudes are likely to persist in later life and be carried into political roles.

Whether we choose to examine the attitudes and behaviour of elites or of the general public, it is clear that much of our analysis must rely on propositions about how individuals acquire and change their images of political life. As to acquisition, first, it might be helpful to draw a few simple distinctions. It is possible, first, to distinguish between long-term or persistent social and political influences on the one hand, and more ephemeral influences on the other. A further distinction can be made between directed and un-directed processes of influence. And finally, we can distinguish between the acquisition of attitudes by communication, on the one hand, and by interaction on the other. Each of these three distinctions can be illustrated with examples from the literature on integration, and from recent European experience.

Among the more persistent social sources of the political attitudes of individuals, are the processes of education and socialization, which occur not only in formal institutions such as school and the family, but through continuous exposure to communications media or working and social groups. A favourite occupation of more impressionistic historians and psychologists has always been to trace the foreign policies of states, the behaviour of political leaders or the 'national character', to such sources, implying that these provide continuous reinforcement for a particular structure of political attitudes.[1] Attempts to develop 'European' universities, to reform European historiography so as to eliminate the more blatant nationalistic biases from textbooks, and the whole functionalist argument about the effects of international cooperation in matters that figure in the everyday life of individuals – such ideas place great weight on the broad psychological effects of these subtle, unobtrusive features of the social environment. But the distinction between efforts to reduce inequities and abuses arising from cultural differences, and a policy of social homogenization, is a subtle but important one. Homogenization and standardization can turn an individual or a group against the idea of integration if these

[1] For a recent study, see R. LeVine, 'Socialization, Social Structure and Inter-social Images', in Kelman, *op. cit.*, pp. 45–69.

policies are perceived as threats to cultural and linguistic identity.[1]

Specific events and issues provide more ephemeral sources of political attitudes. It is common for individuals or sections of the general public to find themselves mobilized or politically engaged for a short period, after which some of the perceptions and judgements produced by this experience remain as part of their image of political life. Clearly much depends here on the actions of leaders and 'opinion-brokers' in presenting and resolving the issues. De Gaulle's campaign against the supranational pretensions of the EEC has left France a legacy of public attitudes which stress the threat to sovereignty and national identity, and which is more institutionalized and widespread than if he had chosen to do battle on other grounds.

In integration theory, more attention is generally paid to these processes on the level of the policy-makers. Among the elites, neofunctionalists in particular have stressed the short-term influences on attitudes arising from personal contacts in negotiations, conflicts and decisions over specific issues. Shared experience of crises and problem-solving, such as has recurred in the marathon negotiations over the EEC's agricultural policy, is often held to leave a residue of new political attitudes in some of the participants. This would seem particularly true when negotiations have resulted in major qualitative changes in the Community, such as occurred with the acceleration of tariff-reductions or with the successful termination of Britain's negotiations for entry.

Our second distinction is between the directed and undirected acquisition of political attitudes. The most obvious form of directed acquisition is, of course, through propaganda. But deliberate attempts to influence the political attitudes of individuals are also made in the processes of education and socialization, and through threats, promises and intellectual argument in more specific situations.[2] The value of propaganda is certainly recognized by most European

---

[1] It is worth noting here that attitude-change need not be a 'zero-sum' problem – that is, it is not a question simply of replacing a set of national loyalties with a set of European ones. LeVine cites sociological and anthropological studies confirming the view that – at least on the intrasocietal level – 'the multiple loyalties of individuals can have a pacifying effect on intergroup relations.' (*ibid.*, p. 54.)

[2] On these techniques, see Brown, *op. cit.*, esp. Chs. 3, 5, 6. Cf. A. R. Cohen, *Attitude Change and Social Influence* (New York: 1964); C. I. Hovland, I. L. Janis and H. H. Kelley, *Communication and Persuasion* (New Haven: 1953).

organizations, most notably the European Communities and the Council of Europe. The information services of these bodies produce enormous quantities of material, ranging from detailed economic data to passionate rhetoric on the purposes of European unity; this material is designed both to neutralize less favourable nationally-oriented propaganda or less optimistic projections, and to keep the 'European idea' salient in the public mind. The other forms of directed influences on attitudes are, of course, the staples of the politics of integration, since in many ways they are the essence of politics. One need only mention such examples as the implicit French threat to break up the Community over the majority-voting issue, or the complex dealing between Germany and the Netherlands over agricultural policy. Threats, promises and arguments of this kind often have several levels, designed to influence different sectors of the elite and the public.

Undirected forms of influence, on the other hand, would include those aspects of the individual's political environment which act on his attitudes without conscious manipulation for that purpose by other actors. Good examples are the subtle effects of kinship, peer-groups and similar associations, as well as the cultural traditions of the society and the individual's perceptions of events occurring in polit-ical life.[1] A French 'technocrat', for example, passing through the Ecole Polytechnique and up the bureaucratic hierarchy, is exposed to a radically different cultural environment from that of a German trade-union leader, and the result is likely to be a very different set of assumptions about the priorities, for example, of 'efficiency' or 'democracy' in creating a European supranational system. Different cultural and political backgrounds, then, can lead to dramatically different expectations as to the performance of common institutions. One British observer, for example, notes with evident astonishment that M. Noel, the Executive Secretary of the EEC Commission, considers fifty written questions from the European Parliament in three months to be a high figure, when the equivalent at Westminster might be several thousand.[2]

The third distinction is between communications and interaction as sources of attitudes. Communication, essentially, is the transfer of information, including transfer by personal interaction. But the

[1] See K. W. Deutsch and R. L. Merritt, 'Effects of Events on National and International Images', in Kelman, *op. cit.*, pp. 132–87, esp. p. 183.

[2] W. Pickles, 'Political Power in the European Economic Community', in C. A. Cosgrove and K. J. Twitchett (eds.) *The New International Actors* (London: 1970) p. 204.

term is used here more narrowly to refer to the manipulation of symbols, as it were, from a distance. Examples are the press and literature, the mass media, advertising and propaganda, and personal communications through the mail. As we have seen, for many theorists of integration, a rise in indices measuring the attention paid by Frenchmen to German newspapers and television, or the frequency with which these two peoples write or telephone each other, is both a symptom of increased mutual friendliness and trust and a source of further increases in such affections.

Interaction refers to actual situations of face-to-face contacts between individuals. Examples of such situations where new attitudes are acquired by at least one party, are the classroom or discussion-group, work and play situations, social gatherings, families, and, perhaps most significant for integration theory, the 'decisional units', or the small groups in which political decisions are made and conflicts resolved both within and between governments.[1] Most theories of integration perceive such processes of interaction as generators of attitudes enhancing integration – functionalists and neofunctionalists relying on the business of collective decision-making in international organizations, and pluralists on the continuous contacts inherent in governmental meetings, conferences of businessmen, scholary exchanges and tourism.[2]

An individual, then, may derive his political attitudes from a great variety of sources. These sources may serve at various times to provide new perceptions or judgements in areas where existing knowledge has been vague or contradictory, or they may reinforce or challenge well-established images. The various approaches to integration often rely on propositions of this kind, although rarely in a theoretically coherent or even explicit manner. There seems, in any case, to be little consensus on the importance of changes in individual attitudes for the success of integration. The debate, in essence, is between those who see political change as a form of gradual mass conversion, and those who see it as the business of ensuring that individuals whose attitudes and behaviour might aid change, have access to, or hold, the important political roles.

If we are to advance the first view, that major changes in the

---

[1] Snyder et al., op. cit., pp. 86–103; Cohen, op. cit., esp. Chs. 3, 6, 7.

[2] See I. de S. Pool, 'Effects of Cross-National Contact on National and International Images'; J. Sawyer and H. Guetzkow, 'Bargaining and Negotiation in International Relations'; C. F. Alger, 'Personal Contact in Intergovernmental Organizations'; and A. Mishler, 'Personal Contact in International Exchanges'; all in Kelman, op. cit., pp. 106–29, 466–520, 523–47, 550–61.

political attitudes of elites and the general public are in fact a central aspect of integration, then it clearly becomes important to know, not merely what the sources and external stimuli for attitudes are, but also what internal psychological processes take place when an individual undergoes a major change in attitudes.

Herbert Kelman suggests that there are three main ways in which individuals, reacting to their social setting, change their attitudes. The first of these is 'compliance', which takes place 'when an individual accepts influence from another person or from a group because he hopes to achieve a favourable reaction from the other'.[1] The favourable reaction sought is usually the giving of a reward or the removal of a threat of punishment. Changes in attitudes so produced may not be very lasting. They are perhaps represented best in the continuously shifting patterns of agreement and disagreement formed by the exercise of influence in small negotiating groups, where personal or national positions, as well as political resources, are constantly changing.

A second type of change involves what Kelman calls 'identification', which occurs 'when an individual adopts behaviour derived from another person or group because this behaviour is associated with a satisfying self-defining relationship to this person or group',[2] in short, with a role congenial to the individual's image of himself. In this case, because it is linked both to a social structure and to a self-image, the sort of attitude produced by this process may be more lasting. An example might be the national civil servant who begins to accept the political norms of an EEC committee because he finds his part in that committee's work particularly gratifying in terms of his judgement of his own professional skills.

The third process of change Kelman refers to as 'internalization'. This takes place 'when an individual accepts influence because the induced behaviour is congruent with his value system. It is the content of the induced behaviour that is intrinsically rewarding here.'[3] This type of attitude-change, again, would seem more permanent than the first, since it is rooted in the personality or value-structure. It might occur, for example, in situations of conflict between personality and role. A national leader who personally favours more rapid progress to supranationality than most of his colleagues in the Cabinet, finds himself persuaded by the arguments of his counterparts

---

[1] H. C. Kelman, 'Three Processes of Social Influence', in Jahoda and Warren, *op. cit.*, p. 152.
[2] *Ibid.*, p. 153.   [3] *Ibid.*, p. 155.

in the Council of Ministers even though his role prevents him from acknowledging this formally by vote. The arguments, however, reinforce his own position, which he advocates subsequently with added vigour in the councils of his own government.

Of these three processes, the first two clearly involve an individual's changing his attitudes because the new attitudes are associated with favourable experiences (rewards) or with groups or roles in which he finds fulfillment. Compliance operates through the promise of economic, political or symbolic reward; identification occurs mainly through the satisfaction of psychological needs. Internalization, on the other hand, might result from the enhancement of any one of a range of personal values, but the main external stimulus is likely to be new information gained through communication or interaction.

Kelman's three processes are three ways in which the social context can influence an individual's attitudes. But this approach does not tell us how the attitudes affected are related to the individual's 'image' or his total pattern of attitudes, and how this relationship might put constraints on change. It is now generally held that the cognitive, affective and behavioural elements of an individual's total attitude-structure are strongly interdependent. Attitudes, as emphasized earlier, are organized, consistent and habitual ways of thinking, feeling and reacting, and a change in one element nearly always puts pressure on the pattern as a whole. From such assumptions about the tendency of attitude-structures to seek consistency, a number of interesting hypothetical models of attitude-change have been derived and tested experimentally by social psychologists. Because of their possible importance for integration theory at this level of analysis, they merit brief consideration here.[1]

In the first of these, the 'congruity' model, the individual's attitudes are described in terms of a numerical scale ranging from high positive numbers, through zero to low negative numbers.[2] At different points along this scale, such 'cognitive objects' as persons, ideas, policies and institutions are arranged, according to the degree to which the individual approves or disapproves of them. Between any two such cognitive objects, an 'associative bond' is said to exist when

---

[1] On the principle of consistency, see R. B. Zajonc, 'Balance, Congruity and Dissonance', in Jahoda and Warren, *op. cit.*, pp. 261–78, esp. pp. 261–3. The best introduction to these theories of attitude-change is R. Brown, *Social Psychology* (New York: 1965) Ch. 11. See also M. Fishbein (ed.), *Readings in Attitude Theory and Measurement* (New York: 1967) Sec. IIIA.

[2] R. Brown, *op. cit.*, pp. 558–73; Cohen, *op. cit.*, pp. 65–9.

each is in a relationship of enhancement, approval or solidarity with the other. A 'dissociative bond', conversely, is a relation of disapproval, denial or attack. When associative bonds exist between two cognitive objects at the same position on the scale, a condition of congruity or equilibrium is said to exist in the individual's mind. If, for example, a British Conservative Party supporter also favours development of the EEC as a trading community, his government's attempt to enter creates an associative bond such that his attitudes to the Party and the EEC are under no pressure, provided he favours each to roughly the same degree. The same is said to be true if dissociative bonds exist between two objects, one of which is disapproved to the same extent that the other is approved.

Attitudes are changed when associative bonds come to exist between two cognitive objects in different parts of the scale, or when a dissociative bond forms between two objects not in mirror-image positions. In the first case, the objects tend to be shifted to the same point, which lies somewhere between their original positions; in the second, they move to mirror-image positions, again in a compromise between the two original values.[1] Thus if a highly favoured national leader praises the EEC, about which the individual is unenthusiastic, the resulting incongruity will be resolved by a 'devaluation' of the leader and an upgrading of the EEC. Or if this leader attacks the idea of European integration, which the individual supports, thus setting up a dissociative bond, the result will be disapproval of one to the measure that the other is approved. With this model it is held that the extent and direction of these changes of attitude are both measurable and predictable.

The 'balance' model, of which the congruity model is really a special case, is older, less quantitative and less predictive.[2] It has, however, the advantage of flexibility. The scale used in this model simply shows cognitive objects as having positive, negative or null value for the individual, and no attempt is made to quantify these values. As with the congruity model, relationships exist between these objects: they can be positively or negatively associated, or have no bonds at all. Balance is said to exist when two positively valued or two negatively valued cognitive objects are linked by positive (or null) bonds, or when any two objects of opposite value

---

[1] *Ibid.*, pp. 560–4. It is also an axiom of this model that the closer the object is to the middle point, or zero-axis, the more its 'pull' on the other; conversely, the farther out the object, the more it shifts under the strain of incongruity.

[2] *Ibid.*, pp. 573–83; Cohen, *op. cit.*, pp. 69–73.

are linked by negative bonds. In all other cases, imbalance exists, which creates a psychological tension to be righted.

According to this model, attitude-change is just one possibility. This comes about when the signs of the cognitive objects or of their bonds are changed. A French farmer, who dislikes the idea of the Brussels Commission for patriotic reasons but who learns from the press that its agricultural policies may have something to do with his recent prosperity, might come grudgingly to approve of the Commission, or, less plausibly perhaps, to feel that his prosperity, at the price of French autonomy, was not such a good thing. But there are other ways in which the tension might be resolved – ways which avoid a change of attitudes. One of these techniques is 'differentiation'. Here the farmer draws a distinction between the Commission as a corporate body, whose supranational intentions he continues to mistrust, and individual Commissioners like Dr. Mansholt, with whom he associates the policy of which he approves. A third way in which the tension might be resolved is simply through a denial of the relationship between the two cognitive objects, or a refusal to think about the matter at all.[1] Inasmuch as it recognizes that personality and social constraints (such as role) may limit or prevent attitude-change, the balance model appears somewhat more sophisticated and sensitive to real political alternatives than the congruity model.

The third model of attitude-change – really more a loose collection of theories and experiments based on a central theme – is that of 'cognitive dissonance'.[2] The proposition at the core of dissonance-theory is that if an individual is constrained to act in a manner inconsistent with his attitudes, the attitudes will gradually come into line with his behaviour. There are many ways in which situations of dissonance might come about. An individual might undertake dissonant behaviour because of a threat or for a reward of some kind; he might be constrained by his role in a particular group or situation to act in a manner uncongenial to his attitudes.

Such situations are familiar to political scientists, and have in-

[1] R. Brown, *op. cit.*, pp. 578–9. For a discussion of four ways – denial, bolstering, differentiation and transcendence – in which imbalance can be righted, see R. P. Abelson, 'Modes of Resolution of Belief Dilemmas', *Journal of Conflict Resolution*, 3: 3, 1959, pp. 341–52.

[2] R. Brown, *op. cit.*, pp. 584–604; Cohen, *op. cit.*, pp. 78–80, Ch. 6; J. W. Brehm and A. R. Cohen, *Explorations in Cognitive Dissonance* (New York: 1962) esp. pp. 3–7, Chs. 2, and 12–14. The basic theory is in L. Festinger, *A Theory of Cognitive Dissonance* (Stanford: 1957).

POLITICAL INTEGRATION AND POLITICAL MAN

teresting implications for theories of integration in particular. In the interaction between national political elites and the European Community elites, threats and promises are of course common currency, as they are in any bargaining situation. One might speculate whether the behavioural limitations forced on the Commission by the French after 1965, have in fact led to a restructuring of some Commissioners' attitudes toward supranationality, producing less lofty ambitions in this respect. The effects of role, too, may be important. The national bureaucrat, seconded to Brussels and obliged to execute and to defend, in memoranda and speeches, integrative policies of which he does not approve, may find his attitudes evolving in the direction of those policies.[1]

These models of attitude-change are obviously still in a very abstract and experimental condition. Nevertheless, their potential application to theories of integration seems clear enough. They attempt to make explicit what neofunctionalists assume about the effects of successful conflict-resolution on the members of the decision-making groups, or what pluralists assume about the impact of international communications on individuals. By introducing the concept of a need for consistency, moreover, they call into question many of the assumptions about purely rational, utilitarian choice on which functionalists rely.

It might well be argued, of course, that detailed analysis of the internal processes of attitude-change is an unnecessary elaboration or a theoretical luxury. If what we really want to know is how individual attitudes and behaviour affect integration, are we not better off simply taking these individual predispositions as given and focusing on how they are expressed in political action? From a static perspective, this might suffice. If, however, we take integration to be a long, complex and dynamic process, it would seem important to examine the full cycle, including the ways in which the experience of political change itself affects individuals' attitudes.

Whichever strategy we choose, it becomes important at some stage to examine the individual as a political actor and to show how his attitudes, however acquired or altered, feed into the political process. An individual's political attitudes become part of the political process when they are expressed in the form of demands and support for policies. How this expression takes place, and the

[1] In experiments along these lines, social psychologists have found that greater change in attitudes took place when the incentives or pressures to act were lower.

weight it has, varies greatly between the general public and the elites. We shall consider each of these in turn.

For individual members of the general public a wide variety of mechanisms exists whereby demands and support can be communicated to the political system. In almost all cases the impact of these individual acts depends on the degree to which they are consciously supported or unconsciously paralleled by the similar acts of others. The vote is perhaps the most obvious example of such a mechanism, although its role and effectiveness clearly varies greatly between societies. As quantifiable and formal types of mass political behaviour – superficially akin to the economist's concept of demand – voting patterns have been studied extensively in Western democratic systems. But even in systems where the choice of policies, parties or individuals is more strictly limited or pre-determined, the vote serves as a crude indicator of popular consensus. It is crude because elections are too infrequent to provide a reliable profile of changes in public preferences over time, and, more important in this context, because it is always difficult to tell the weight of a single issue – such as European integration – in the complex of elements leading to a voter's decision. In the particular case of integration, too, it is sometimes difficult to assess the impact of voting since domestic issues have tended to dominate Western European elections.

In the French presidential elections of 1966 and 1969, however, there is clear evidence that the European issue intruded forcefully. In 1966, the surprising result produced some adjustment of de Gaulle's tactics, notably a willingness to resolve the impasse over agricultural policy and majority voting in the Community.[1] In 1969, M. Pompidou was more careful than his predecessor to appeal to the 'European' as well as the nationalist wings of the potential Gaullist vote.

On the whole, however, the average European might well feel a weary cynicism on hearing the federalist argument for a directly elected European Parliament to increase popular participation in the Community. He would observe the apparent acquiescence of his fellow Europeans to the present technocratic remoteness of the Community in its daily workings. And he would note the propensity of national governments to avoid rather than encourage public participation when major decisions are being made concerning the Community's future. In the British election of 1970, the European

[1] F. R. Willis, *France, Germany and the New Europe 1945–1967* (London: 1968) pp. 346–51.

issue was kept well in the background. In the subsequent national debate over entry to the EEC, the Government has made it clear that that other instrument for expressing popular preferences, the referendum, will not be used.

The political attitudes of individuals may also feed into the political process through their participation in interest groups or political parties. Individuals can become attached to these organizations for a variety of reasons – occupation, family, class, social pressure, or on the basis of single, specific issues. There are many different types of interest groups, too with different degrees of permanence, breadth of concern, bases of membership, and points of access to the decision-making process. The various issues of European integration have seen the involvement of a wide selection of interest groups in most countries, particularly business groups (the Patronat, the Confederation of British Industries) and trades unions (the Deutscher Gewerkschaftsbund, the Trades Union Congress and other national confederations, as well as individual unions). Besides these broad organizations there are many pressure groups whose sole concern is European integration, such as Monnet's Action Committee, the federalist groups all over Europe and such opposition groups as the Common Market Safeguards Campaign in Britain. In most of these groups, of course, it is the leaders who articulate policy and interact with governments; other groups, such as the Action Committee, consist of influential leaders throughout. Others are more likely to have the illusion rather than the reality of participation and influence in decision through such groups.

A political party can be seen as a particular type of broad interest group, usually designed to aggregate political demands and support in the form of multiple interests, and not merely to influence but to control the governmental process. In such organizations individual attitudes are expressed through conference resolutions, in meetings of local groups such as constituency associations, and less formally in day-to-day administration. Characteristically, the mass of political information represented by these individual contributions is filtered out and refined as it passes up through the hierarchy of the party or group to the point where expressions of collective policy emerge. Again we would expect that individual expressions of opinion count for relatively little in the routine operation of the party. But when a party is badly divided or in the throes of changing its collective mind – as Britain's Labour Party was over Europe in 1971 – those at the grass roots are likely to be cultivated assiduously by competing, insecure elites, and thus to have unusual influence.

In addition to these more formal processes, there are many informal ways in which individual's attitudes can have an impact on the political system. Among these are the periodic expressions of public opinion in polls and interviews published in the press, individual communications to the media and to political leaders and other representatives, public demonstrations, and even organized or anomic violence. In many cases, too, inattention, lack of action and general silence can be telling expressions of the state of public opinion and attitudes on political issues. Certainly, if an attentive general public, whose members feel that they can and should participate in political decisions, is one quality of a well-developed political system, the European Community has a long way to go.

By definition, the elites have not only a greater range of opportunities than the general public for influencing policy, but also a greater effect in employing many of those means of influence they have in common with the public. In political parties and interest groups, the elites both shape and interpret patterns of demand and support for policies. Bureaucratic elites apply specialized knowledge and skills, and the accumulated resources of continuity, in feeding their own influence into the policy-process. Communications elites have a mediating role between the policy process and public opinion which often gives them an influential position in both.

More important than the more or less formal channels of influence open to the general public are the less formal and less obvious means open to the elites because of their organizational positions and social status. The ability to control the horizontal and vertical flows of information, possessed by certain elites in political, administrative and communications structure, amounts to a capacity to impress attitudes on policy. For example, the central position of the Commission in the European Communities system and its dominance of the sources of information magnify the effect of individual Commissioners' attitudes and demands immeasurably. In the policy processes of states, too, the attitudes toward integration held by politicians and bureaucrats who control either the formal or the informal information-structures of government, tend to have disproportionate weight. Hence the importance placed by some students of integration on such processes as bureaucratic interpenetration and cross-national elite-contacts, as means of creating

'European' attitudes in policy-makers likely to end up in such central positions.[1]

It is often claimed – frequently by way of criticism – that the movement for European integration since the last war has had an unusually elitist quality. The elites referred to in such observations are not, however, the men at the pinnacles of political power so much as those at the middle and upper ranges of bureaucracies and political parties, and the leaders of industry, the unions and the media. Recent criticisms of the European Community, as the leading edge of integration, place particular emphasis on the bureaucrats, technocrats and economists who seem to dominate policy-making. Are these 'Eurocrats' – men such as Jean Monnet, Walter Hallstein, Jean Rey, Franco Maria Malfatti, Louis Armand, Pierre Uri, Etienne Hirsch – to be seen as early models of the emergent European Man? Are the values of efficiency, rationality, productivity and technological innovation, with which many of the more technocratic members of the Commission have seemed obsessed, to have priority in tomorrow's Europe over such values as political participation, representation and regional cultural identity?

However one chooses to answer this question, it is clear that the Eurocrats, in the form of brilliant administrators and political innovators and in the form of middle-range functionaries, have steadily and inexorably built a solid functional foundation for European integration. The political leaders – those at the pinnacles of power who are accountable to electorates – have been on the whole less consistent, and one quickly becomes aware in looking back at postwar European history how much has at times turned on their acts. Some, such as the succession of postwar British Prime Ministers (and Opposition Leaders) until the 1960s could legitimately plead the restraints of an insular public, while of course aware that little could stop a Government if it chose to lead the country into Europe. The French leaders, on the other hand, seem to have specialized in brilliant 'coups' – Schuman to one effect with his Plan of 1950, de Gaulle to quite another in the 1960s. It would be wrong, of course, to see the progress of integration purely as a series of dramatic, autonomous acts at the summit. Nonetheless, such acts as Adenauer and de Gaulle's negotiation of the Franco-German Treaty of 1963, Brandt's initiative at the Hague Conference of 1969 and the meeting of Heath and Pompidou over

[1] On the 'Europeanization' of bureaucrats, see D. Coombes, *Politics and Bureaucracy in the European Community* (London: 1970).

British entry, have provided unmistakable catalysts for the process of integration.

Having discussed in some detail the nature of attitudes, how they are acquired and altered, and how individuals, as members of the general public or of the policy-making elites, influence the progress of integration, it would be useful now to return to the literature on integration in search of a pattern in the main arguments and assumptions it contains on this level of analysis. It is possible to discern, running through this literature and emphasized to varying degrees by each approach, four main groups of propositions, or 'grand hypotheses' about the circular relationship of individuals' political attitudes and the process of political integration.

The first of these 'grand hypotheses' has to do with the social, political and institutional context in which decisions pertaining to integration are made, both in governments and in international organizations. The general proposition is that the pressures and experience of decision-making, problem-solving and conflict resolution will produce gradual shifts in the attitudes of participants which, in the next round of decisions, will make it somewhat more probable that solutions favouring integration will be found. As has been argued earlier, such ideas are central to neofunctionalist thinking in particular. But the learning of cooperative habits (functionalism), the effects of elite-interactions (pluralism) and the formative influence of institutions (federalism) – all such notions rely on similar assumptions.

Within this 'grand hypothesis' are subsumed a number of more specific propositions, some of which can be spelled out in more detail. In the first place, it is claimed that successful problem-solving and conflict-resolution creates and enhances a spirit of cooperation and a shared commitment to certain goals among the participants. To this end, a deep political crisis, paradoxically, is potentially, more productive than a technical disagreement.[1] Attitude-change is aided by the existence of a common pressure to come to a decision by a certain time, or not to fail to agree; this is assumed to create a sort of corporate, club-like state of mind among participants, although clearly the degree to which this is possible will depend also on the definition of the situation with which each begins.

[1] Cf. R. C. North, H. E. Koch and D. A. Zinnes, 'The Integrative Functions of Conflict', *Journal of Conflict Resolution*, 4: 4, 1960, pp. 355–74; L. A. Coser, *The Functions of Social Conflict* (New York: 1956).

In the second place, a decision-making or bargaining situation is seen as setting up, like any small-group process, pressures on individuals to conform to certain norms and play certain roles. In such cases, cognitive dissonance might be produced, or at least opportunities would exist for the social influences on attitudes which Kelman describes.[1] Third, the organizational structure which grows up where there are continuing conflicts and decisions, is said not only to provide a pacifying and ordering solution; it also manipulates symbols and, by controlling communications, shapes individuals' perceptions of each other, the issues, the urgency of the situation, their roles, and the organization itself. All three hypotheses, then, refer to certain properties of decision and conflict-situations which create attitudes favouring further integration among elites. These changes of attitudes will often have less to do with rationality than with the individual's need to restore consistency in his cognitive structure. These attitudes are self-reinforcing in a continual bargaining situation such as that of the EEC; in time they also filter down to national government and public opinion.

The second group of propositions discernable in the literature on integration centres around the argument that the process of change advances to the extent that both elites and public perceive it to be of continuing benefit in meeting their basic needs, particularly those of welfare and security. These ideas, which are more purely rationalist than the first group, are developed most explicitly in functionalist literature, where loyalties and support for cooperation are assumed to be based largely on utilitarian assessments of the degree to which the institutions in question satisfy the individual's needs. In neo-functionalist writings the concept of interest is transferred from the needs of the individual and society to the demands of groups, which give support to policies, seek access to decision-processes and develop loyalties according to where these demands are met. Federalists and pluralists too, associate loyalties with the capacity to provide security; Deutsch also notes the integrative effects of benefiicial communications.[2]

Among the more specific propositions which can be found in this

---

[1] Kelman, 'Three Processes of Social Influence', *op. cit.*; Cohen, *op. cit.*, Ch. 7. Cf. E. B. Haas, *Beyond the Nation-State* (Stanford: 1964) p. 112, for a suggestion that cognitive dissonance may be a helpful explanation of self-reinforcing integration in international organizations.

[2] See Deutsch, 'Transaction Flows as Indicators of Political Cohesion', *op. cit.*, pp. 77–83, 86–7 for some formulae purporting to measure these communications and their effects.

general group, four are of particular interest here. The first of these is that when members of the general public become aware of the material benefits of cooperation, they will develop a stronger cooperative ethos – changing both their perceptions of political life and their feelings toward each other – which will lead in time to a large-scale social transformation, perhaps of global proportions. This would be a pure example of learning by 'association', attitudes being adopted because they are associated with concrete benefits. A second related proposition is that the leaders of interest groups will support policies enhancing integration not out of general principles or ideologies, but on the basis of advantages perceived in specific situations. In addition, they may seek access to political processes operating beyond the national level. In both cases, while loyalties may not change fundamentally, perceptions of political institutions and processes do. The common organization, for instance, may gradually come to be seen as the most important source of benefits.

A third proposition in this group has to do with the general belief – among elites especially – that the parochialism of political structure in some sense deprives men of the benefits of the internationalization of technology and economics. Tensions are thus created to internationalize these structures, and a new political world-view gradually emerges to support such changes. The fourth proposition, familiar to federalists in particular, holds that common needs or fears have the effect of producing common perceptions of the sort of political solution required, as well as the common loyalties to support it. A form of cognitive dissonance may be involved in both these cases: the pressures of needs (such as security from a common enemy) force the leaders and peoples of two states into forms of cooperation which, by requiring rationalization, lead to attitude-change.

The third 'grand hypothesis' refers to the psychological effects of communications and interactions between the members of different states on all social levels. The general argument is that communication and interaction form the basis of a collective learning-process: the more contact there is between people, the more accurate their perceptions of each other become; in addition, the more such contacts are seen to have mutually beneficial results, the more that mutual feelings of trust and loyalty are created. This increased mutual awareness and affection is assumed to be self-reinforcing, rather like the ascending spiral of 'escalation'. This idea of the growth of 'community' has been most elaborated by pluralist writers such as Deutsch and Russett.[1] On the elite-level, federalists and neofunctionalists also assume the existence of such a process, while the same could be said of functionalists with respect to the general public.

A number of more specific propositions can be drawn out of this general argument. First, attitude-change consists of two distinct processes. One involves, almost exclusively, what is called 'transfer',[2] or pure learning by the absorption of new information and the readjustment of cognitive structures. This comes about through the act of communication and interaction with other people and societies, in governmental meetings, business conferences or travel. The second stage really involves the type of attitude-change discussed with respect to functionalism – that which results from need-satisfaction. The difference is that, at least initially, the new loyalties are directed not to a common organization, but to other peoples. Frenchmen, for example, might respond to the benefits of European cooperation more by liking Germans than by liking the EEC.

A second proposition would be that attitude-change depends on the continuing expansion of channels of communication to handle the increased flow of messages. As 'community' grows, therefore, common institutions, common languages and transport facilities must emerge to guide and regulate communications, or else the process will be frustrated or choked off. A third proposition emphasizes the mediatory role of 'images', which may inhibit or encourage this type of social communication and learning. The individual travelling in a new country or meeting with foreigners tends to select data which confirm this image or which satisfy deep psychological needs. To the extent that this image is hostile, clearly the effects of social communication and interaction are likely to be limited or even counter-productive.[3] A de Gaulle, then, is able to retain through the 1960s an image of American and British hostility based on the 1940s.

A final 'grand hypothesis' has to do with the effects of symbols on political attitudes. It refers not only to the conscious manipulation of symbols by those in authority to change the awareness and loyalties of the public, but also to the less directed responses of individuals to acts, institutions and persons they may take as symbols.

[1] See esp. K. W. Deutsch, *Nationalism and Social Communication* (Cambridge, Mass.: 1966) esp. Chs. 4 and 5; B. M. Russett, *Community and Contention* (Cambridge, Mass.: 1963).

[2] Lambert and Lambert, *op. cit.*, pp. 61–3.

[3] Klineberg, *op. cit.*, Chs. 4 and 5.

Foremost among writers on integration who stress this idea is Etzioni, who points to the importance of control of 'identitive' power by the new central institutions as a means of creating a consensus underlying the new system.[1] Federalists and neofunctionalists, who look to the formation of a new supranational state, imply this sort of governmental activity, to create cohesion through encouragement of a new common political culture. Symbols, as Merritt has shown, also have a role in the pluralist concept of integration through social communication.[2]

There are a number of interesting specific propositions related to this idea. In the first place, general support for integration can be encouraged through the invocation of myths of historical unity and through constant references to shared cultural memories. Such techniques may not create new loyalties, but, like any form of advertising, can at least have a cumulative impact on popular perceptions – in this case perceptions of the available political solutions. Secondly, similar public relations operations can supplement common functional activities to create or reinforce the belief that the new benefits have derived largely from the advances of integration. As a number of recent studies of political behaviour have shown,[3] people act more on the basis of what they believe to be advantageous to them than of what really is. The nation-state has been the chief beneficiary of this phenomenon: no matter what the real, utilitarian value of common institutions, the state remains the symbolic source, and hence the salient one. The progress of integration thus requires efforts to make the symbolic, as well as the concrete, benefits of common institutions, as salient as those of the nation-states. A third proposition refers more to the elite-level. The symbolic trappings of leaders' activities can become an important source of integrative behaviour. Dubious outcomes are thus invariably presented as successes, clocks are stopped at midnight, and everything is done by Community officials to maintain the public impression that the bicycle of integration – however it may in fact be tottering – is rolling forward.

The propositions related to each of these four 'grand hypotheses' vary somewhat in precision and testability. But this brief review of the literature on integration should have at least made it clear that

---

[1] A. Etzioni, *Political Unification*, (New York, 1965) pp. 39–41, 71–2.

[2] R. L. Merritt, *Symbols of American Community 1735–1775* (New Haven: 1966) esp. Preface, Chs. 2 and 9.

[3] See esp. M. Edelman, *The Symbolic Uses of Politics* (Urbana, Ill.: 1964).

some explanatory depth and breadth is to be gained by attempting to apply social-psychological insights to the study of political integration. In order to do this, however, we need techniques of assessing and measuring the political attitudes of individuals.

One traditional method, of course, is to work backwards, inferring the political attitudes of leaders or even the general public, from expressions of government policy. Indeed, commentators often talk of the British or French 'attitude' to European integration when, strictly, what they mean is 'governmental policy'. But it is also possible, in some cases, to argue that policy does in fact reflect the attitudes of certain individuals – as, for example, French policy toward Europe was seen primarily as an expression of President de Gaulle's personal view of the world.[1] The difficulty with this type of analysis is that it tends to be *post facto* or tautological. Once we know the policy, we need not be concerned about the private opinions of leaders, while knowing these opinions does not always enable us to predict behaviour. For this latter purpose it is more useful to have a full picture of the whole policy-process.

A second way of assessing attitudes is to infer them from objective indices of political and social behaviour. Measures of social communication, such as the flow of trade, mail, tourism, investment and mass media may serve, like coloured dyes in a seemingly static, calm ocean, to show up currents and patterns of attitudes. But inferring these attitudes from such aggregated behaviour requires the prior and hardly self-evident assumption that political attitudes always exist in or aspire to a strict correspondence with behaviour. This type of inferential problem bedevils such of Deutsch's work on social communication.

A third method of assessing patterns of political attitudes is content analysis, which focuses on the verbal behaviour of individuals and collective communications media. The researcher assembles a coded set of symbols and statement-units which he takes to represent the sorts of political attitudes he is seeking. He then counts how often they appear in editorials, articles, speeches, policy-statements, memoranda, debates and other samples of verbal behaviour. Comparing these frequencies with normal patterns of attention, and tracing them over time, he can arrive at a picture of

[1] The reification of foreign policy is encouraged, of course, by the dramatic necessities of mass communications. For an attempt to assess the importance of personality in foreign policy, see J. N. Rosenau, 'Pre-Theories and Theories of Foreign Policy', in R. B. Farrell (ed.), *Approaches to Comparative and International Politics* (Evanston, Ill.: 1966) pp. 47–8. Cf. Inglehart, *op. cit.*, pp. 777–83.

the historical development of a political community.[1] At its most rigorous and systematic, this method requires a computer, since it relies on a great quantity of data; but rougher, more impressionistic techniques have been used as well. A more serious problem, particularly in the sort of costly and elaborate operation involved here, is to assure correspondence between the indices and the patterns of attitudes they are taken to represent. The verbal behaviour of diplomats and politicians, after all, is notoriously unreliable.

Public opinion polls are perhaps the best known method of assessing attitudes toward political issues and institutions. Ideally, of course, the researcher should formulate his own questions and conduct his own survey. But very often, since this can be expensive and requires special skills, he must make use of polls taken by other people, often for other reasons, and merely make a 'secondary analysis'. In this case, distortions are liable to creep in. Another problem, applying to public opinion polls generally, is that most questionnaires tend to structure the respondents' mental picture for him so as to elicit more or less predetermined answers. Once again, to use a more flexible, open-ended form of questioning raises costs dramatically. And finally, of course, such polls, if they are to show change, must be repeated over a period of time with consistent questions. Nevertheless, patterns of opinion, grouped by such categories as region, class, age and ethnic origin, can provide a useful background for research on integration.

In principle the most valuable and sensitive method of assessing political attitudes is the open-ended or 'depth' interview, carried out in a representative sample of the elite or the general public.[2] This is, of course, an expensive and exhausting procedure, requiring a great deal of methodological sophistication and some tenacity in recording interviews with important and frequently impatient people. The data so derived can be used to substantiate arguments based on other sources, or it can be treated by content analysis to yield more systematic patterns of attitudes. This method would appear to offer the most potential for reaching the core-attitudes of individuals. Nonetheless, many of the problems raised in

[1] Merritt, op. cit., Ch. 2.
[2] A good example of a study based on this technique is Almond and Verba, op. cit., for which approximately 5000 interviews were conducted. Cf. K. W. Deutsch, L. J. Edinger, R. C. Macridis and R. L. Merritt, France, Germany and the Western Alliance (New York: 1967) which is based on interviews with 147 French elite-members and 173 West German leaders. See Ch. 1 for a description of the method.

POLITICAL INTEGRATION AND POLITICAL MAN

connection with opinion polls and content analysis, can also occur in this last case.

These five methods all have their strengths and weaknesses. As Deutsch has demonstrated, it is possible to use them jointly, strong correlations often becoming evident between the patterns measured in each way.[1] It seems fair to say, in conclusion, that political attitudes are inherently no more elusive than many of the other phenomena with which theorists of integration have to deal. It is doubtful if the behaviour and attitudes of individuals will ever yield up the full and sufficient explanation of political integration. But to ignore these variables as unmanageable or unimportant may be to seal off a whole area of fruitful inquiry. In a sense it is ironic that theorists of integration have devoted such a great proportion of their attention to the transformation of systems and the behaviour of states, passing over the role of the individual political actor. The views of many of these theorists, after all, conform to those of the Victorian novelist and critic George Gissing: 'It is because nations tend to stupidity and baseness that mankind moves so slowly; it is because individuals have a capacity for better things that it moves at all.'[2]

[1] *Ibid.*, pp. 215–17.
[2] *The Private Papers of Henry Ryecroft* (London: 1903) p. 42.

Appendix I
Explaining Integration: The Three Levels of Analysis (Chs. 6–8)

I. System: Conditions for change (Ch. 6)
   A. Decision-making dimension
      1. Background – e.g. external threat to regional security or autonomy
      2. Process – e.g. skills of negotiators and organizational officials in bargaining situations over integration

   B. Functional dimension
      1. Background – e.g. level of technological and economic development in the system
      2. Process – e.g. specific social and economic problems, calling for actions on system-basis
   C. Behavioural dimension
      1. Background – e.g. ethnic and linguistic origins of system's peoples
      2. Process – e.g. growth of new institutions to facilitate communications and consultations in system
   D. Attitudinal dimension
      1. Background – e.g. shared cultural traits and values in system's peoples
      2. Process – e.g. social and institutional pressures on perceptions and loyalties of participants

II. States: Sources of 'community policy' (Ch. 7)
   A. Needs and constraints from the general, non-political environment – e.g. geographical factors
   B. Influences from formally external political systems
      1. Global international system – e.g. alignments of states, policies of superpowers
      2. Integrating system – e.g. policies of system-wide organizations

3. Domestic systems of other states – e.g. 'informal penetration' by interest groups

C. Influences arising in the domestic political and social system
 1. Economic – e.g. size of public sector
 2. Social – e.g. degree of pluralism
 3. Cultural – e.g. ideological basis of society
 4. Political institutions and processes
  a. input-stage – e.g. groups, parties, public opinion
  b. decision-stage – e.g. roles, institutional pressures, personality
  c. output-stage – e.g. capabilities of bureaucracy, diplomats, agencies

III. Individuals: Conditions changing attitudes and behaviour (Ch. 8)
 A. The social context of decision-making and bargaining – e.g. time-pressures, group dynamics
 B. The effects of need-satisfaction – e.g. utilitarian gratification, group interests and access
 C. Communications and interaction – e.g. social learning, cooperative habits
 D. Symbols – e.g. effects of myth, propaganda

Appendix II
List of Abbreviations

AEF	Action Européenne Fédéraliste
CEEC	Committee for European Economic Cooperation
CERN	European Nuclear Research Centre
Comecon	Council of Mutual Economic Assistance
ECE	Economic Commission for Europe (UN)
ECSC	European Coal and Steel Community (in French, CECA)
EDC	European Defence Community
EEC	European Economic Community
EFTA	European Free Trade Association
ELDO	European Launcher Development Organization
ENEA	European Nuclear Energy Agency
EPC	European Political Community
EPU	European Payments Union
ESRO	European Space Research Organization
Euratom	European Atomic Energy Community
GATT	General Agreement on Tariffs and Trade
IAEA	International Atomic Energy Agency
ILO	International Labour Organization
MFE	Mouvement Fédéraliste Européen
NATO	North Atlantic Treaty Organization
OECD	Organization for Economic Cooperation and Development
OEEC	Organization for European Economic Cooperation
UEF	Union of European Federalists
UN	United Nations
WEU	Western European Union

Index of Persons

Abelson, R. P., 255 n
Acton, Lord, 154
Adenauer, K., 58, 133, 173, 242, 260
Aikin, C., 153 n
Alger, C., 115 n, 251 n
Alker, H., 43 n, 44 n, 205 n
Allport, G. W., 245
Almond, G. A., 67, 86 n, 116, 197, 200 n. 207, 225, 235 n, 236, 245, 246 n, 247 n, 267 n
Althusius, J., 70 n, 153, 160
Amiel, H. F., 84 n
Anderson, C. W., 232 n
Apter, D. E., 67
Armand, L., 66, 69, 70 n, 77–8, 79 n, 85 n, 87, 89 n, 152 n, 260
Aron, Raymond, 18 n, 33 n, 34, 37 n, 60, 115 n, 142, 144, 153 n, 156 n, 158 n, 170 n, 181 n, 219
Aron, Robert, 157 n
Asch, S. E., 244
Attlee, C., 58

Balassa, B., 135 n
Banfield, E. C., 243 n
Barber, W. J., 20 n
Barraclough, G., 226 n
Barrera, M., 120 n
Bay, C., 111 n
Bell, D., 110 n
Beloff, M., 32, 115 n, 144 n, 153 n
Bennett, W. H., 151 n, 159 n
Berger, G., 152 n, 157 n, 159 n, 160 n
Berle, A., 152 n
Birch, A. H., 151 n, 161 n
Bismarck, O. von., 39 n
Bodenheimer, S. J., 33 n, 57 n, 108 n, 176 n
Bodin, J., 158
Bonnefous, E., 96

Bottomore, T. B., 246 n
Boulding, K. E., 17 n, 37, 48 n, 244
Bowie, R. R., 176 n, 180, 181 n
Bozeman, A. B., 30 n, 158 n
Brams, S. J., 41–2 n
Brandt, W., 56 n, 58 n, 260
Brecht, A., 18 n
Brehm, J. W., 255 n
Brown, G., 186 n
Brown, J. A. C., 244, 249 n
Brown, R., 253 n, 254 n, 255 n
Bruck, H. W., 130 n, 209 n, 225 n, 245 n
Brugmans, H., 149 n, 152 n, 156 n, 157 n, 158 n, 159 n, 160 n, 165 n, 166 n, 171–2 n, 174 n, 176 n, 177 n, 178 n, 179, 180, 182 n, 183, 185 n, 186
Buchan, A., 195 n
Bull, H. N., 18 n, 39 n, 50 n
Burton, J. W., 37, 47 n
Butterfield, H., 39 n

Camps, M., 34 n, 72 n, 176 n
Châtenet, P., 97
Chevallier, J. J., 157 n
Churchill, W. S., 52, 58, 59, 242
Clark, W. H., 117 n, 125 n, 134 n
Claude, I. L., Jr., 19, 29, 31 n, 33 n, 37 n, 69, 71 n, 74, 79 n, 81 n, 86 n, 102 n, 155 n, 156 n, 164 n, 168 n, 169, 171 n, 201, 218, 219
Clausewitz, C. von., 36
Cobden, R., 45
Cohen, A. R., 249 n, 251 n, 253 n, 254 n, 255 n, 262 n
Cole, G. D., 160
Cole, T., 159 n
Coleman, J. S., 67 n, 116, 197, 225 n, 235 n
Comte, A., 65
Coombes, D., 260 n

273

Subject Index